Parrots
and
Parrot-like
Birds

By
The Duke of Bedford

Diseases of Parrots
By
David L. Coffin, D.V.M.
Angell Memorial Hospital

Published by T.F.H. Publications, T.F.H. Building, 245 Cornelison Avenue, Jersey City, N. J. 07302. Distributed in the British Empire by T.F.H. Publications (London) Ltd., 13 Nutley Lane, Reigate, Surrey, England. In Canada by Clarke, Irwin & Company Ltd., Clarwin House, 791 St. Clair Avenue West, Toronto 10, Ontario, Canada. Printed in the U.S.A. by the lithograph process by T.F.H. Lithograph Corp., Jersey City, N. J. 07302.

Distributed to the Book Trade in the U.S.A. by Crown Publishers, Inc., 419 Park Avenue South, New York, N. Y. 10016.

Preface

Shortly before his tragic death, the Duke of Bedford completed the revisions necessary to bring "Parrots and Parrot-like Birds" up-to-date. Although the importation of birds of the parrot family into the United States is under certain restrictions at the present time, the notations regarding the importation of various species have been retained as an indication of their population in captivity. The practical approach of the book has been carried out by including all, but only, those species likely to be encountered in captivity. Any species not treated specifically may be assumed to be identical in habits and care to close allies. The inevitable confusion of popular names has made it necessary to include more than one name for some species, but the inclusion of the Latin name makes positive identification possible.

The charm of His Grace's prose is intact; even the English spelling has been retained. It must be kept in mind by American readers that all climatic descriptions relate to England. Consequently, bird-keepers in various climates should translate remarks concerning the hardiness, etc., of various species to conform to the climate of their own area.

His Grace would wish to express his appreciation for the chapter on diseases by David L. Coffin, D.V.M., of Angell Memorial Hospital. Dr. Coffin has made a thorough clinical study of the diseases of the parrot family, and studied the birds in the field in South America.

The assistance and co-operation of many members of the fancy has permitted the compilation of a complete, yet concise, work. Among those whose assistance has made this book possible are: Malcolm Davis, Curator of Birds, Washington Zoological Park, Smithsonian Institute; Karl Plath, Curator of Birds, Chicago Zoological Park; C. Ragan, Southern Bird and Pet Exchange; Earl Rappaport, Tri-State Aquarium; Allen Silver; W. Watmough, Poultry World, Ltd.; David West; and Jack Young, Parrot Kings.

In Memoriam

The tragic death of the Duke of Bedford on his Devonshire, England, estate near Tavistock, discovered on October 11, 1953, shocked the avicultural world. The loss will be keenly felt not only by the thousands of bird-keepers who knew him personally but also by the vast number of aviculturists throughout the world who were familiar with his life-long devotion to aviculture, his many articles on the subject, and this book.

On October ninth, His Grace, who had previously travelled down to his home with some Budgerigars he planned to add to his group of homing Budgerigars, went out with his shotgun to hunt a Sparrowhawk which was menacing his flock of one hundred birds. While forcing his way through some bushes he seems to have stumbled and the gun accidentally fired, inflicting fatal wounds.

When his disappearance was reported, commandos, police, and volunteers scoured the moors of Devon. Commandos from a near-by Royal Marine school used walkie-talkie sets and mine detectors. In all, two hundred men joined in the search. Saturday night, October tenth, workers drained a large pond on the duke's twelve thousand acre estate.

A gamekeeper's hunch finally led to the body. Estate workers found the Duke lying in undergrowth near a favorite beauty spot. Death was believed to have been instantaneous.

Both at Endsleigh and Woburn it was the Duke's practice to release his homing Budgerigars early in the morning where they could fly at liberty in the garden and return to the aviary to roost, feed, and breed.

His early interest in aviculture was fostered by a boyhood of unique opportunity, for at Woburn Abbey his father's collection of birds and animals was unequalled in Britain for number and variety.

While at Oxford he bought two pairs of Madagascar Lovebirds, which he put at liberty at Woburn. They stayed in the grounds and reared young. Later, the Duke decided to specialize in parrot-like birds, and prior to World War One he bred at complete liberty the Roseate Cockatoo and the following parakeets: Red Rosella, Mealy Rosella, Pennant, Adelaide,

Barnard's, Redrump; and later, the Passerine Parrotlet and Peach-faced Lovebird. Among the finch-like birds the Duke bred at liberty the Common Waxbill, Orange-cheeked Waxbill, Avadavat, Orange-breasted Waxbill, Cordon Bleu, Lavender Finch, Diamond Sparrow, Rufous-tailed Finch, Parson Finch, and Long-tailed Grass Finch.

A fellow of the Zoological Society, member of the British Ornithologists' Union, and a member of the Council of the Avicultural Society, His Grace was also associated with the Avicultural Society of America, and a life member of La Societé Nationale d'Acclimation de France.

He was seriously connected with religion, monetary reform, and work for international peace. Among the books and pamphlets he wrote is an autobiography, "The Years of Transition," which includes a description of the animals found at Woburn. With the object of making Christianity intelligible to people who have not had the benefit of education, he wrote "The Road to Success." "Poverty and Over-taxation; the Way Out," is a treatise on monetary reform, and "Public Enemy Number One; Hate and Hysteria," was written with the hope of reducing prejudice and misunderstanding between Communist and non-Communist countries.

The Duke always had a keen interest in natural history, and he made a special study of the deer and birds of which he once had a large collection. Apart from politics, his main interest was his private zoo. Herds of bison and rare deer roamed his parklands at Woburn. Tame fish rose to be fed when he rang bells beside their pond—the big ones to a large bell, middle-sized ones to a middle-sized bell, and so on.

The Most Noble Hastings William Sackville Russell, twelfth Duke of Bedford, Marquess of Tavistock, Earl of Bedford, Baron Russell of Chenies, Baron Russell of Thornhaugh in the county of Northhampton, Baron Howland of Streatham in the county of Surrey, was born in Scotland on December 21, 1888. He was educated at Eton and Balliol.

The Duke married at twenty-six and at his death left two sons and a daughter.

The Duke of Bedford's untimely death was a severe loss to aviculture, but his expert advice on the keeping and breeding, feeding and management of birds will be closely followed by succeeding generations of aviculturists.

Table of Contents

Color Illustrations

Introduction

The parrot family has occupied a deservedly high place in the favour of bird-keepers ever since the days when the Romans began to import from the East, Plumheaded and Ringnecked, or Alexandrine, Parakeets. The intelligence of parrots and their affection for their owners, their power of imitating the human voice, their longevity and gorgeous plumage, all combine to place them in the front rank as pets or aviary inmates. Some critics, it is true, argue that the colouring of psittacine birds is gaudy rather than beautiful, that their natural cries are disagreeable, that they are destructive to growing plants, and that they are unpleasant to handle without strong gloves; but we may reply that there are some species to which none of these objections apply and many to which only one or two can be made.

As compared with the science of breeding and managing domestic animals, aviculture is as yet in its infancy; much ignorance still prevails and a good many foreign birds in confinement are subjected to unnecessary suffering through the lack of knowledge and thoughtlessness of their owners. Parrots are no exception, and it is in order to remedy this state of affairs, as well as to increase the pleasure which may be derived from the study of a fascinating group, that this book has been written. It will, perhaps, serve as one of the milestones which mark the road of avicultural progress.

To prevent disappointment and confusion it may be well to add that "Parrots and Parrot-like Birds" is not a complete monograph of the family, but only an attempt to include the majority of those species that have been imported or kept in confinement. Many species and a few sub-genera are not mentioned at all. Of these several are very unlikely to be imported alive by reason of their extreme delicacy in confinement; others, however, we may hope some day to see in our aviaries.

The writer has made use, as far as possible, of the most recent scientific nomenclature. While this may result in many well-known birds appearing under strange and unfamiliar Latin names, modern classification has at least this merit from an avicultural point of view: that it tends to associate in the same sub-genus only birds that are exceedingly closely allied. The reader will therefore be fairly safe in assuming that when little information is given about a rarely imported species it will, in habits, disposition and requirements, be almost identical with better-known and more fully described birds bearing the same sub-generic title.

I

Cages and Aviaries

The average parrot cage would appear to be constructed with the express object of causing the maximum degree of discomfort to the parrot and of inconvenience to its owner. In the first place it is almost invariably at least half the size it should be for the bird it is expected to contain. It is now, I believe, the law of the land that no bird, except when on a railway journey or at a show, may be kept in a cage which does not allow it freely to stretch its wings. From the protection of this beneficient law it would appear that, for some unknown reason, parrots are exempt. Up and down the country one meets with hundreds of parrots in cages so small that they cannot possibly flap their extended wings; yet no parrot cage is admissable which does not permit this form of exercise to the inmate. A very large and lucrative trade is done by dealers who sell a parrot and cage at "attractive" prices. The cage on these occasions is always far too small, for the provision of a decent-sized cage would eat up the margin of profit. Owing to its cramped environment, the parrot's days are considerably shortened; the owner, therefore, has to buy a new parrot. This is good for the bird trade, but bad for the unhappy birds.

A parrot cage is usually fitted with a swing at the top and a metal grating at the bottom. The former gets in the way of the bird's head when it is sitting on the perch and prevents its flapping its wings; the latter prevents its resting its feet on the flat surface of the cage bottom and collects quantities of dirt, materially increasing the trouble of cleaning the cage. Both these stupid devices should be removed at once.

The tray at the bottom of the average parrot cage is made of very thin metal covered with a thin coat of white enamel. The first time the cage is washed the enamel begins to come off the bottom, exposing the metal, which is specially chosen for its liability to rust. In a very short time it has rusted right through and can then be replaced by a serviceable tray of very solid metal, which will neither rust nor split at the corners. The tray at the bottom of a parrot cage should be thickly covered with gritty sand — sea-sand is excellent when obtainable. If, as most people do, you

1

sand the tray as sparingly as though you were sprinkling gold dust, there will tend to be an unpleasant smell from the unabsorbed moisture of the droppings, the bird's feet will constantly be fouled and the difficulty of cleaning the tray will be much increased, as the droppings will adhere firmly to the metal and solidify.

A parrot's cage should not be covered with a cloth at night.

A caged parrot, in addition to food and drinking water, should be frequently supplied with a small bit of turf, a small twiggy branch of any non-poisonous deciduous tree — oak, ash, elm, lime, beech, hazel, etc. — to bite up, and with a bath. The latter should be fairly shallow, too heavy for the bird to tip over, easy to step into, not too slippery, and of sufficient size. It should be placed, if possible, in such a position that the droppings from the perch fall clear of it. If a parrot is slow in taking an interest in turf, twigs, bath, or for that matter any kind of food that would be beneficial to it, do not be discouraged, but continue to offer them at regular intervals, for months if need be. Sooner or later they are pretty sure to be patronized. It took me nearly two years to induce my Bourke's Parrakeets to partake of any green stuff.

Many parrots which do not bathe freely love to be stood out in a shower of warm rain, or, in winter, to be sprayed with tepid water. But never force a shower bath on a bird that not only objects to the first few drops that fall on it, but continues to object after a minute has passed.

The only really effective way of disinfecting a parrot cage is to scorch every part of it with the flame of a blowtorch. You can never quite trust disinfectants to do their work.

A rectangular cage two feet ten inches long, two feet wide, and one foot eight inches high of wire netting on a good solid metal frame with an equally substantial metal tray at the bottom is useful for newly-arrived parakeets, as it allows them a certain amount of wing exercise. Put the perch as near to one end of the cage as will permit the bird's tail just to clear the wire when it is sitting with its back towards it. That will leave a foot or two of flying space from the perch to the wire of the further end. With delicate birds it is a good thing to have a sheet of zinc to hook on to the back and ends of the cage to keep off draughts. The sand tray must be fairly substantial and of a good fit. Nothing is more maddening than trying to push a tray that has buckled out of shape and split at the corners in or out of a cage containing a nervous bird. If the parrakeets in the cage are small, be careful, when you are cleaning, to stop up the space where the tray goes in; otherwise you will return to find them loose in the birdroom, or, if a window or door be open, in the garden.

Never put any kind of paint or varnish on any parrot cage or aviary, or the birds will nibble it and get poisoned. Creosote, when dry, is, however, a safe dressing for woodwork.

Scarlet Macaw. The Scarlet Macaw, also called Red and Yellow Macaw, is offered for sale more frequently than any other Macaw. This large bird makes a good pet but requires a very roomy aviary strong enough to stand up to its destructive beak. Photo by Horst Mueller.

A pair of Abyssinian Love Birds. The male is at left. Drawing by R. A. Vowles.

Blue Eared Lorikeet. Photo by Horst Mueller.

African Grey Parrots make very friendly and affectionate pets if they are handled properly. Photo by Sam Fehrenz.

African Grey Parrot. Although the configuration of the African Grey Parrot is less pleasing than that of other good talkers, the alertly curious expression of a good African Grey makes it look especially intelligent. Photo by Horst Mueller.

There are two types of outdoor aviaries which can be considered really satisfactory — movable aviaries and fixed ones with the floor, both of shelter and flight, made of brick, concrete, or similar hard material which is as easily washed and disinfected as the floor of a well-made dog kennel. The usual type of outdoor aviary — a fixed one with an earthen floor to the flight — is a disease-trap which gets steadily more destructive the longer it stands. No experienced pheasant breeder would think of trying to rear his stock year after year in the same run, yet far more delicate birds are treated as though they were immune from the harmful effects of stale ground. Of course, if you like, you can keep such an aviary filled by buying six times as many birds of a certain species as you would need to do if you housed your first pair in a healthy fashion so that there was no need to constantly replace casualties; or, when the ground becomes "sick" to one species, you can try new ones that for a time do not suffer so much. But this is hardly good aviculture, nor even particularly humane treatment of animals. Re-turfing and disinfecting the ground with lime may be a palliative to the evils of a fixed site, but in practice I have found it a poor one.

A rectangular movable aviary, twenty-four feet by eight feet by eight feet, gives very good breeding results with parakeets not larger than a King and also with the smaller cockatoos. The aviary, including the whole of the floor, is covered with strong half-inch mesh wire netting and the wooden framework of the flight is on the outside of the wire and not on the inside. The object of covering the floor is to exclude rats and other burrowing animals. Grass quickly grows through the meshes and makes the wire invisible. Young mice can get through even half-inch mesh, but full grown ones have difficulty in doing so and frequently share the fate of the vegetarian weasel in the fable which entered a barn by a small hole when he was thin and found egress impossible when he had fattened on the farmer's store. The advantage of having the wooden framework on the outside is that the birds cannot bite it, nor can they sit on it and soil it with their droppings.

In the top left-hand corner of the aviary flight is a small hinged door that opens inward and upward. This door can be propped open at any time when it is desired to set a bird at liberty; it should have a fastening on the outside as well as on the inside or a playful bird may undo and open it. The same door is used when the catching box is brought into operation. This catching box is a rectangular box of wire netting two feet six inches by one foot six inches with an inside lining of taut string netting to keep the birds from knocking themselves against the wire and hurting their heads and nostrils. It is made to hook to the top of the aviary in front of the small top corner door and it is itself fitted with a wooden door, corresponding in size to the aperture of the top door, which slides in a groove from left to right. When you desire to catch a bird, hook the catching box onto the aviary, push back the slide of the catching box, undo the fastenings of the little top door, and tie one end of a longish bit of string round the base of the top door (the top door should be of wire on a wooden frame). Pass the other end of the string through a mesh of the wire in the aviary roof so as to supply leverage for pulling the top door open against the roof of the aviary. Then take your stand about half way back in the aviary flight, still holding the string in your hand, and then either yourself, or with the help of an assistant, gently drive the bird you wish to capture into the catching box. As soon as it enters the box, slacken the string you are holding and the top door, if properly oiled and working freely, as it should be before you start operations, falls downward of its own weight, making the bird a prisoner. You then mount a pair of steps, push forward and fasten the slide of the catching box, close and fasten the top door, and the capture is safely effected without any chasing about with a net. It is very important in the hurry of the moment, not to forget the catching box slide. If you do, as soon as you unhook the catching box the bird darts out to freedom and the catching has to be done over again — under much more difficult circumstances! Of course a very wary bird may refuse to enter the catching box, especially if it has been caught in it before; in that case, other methods have to be adopted. When a net is used, always cover the rim with thick, soft padding.

In the bottom left-hand corner of the front of the aviary flight is an entrance door four feet six inches by two feet six inches. In the centre of the front of the aviary flight, three feet six inches above the ground, is a small door one foot two inches by one foot; just inside this door and practically on a level with it is a metal bracket holding the bath and fruit dish, and when necessary, a seed dish as well.

The wire roof at the front end of the aviary flight is covered with corrugated metal to give some protection from sun and rain, and further protection is afforded by other sheets of corrugated metal which cover the shelter and project about two feet over the shelter end of the flight.

In addition, a flat circular piece of wood four feet in diameter is fixed on the outside of the centre of the wire roof of the aviary flight. Four perches diverging to the four corners of the aviary flight are fastened at one end to a stout piece of wood two feet six inches in length in the centre of the flight, this piece of wood being attached to the circular shelter disc above, as the stalk of a mushroom is attached to the umbrella portion. The other end of the left-hand front perch runs up to the bottom end of the little top door in the left-hand corner, thus leading a bird up to the catching box when the door is open.

The aviary shelter itself is two feet six inches deep from back to front and the same height as the flight. In the centre of the front of the shelter, eleven inches from the top, is a window one foot eight inches long and one foot high. In the right-hand corner, ten inches from the top and nine and one-half inches from the side, is a circular entrance hole five inches in diameter. This entrance hole can be closed by a down-dropping slide eight inches by six and one-half inches, which runs in a groove and is raised by a twenty-five foot length of picture wire running through brass screw-eyes and a pulley at either right-angle bend. The wire terminates in a length of cord, and a loop is made in the cord to slip over a check on the outside of the front of the flight when the slide is pulled up. In addition to the large window in the front, the shelter has four other small windows eight and one-half inches by six and one-half inches, covered with wire netting on the inside, as are the whole of the back and two sides of the shelter. Two of these windows are in the sides of the shelter seven inches from the top; one is exactly opposite the entrance hole so that its light may encourage a bird to pass through and the other is in the same relative position on the other side of the back of the flight. In the right-hand side of the shelter is a small door one foot square on the inside of which is fixed a stout bit of wire to hold the seed dish and another to hold a small receptacle for water which is only needed when birds are confined to the shelter and have not access to the bath in the flight.

The shelter has three perches one foot six inches from the top, running from back to front and so arranged that no droppings fall into the seed dish. One of these perches leads up to the entrance hole and a corresponding perch in the flight also leads up to the entrance hole, care being taken to fasten the ends of the perches as close as possible to the lower edge of the entrance hole, so that birds do not have to jump up and jump down when passing through.

The floor of the shelter should be of metal and sufficiently strong for the person cleaning out the aviary to tread on it without causing damage. It should be thickly covered with dry sand. On no account use damp sand, as this is liable to cause chills.

The roof of the shelter should be made waterproof and mouseproof with corrugated metal on top. The corrugated metal should project somewhat into the flight so as to overhang the cross perch in the flight, already mentioned as being nine inches from the front of the aviary shelter. The aviary shelter itself should always be boarded with tongue-and-grooved lumber. Where hard-biting birds are kept, such as the bigger broadtails, Ringnecks, and parrots, the woodwork of the front of the aviary shelter must be covered with wire netting, but for the smaller broatails and Asiatic parakeets, lovebirds, etc., this is unecessary. In the case of cockatoos, pileated parakeets, and other hard-biting birds, an inner layer of very strong wire netting of the thickest possible gauge must be used throughout the aviary inside the fine mesh wire netting, an outer covering of which is required to exclude mice.

II

Aviary Management

With accommodation of the type described in the last chapter, even a very large collection of forty or fifty aviaries, containing as many breeding pairs, is easily managed and for the greater part of the year involves but little labour.

First thing in the morning the aviary attendant goes 'round pulling up the slides if the birds have been shut into the shelters for the night. He then takes a box of mixed seed on his arm (with two or more divisions, if two or more seed mixtures are in use), unlocks the little side door of each aviary shelter and replenishes the food dish, at the same time carefully observing the birds to which the aviary belongs to see that they have come through the night in health and safety.

After breakfast he goes along the front of the aviaries with a can of water and a supply of apples, opens each little front door communicating with the bath and fruit dish bracket, tips the contents of the bath, if clean, into the fruit dish to wash it out, and refills the bath. When the watering is finished, he shuts one pair of birds into the flight by dropping the slide, opens the door at the back of the shelter, and cleans the interior. When the interior of the shelter has been thoroughly cleaned with the aid of a non-poisonous disinfectant, the seed dish is also taken out, washed, and refilled with fresh seed. When the shelter is finished, the attendant goes 'round to the front of the flight, pulls up the slide to re-admit the birds to the shelter, gathers a bunch of twiggy branches of some non-poisonous, deciduous tree that the birds enjoy nibbling, ties it up in the flight, and removes any old sticks that may be left from last time. Since the birds occupy only the aviary shelter to a great extent at night, it is usually sufficient to clean one shelter a day in rotation, unless a bird has fallen ill. In which case it is prudent to clean and disinfect the shelter at once, even if it be out of its turn. When the cleaning of the shelter is finished, the work for the day, apart from looking the birds over, is normally ended unless there are heaters to be attended to. In the right-hand bottom corner of each aviary shelter, three feet six inches from the ground, is a wooden

6

box with a zinc top; a door one foot two inches by ten inches at the left-hand end; an open wire front facing inwards and separating the interior of the box from the interior of the aviary shelter. In the box is placed any brooder lamp or other heating apparatus which experience has proven to be safe and which will neither produce fumes nor cause an outbreak of fire.

The zinc top of the heater box should have an air space of one inch separating it from the outer wooden top so that if it becomes too hot it will not char or set fire to the wood. In mild climates, no heating provision may be necessary, but in districts where the winter is very severe, some form of electric heating servicing the entire range of aviaries which will, of course, be on a fixed site will have to be installed.

For very large parakeets, such as Red Shinings, a twenty-four foot aviary may not be long enough to provide the wing exercise necessary to secure fertility in the cocks. An extension of twenty feet may be made to the end of the flight, detachable from the rest, for a forty foot aviary would be too long and cumbersome to move in one piece.

Where a number of cock Barrabands and Rock Peplars are kept as day-liberty birds, a communication passage of wire netting three feet nine inches by two feet by one foot nine inches may be constructed to join two or more aviary flights together, but it is advisable to have some means of closing these passages by a sliding partition pulled by a string from the end of the aviary in case any birds behave in a tiresome fashion and dodge to and fro when you want to shut them into the shelters for the night. The shelters themselves, in order to accommodate more birds in comfort and without quarreling, should be about a foot wider than the ordinary ones and should have a few extra perches.

When the aviaries are to be moved onto fresh ground, the grass at the bottom must first be cut and torn up so as to free the wire bottom. This is a rather dirty and tedious job and a pair of canvas gloves is desirable, as well as a flat board to kneel on. When the wire is quite free of the ground, the aviary is raised on wooden rollers ten feet long and seven inches in diameter by the aid of blocks and crowbars and is slid forward onto a fresh site. Four handy men can move a twenty-four foot aviary bodily with tolerable ease and as it is unnecessary to enter the aviary during the actual process of moving, the birds are not unduly alarmed. The use of blocks and tackle would probably facilitate the process even more. October is the best month to begin moving. If the vacated site is ever to be occupied again, it should receive a good dressing of lime and agricultural salt. The former improves the quality of the herbage by making the droppings assimilable as plant food. The salt acts as a useful soil disinfectant. Lime as a disinfectant is perfectly useless and is never to be relied on to destroy germs or parasitic worms.

When a bird dies of an infectious complaint, such as tuberculosis, the

whole of the aviary should be scorched with a blowtorch, particular attention being paid to the wire bottom and sand trays. The perches should be
burned and the woodwork re-creosoted. The aviary should be moved onto
a fresh site and the vacated site given a very heavy dressing of salt—heavy
enough to kill temporarily the grass completely. When rain has washed
the salt sufficiently far into the ground for it to be no longer injurious to
plant life, the ground may be re-seeded with rye grass.

The time of moving is also a good opportunity to give the outside
woodwork of the aviary and particularly the bottom frame a dressing
with creosote. Do not put wet creosote where the birds are likely to stain
their plumage, and be careful to keep it off the wire, for creosote on wire
netting remains wet and sticky for weeks. Ordinary workmen are often
very careless in this matter.

While I do not advise a smaller aviary than a twenty-four foot by eight
foot by eight foot, one for breeding young of the medium-sized parakeets
of a quality equal to their wild parents, it is possible to keep birds for a
good number of years in excellent plumage in much smaller and consequently less expensive quarters. They may even breed, anyhow for the
first few seasons, but their offspring should not be sold at the price of
imported birds.

It is very unfair to ask a fellow aviculturist a biggish price for birds
which may look all right, but will only be a source of vexation and loss
as breeders by reason of their lack of stamina, the cocks proving infertile
and the hens getting egg-bound, or at best producing nothing but weak
and deformed young.

These degenerate birds, bred in very small aviaries, are best given
away as pets to people who cannot afford to buy parakeets. If a letter be
sent to some well-known fanciers' paper offering to give the birds to a
good home and stating their needs and also their drawbacks, a very large
number of applications will be received — so large, in fact, that it is wise
to stipulate that no telegrams nor stamped envelopes be sent and no replies
expected by unsuccessful applicants. From these applications it is easy
to make a satisfactory selection and you have the pleasure of knowing
that not only have the birds gone to a place where they will be cared for
as priceless treasures, but you have given great joy and interest to a bird
lover in a less fortunate position than yourself.

Any bird can be disposed of in this manner, no matter how common,
uninteresting, or even defective, and it is a thousand times better to send
it where it will be really appreciated than to bestow it on some rather
unenthusiastic friend or neighbour, or worse still, dump it at a zoo where
it is even less welcome. When the bird is despatched, full directions as to
its treatment should be sent with it; in this way sound knowledge as to
correct management can be extended — a very desirable thing in an age

when people still exist who think it may be right to slit a parrot's tongue in order to encourage it to talk!

Where lack of space or the unevenness of the ground makes it impossible to put up movable aviaries, there is nothing for it but to erect fixed ones with a concrete or tiled floor. In the hard material a hole should be left so that the nesting tree trunk can stand on earth and if there is any risk of rats finding their way up through the hole it can be covered with wire netting. It is most important that the floor of a fixed aviary have a slight slope and a drainage trench which runs off all rainwater immediately. If it collects in pools at the middle or at the sides, the birds will constantly be drinking water fouled by their own droppings.

The shelter should contain as little unnecessary lumber as possible so that it can easily be cleaned and disinfected. Be careful to see that the partition between aviary compartments does not allow birds to damage each other by fighting through the wire. Two large parakeets cannot do much harm to each other through half-inch mesh, but it is dangerous to put a small-beaked species next to a large, quarrelsome neighbour. I once had the upper mandible of a fine cock Hooded Parakeet completely torn off by a Barnard fighting him through half-inch wire. Two Barnards could not have got a grip on each other, but the Hooded's slender beak went right through the mesh. Double wire partitions are therefore essential to protect beaks and toes.

When birds are kept in a fixed aviary it is a good plan to keep a large tray of fresh turf in the flight and another of earth on which oats are thrown to sprout. Green food must also be provided. This, either in cage or aviary, should have its stalks pushed firmly into a vessel of water that is not easily upset. In this way it keeps fresh much longer.

When new birds are turned into an aviary for the first time, keep them shut into the shelter for a few days until they become used to it and know where to find the food. Some species are at first very stupid and obstinate about allowing themselves to be driven into the shelter for the night. For very difficult cases it is well to keep in readiness a wing of netting on a wooden frame which can be hooked onto the wire mesh of the top of the aviary flight so as to form a blind alley leading up to the entrance hole into the shelter. This will make it less easy for them to keep on breaking back towards the front of the flight. Shutting up can be left until a quarter of an hour before sunset, but when you have new birds allow ample time for getting them in in case they give trouble. Never leave shutting up until it is getting dark as the birds are then apt to knock themselves about if disturbed. Never, also, when driving birds in, forget to close the door of the flight properly behind you. I once lost a Bourke's Parrakeet through neglect of this precaution.

A collection of birds should be looked over carefully after daybreak and at 2:30 p.m. in winter, and after daybreak and at 5:30 p.m. in summer, to see if they are showing signs of incipient illness. Never leave a bird that is showing signs of illness, however slight, where it is until the following day. If you do, it will certainly be dead or dying next morning. With sick birds a stitch in time saves not nine, but ninety-nine. When a bird has recovered from an illness, never return it to exactly the same surroundings in no better condition than it was in when it fell ill; if you do it is sure to get ill again. Either wait till it is in better health, or give it more protection.

A parrot when ill partly closes its eyes and usually, though not invariably, ruffles its feathers and is inclined to put its head "under its wing." A bird which sits with its head "under its wing" and both feet on the perch is practically always ill, but if it has one foot tucked up it is only sleepy. A sick bird has the lower breast and abdomen more puffed than a sleepy one.

Some birds when dozing may be seen to ruffle up a lot on the back and wings, but if the feathers of the breast and belly are fully tight, probably all is well. A bird that stretches itself has seldom much the matter; neither has one that cocks its head sideways to look at an object above or below it. Vomiting is a common sign of chill. The action is quite different from that of a bird in breeding condition bringing up food from its crop and either re-swallowing it or feeding its toes, the end of the perch, or its owner. When a parrot vomits, it allows the food to run from the beak onto the ground, or gets rid of it with a shake of the head and the head feathers usually get more or less messed up. Occasionally a parakeet will vomit to get rid of some objectionable substance in the crop without being really unwell, but in ninety-nine cases out of a hundred vomiting means a chill.

Newly-imported birds, are, of course, usually very sensitive to cold and sudden changes of temperature, but do not forget that the main cause of illness in acclimatized birds, i.e., those which have had a complete moult in an outdoor aviary, is not cold and wet but weather, or other conditions, which favour the rapid multiplication of, and assumption of, a virulent nature by bacteria inimical to birds. You may, therefore, expect the largest number of cases of sickness during the summer and autumn and during mild spells in winter. Periods of extreme cold and wet may lower the birds' vitality but they are even harder on our enemy, the microbe, so during the most inclement winter weather, if the birds are reasonably housed and fed, there is seldom any sickness among acclimatized stock. For the same reason, large and sudden drops in temperature are more dangerous in relatively high temperatures than in relatively low ones. A drop from eighty-six degrees Fahrenheit to fifty-five degrees is more likely to produce casualties than a drop from fifty-five degrees to twenty-five degrees.

When looking birds over, never make the mistake of not troubling to get a sight of some individual because it has always seemed so robust that you are sure no illness could possibly overtake it. More than once I have lost an old favourite, which has braved the storms of many winters, through rashly assuming, on a lovely June day, that it could not possibly have got ill and must only be in the shelter feeding.

Birds are very regular in their habits and tend to do the same thing at the same time in the same way. An observant bird keeper soon gets to know the ways of each individual in his collection and any deviation from its normal custom should at once be enquired into as a possible indication of sickness. Do not make up explanations in your head as to why that bird was not in its accustomed place or flew from an unusual corner. Look for them.

An indispensable adjunct to any large collection is a hospital room where the temperature can be maintained at an even eighty-five degrees even in the coldest weather. The hospital need not be large, as it will not have to accommodate any great number of birds at one time, but it must be well-insulated so as to be as little affected as possible by the outside temperature. If it is a wooden building, it must have double boards with a sawdust-filled space between and double windows. Vita-glass is to be preferred for all hospital, birdroom, and aviary shelter windows.

For heating hospital or birdroom, nothing equals thermostatically controlled electricity, which has only one serious drawback — that of being at times rather expensive. There are various makes of electric heaters which are movable and can be placed beside a sick bird's cage in such a way that it can have a nice choice of temperature. If it wishes to sit on a perch close to the side of the cage nearest to the heater it can enjoy an even temperature of nearly ninety degrees, or it can move away, if the cage is not too small, to a temperature or eighty degrees or less. If you have a very valuable bird very dangerously ill, such an arrangement is of priceless advantage. The vagaries of all forms of heating dependent on stove or furnace are in such circumstances maddening. No stove or furnace (oil stoves excepted) can be trusted to keep an even temperature for more than five hours without attention. In the evening it will half roast the bird and before morning, if you do not get up two or three times in the night to attend to it, it will be dangerously low and your patient will be in extremis. Gas heating is not quite so bad, but unless you can by some means prevent the fumes getting into the room, your whole collection may be asphyxiated.

If you cannot afford a proper hospital, you may be able inside a room to construct something of boards and glass which will hold a cage or cages, and which can be kept at an even eighty-five degrees by means of one or more of the heaters already referred to as being useful for warming an aviary shelter. Hospital cages for sick birds are also sometimes on the market. If you decide to dispense with all high-temperature appliances and make use of the kitchen or the greenhouse with its immense variation of temperature, you will lose about three-quarters of your sick birds instead of saving about three-quarters.

Another indispensable adjunct to a collection is a quarantine room, also well heated, where new arrivals can be kept for at least two weeks to make sure they are not suffering from some dangerous infectious ailment You may neglect the precaution for months or even years without mishap, but sooner or later you will regret it.

Many years ago at my old home, I received an apparently healthy Bauer's Parakeet and turned her with a cut wing into a small walled garden. About four days later she developed septic fever of the most virulent type. Not only did every bird which was at all susceptible to the disease in that enclosure die, but full-winged liberty birds that occasionally came in to feed also caught the infection and spread it about the garden. I lost every King, Crimson-wing, Redrump, Blue Bonnet, Grass Parrakeet, and Many-colour in my collection, and I could never from that day onward, for years after, keep any of the four last mentioned species either in cage, aviary, or at liberty, without their falling victims before many months had passed.

Birdrooms necessarily vary enormously in size, shape, and arrangement; but a good birdroom should always be easy to keep scrupulously clean and should be very light. It should get plenty of winter sun, but should have arrangements for shading in summer, as parrots hate very hot sunshine and often fall victims to sunstroke if unable to escape it. Apart from perches, the less wood and the more metal there is about the structure of a birdroom, the better. Natural perches are best for flight cages and they can be removed and burned as they get dirty or worn out. Do not crowd a flight cage with too many perches, but allow the birds the maximum of room for wing exercise. An even temperature in a birdroom is very desirable. We hear a lot about birds being able to stand cold at night because even in the tropics the nights are very chilly, but all I know is that if you allow this sort of tropic night to be produced in your birdroom you are likely to be the possessor of a good many corpses.

If a bird accidentally escapes, the first thing to do is to put food on the top of the aviary or aviaries it is most likely to visit, and to keep the whole place as quiet and free from disturbance as you can until it has come down and fed. A bird that has found your artificial food after escaping is already more than half caught. You can gradually work the food under or into some sort of trap and a capture will soon be accomplished. If you locate the stray at some distance, go in pursuit of it with a trap feeding tray and a decoy — its mate for choice. A very good form of trap feeding tray consists of a kind of hinged dish-cover arrangement of wire netting two feet nine inches by two feet three inches and one foot three inches high at the apex, and provided with an inner lining of taut string netting one and one-half inches from the wire, to prevent the bird hurting its head should it fly up in alarm as the trap falls. The dish-cover part is propped up on a short bit of stick to which a long line is attached and well inside is placed a dish of seed containing no peanuts.

When you set the trap close to the decoy's cage be careful to see that the prop pulls away easily and the trap falls quickly. A hanging fall of the trap may alarm the bird and it may get caught and severely injured by the descending rim as it tries to escape. The shorter the stick the quicker, and consequently the safer the fall, so the trap should be propped up no higher than is necessary to allow the bird to enter. Do not pull the moment the bird is inside, but wait till it settles to feed and is unsuspicious. In the front of the dish-cover part of the trap is a small door of just sufficient size to admit the arm through which the bird can be driven into a cage or caught by hand.

If you intend to keep birds at liberty, send a courteous note to neighbours whose property they are likely to visit, asking them to use their influence to prevent their being shot. A similar notice in the local paper is also desirable. There are, unfortunately, a good many persons about who will shoot a strange bird to find out what it is, or in mistake for a hawk; but very few are so utterly lacking in good feeling as to shoot a neighbour's pet bird knowing that it belongs to him. People who get their birds shot have often only themselves to thank for neglecting to make it widely known that they keep foreign birds at liberty.

Never let your birds be a nuisance to your neighbours, but keep fruit-eating species and fruit bud-eating species shut up at those seasons of the year when they are inclined to be mischievous. If damage is done, compensate liberally.

Keep also on good terms with the children and youths of the district and when you send a subscription to Scouts, Guides, football teams, etc., ask that they will do you a good turn by using their influence to prevent ignorant or mischievous persons from injuring your birds.

Never keep quarrelling birds together. There is no greater or commoner form of cruelty which aviculturists indulge in through their greed than to cram as many birds as possible into an aviary. How would they like it, I wonder, if they were confined, without means of escape, with some savage bully who was perpetually seeking to injure or destroy them? If one bird dislikes another sufficiently to fly the whole length of the aviary in order to attack it, those birds should be separated at once.

Vermin, of course have to be dealt with. Mice are always a nuisance, but an aviary of one-half inch mesh netting kept in good repair with a mouse-proof shelter should not give them much chance. If, however, you can obtain an even finer mesh, get it. Rats and weasels can be excluded by seeing that the netting is kept in good repair, particular attention being paid to the floor netting at the time of the annual shift of movable aviaries. For weasels, unbaited tunnel traps of bricks and turf with the trap set in the middle are often effective. Hawks and other predatory birds are at times a nuisance and though parakeets are usually too wide awake to allow themselves to be caught, a hawk scares them badly and Barrabands frightened by a hawk in the afternoon will sometimes refuse to return to the feeding aviary and roost out, thus exposing themselves to a far more deadly enemy, the owl. Hawks are usually rather punctual and regular in their habits when one is not carrying a gun, appearing at the same time each day and following the same line of flight. When one is armed they are extremely irregular and unpunctual, but now and then they forget and one has one's chance. A very long shot should be taken if a nearer one is not offered and if they take themselves off for good your object is gained. Rooks and Jackdaws occasionally show a disposition to mob cockatoos and large parakeets. A shot or two will teach them to mind their manners for a considerable time. Starlings are a great plague in the breeding season as they occupy every available nest box and nest hole. Some pairs are extremely savage and determined, and I have known them to defeat even such powerful birds as Pennants and Mealy Rosellas when the latter have been trying to nest at liberty. Constant persecution of the starling population with an air rifle or walking-stick gun is the best remedy.

The owner of a collection of foreign birds should cultivate a lively imagination, combined with an ability to foresee coming evils, equal to that of the prophet Jeremiah. Whenever you make any disposition with regard to a bird, always try to think of all the catastrophes that may result in consequence and endeavor to guard against them. There is generally just one you have not thought of, but if so, you will remember it next time! In the same way, consider the possible evil effects of any changes in the environment of your birds, for which you are not responsible and, if you can, meet them also. For example, if the temperature drops to twenty degrees below the freezing point in May when you have a valuable hen nesting in a shelter, put in a heater to stop her from getting egg-bound. Do not wait until she gets egg-bound, for even if by treatment you save the bird you will lose the eggs, for a parakeet, once egg-bound, hardly ever sits.

While experience is naturally of the greatest value, it is true to say that good aviary attendants are born and not made. An aviary attendant must possess the gift of being able to detect the very earliest signs of illness; he should be painstaking and clean in his work; it should be possible to trust him to carry out implicitly in one's absence even orders of which he does not himself see the sense. He should possess the prophetic vision of possible evil already alluded to. He should be keen enough on his job to be willing in time of emergency to sacrifice, without being ordered to do so, a Saturday afternoon or Sunday to recapturing a strayed bird, and he should be ready to get up in the middle of a winter night to attend to a sick one because he feels the threatened loss as keenly as the owner.

Sometimes talent appears in very unlikely quarters, quite elderly men who have never had anything to do with foreign birds quickly attain a skill and reliability that is hard to beat.

Women also make good aviary attendants, often showing quickness of observation and great devotion to their charges, coupled with scrupulous care in carrying out instructions.

The worst possible type of aviary attendant is a lad — particularly a country one. There may be honourable exceptions, but boys present, as a general rule, an almost perfect combination of all the qualities least to be desired. Even people of moderate means who cannot afford a whole-time aviary attendant, but include the care of the aviary with other work, would be very well advised to pay the difference between a man's and a boy's wages in order to secure someone who will discharge all his duties with far more intelligence, trustworthiness, and care than the average youngster.

Occasionally circumstances compel one to take charge of nestling birds which have not yet fed themselves. If young enough to have no fear and open their beaks for food, the larger species may be reared as recommended in the article on Rock Peplars on page 189. The degree of heat supplied must be in proportion to the age and development of the brood. Very tiny babies may need a temperature of eighty-five degrees. Older nestlings which are fledged and have learned the fear of human beings will usually begin to feed themselves as soon as they get really starving. They should be placed in a box cage in a very warm situation. Blotting paper should be substituted for sand on the cage floor, as sand gets into the birds' eyes and beaks as they are struggling to get out. The floor of the cage should be sprinkled with well soaked canary and millet seed, shelled soaked sunflower, cracked soaked hemp, and stale brown breadcrumbs almost as fine as powder. The food should be constantly renewed as it gets dry, or is scratched into corners.

If the young bird is growing dangerously weak, or appears to have caught a chill, forced feeding must be resorted to. For emergencies of this kind, there is nothing better than a raw egg beaten up in half a cupful of new milk and administered, a drop at a time, from the end of a small camel-hair paintbrush. Wrap the bird in a handkerchief and hold it gently but firmly in the left hand, the first finger and thumb keeping its head as steady as possible. Place the drop of milk at the side of the upper mandible, near the lower edge, and towards the tip. If it keeps its beak firmly closed you will need an assistant to hold the bird while you open its beak and administer the food in very small quantities at a time. Do not give more than three or four drops at the first feeding, as too much milk given before a bird is used to it, is liable to induce vomiting, and it is better to give a little which is kept down than a larger quantity which reappears. As soon as possible mix some whole wheat, rye, or a dark bread with the milk and get the bird onto a more natural and less liquid diet.

Take great care not to mess the bird's plumage, either with the milk or with the perspiration from your hand, as a bird with its feathers messed up is liable to chill and also feels uncomfortable and wretched. A meal should be given not less often than once in three hours and if possible once or twice during the night if the patient is in a weak state. As soon as it starts to eat seed or breadcrumbs, the milk can be soon discontinued, as it is too stimulating for a bird that is well nourished. The young of very small species, even when healthy, are often easier to feed from the tip of a camel-hair paintbrush than from the mouth or fingers, especially when they are only beginning to get used to their human foster parents.

The requirements of parrot-like birds in the matter of nesting accommodation are of so varied a nature that little general advice can be given. It is always, however, wise to have the entrance holes facing north, as some species are very particular that their front door should have this aspect, possibly because it is cooler in tropical countries.

In wild birds what may be termed the mental factor is often almost as important as the physical, where success in breeding is to be achieved. A nest that takes a hen's fancy is a powerful incentive to her to lay and conversely the lack of an attractive nest is likely to keep her from laying, even if by good management her reproductive organs have been brought into a state of pronounced activity.

It is a good sign if, very soon after the nest is put in, the hen is seen to go right inside, although it may only be for a few moments.

It is a bad sign if she repeatedly flies off after a hurried glance at the entrance hole; if she pointedly ignores the entrance and for days searches every other part of the nest but the right one for a way in; or if, after showing some interest in the nest for the first few days, her visits of inspection grow steadily fewer and shorter; all these evidences of dissatisfaction should point to the immediate need of providing other types of nest that may prove more attractive. King and Crimsonwing Parakeets like a tremendously deep nest box in which they can climb down from a height of about six feet nearly to ground level. Always, of course, make the interior of a nest climbable by a strip of wire netting tacked to the side.

Cactus Conures. The Cactus Conure, from southeastern Brazil, makes up for its lack of gaudy color by its friendly, outgoing personality. Kept with other Conures, it is reasonably peaceful. Cactus Conures reach a length of about eleven inches. Photo by Horst Mueller.

Bee Bee Parrot. The Bee Parrot, also known as Tovi Parrakeet and Orange Chinned Parrakeet, is a peaceful and sociable dwarf parrot; some individuals become proficient at talking, but most Bee Bees are not good talkers. This common and inexpensive species reaches a length of about six and a half inches.

Top to bottom: yellow variety of Redrump Parrakeet; lutino variety of Nyassaland Love Bird; blue variety of Masked Love Bird. Drawing by R. A. Vowles.

III

Notes on Breeding

Although there are a few exceptions, most members of the parrot family, when breeding, are very intolerant of the presence of their own and allied species, and each pair must be kept separately.

Most parrot-like birds, also, are unsafe companions for birds of other orders and most use no nesting material, laying their white eggs at the bottom of a hollow in a decayed tree trunk. Nearly all like their nest to be a little on the small side and the entrance hole leading to it to be also rather small, but care must, of course, be taken not to provide boxes so small that the young cannot develop properly and not to provide entrance holes so narrow that birds cannot get through them, especially if they are weak-billed species which cannot enlarge the holes by biting the wood. The interior of nest boxes must be made climbable by tacking a strip of wire netting to the side below the entrance. Although they are rather heavy to move in some cases, natural hollow tree trunks make good and attractive nests, especially for the larger species, such as cockatoos. They can be made a little more easy to handle if they are cut in transverse sections, the sections being fastened together temporarily when the nest has been erected in a suitable position.

Wooden nest boxes are of two kinds; hanging boxes with a wooden bottom; and "grandfather clock" nest boxes seven or more feet in height. These latter have a bottom of fine mesh wire netting to exclude mice and are filled to the necessary height with peat moss, on the top of which a handful or so of soft decayed wood is placed. The bottom of the nest should be, in most cases, about eighteen inches below the entrance hole. In the case of grass parrakeets a rather shorter "climb-down" is desirable, while in the case of King and Crimson-wing Parakeets an extremely long climb-down is preferred, the nest being only a few inches above ground level. One reason why so many people find that their Kings and Crimson-wings do not take to the nest box, but prefer to lay on the ground, is that they have not provided anything like a long enough climb-down. If possible, provide a pair of birds with more than one nest box and give the different

17

boxes different aspects, as some birds like a northerly aspect for the entrance hole and others a southerly one.

Always, if you possibly can, place the nest boxes in the flight and not in the shelter, as young bred in an aviary shelter are far more likely to be rickety. You can provide a little overhead shelter from sun and torrential rain, but a certain amount of rain falling on a nest box does not matter if it has a good lid, especially if it be the grandfather clock type.

Some hen birds, however, do not take kindly to a grandfather clock nest and tend to burrow about too much in the soft material at the bottom, sometimes burying their eggs. Such birds need to be provided with nest boxes with hard wooden bottoms, these bottoms being always concave to prevent the eggs from rolling about.

A few inches above the level of the actual nest it is a good plan to have a little inspection door cut in the side of the box, but the greatest care must be taken that this door cannot get opened accidentally, or be opened by the birds themselves playing with the catch.

If a hen bird apparently in breeding condition does not settle down as she should to a nest box, or, after an initial interest in it, seem later to grow tired of it and to want something different, try, if you can, to meet her fancy by providing other boxes of a different type. With birds the psychological factor is nearly, if not quite, as important, where breeding success is concerned, as the physical factor of good health. A box that takes a hen's often capricious fancy, is a most powerful inducement to her to go to nest. Double brooded parakeets should always be provided with at least two nest boxes of similar type, for many of them have the Budgerigar's habit of laying again before the young of the first round have left the nest, the cock taking sole charge of their feeding.

Some cock parakeets, particularly Redrumps and their near allies and certain grass parrakeets, such as Turquoisines, very quickly tire of their offspring. The males, especially, must be watched most carefully in case they should turn on their sons and kill them. I have even known a cock Barraband do this though the habit is very rare in members of that sub-genus. The larger broadtails, Rosellas, etc., may also need watching though they do not usually tire of their offspring as quickly as the Redrump family.

Most parrots and cockatoos are tolerant of the presence of their young for a long period after they have left the nest but some breeders have found that in this respect Leadbeater's Cockatoo is an exception.

If young parakeets have to be taken away from their parents at a rather early age, keep them at a comfortably warm temperature and scatter seed, both soaked and dry, all over the floor of the cage. On no account place the seed only in a dish. It is usually the smaller seeds such as canary, that the young of even the larger parakeets will first begin to pick up. A little soft food in the shape of milk-sop made with whole meal bread and mashed up apple may also be offered. This, for cleanliness sake, can be put in a dish; but the birds will take it more readily if at first it is scattered about in little separate pieces instead of being left altogether in a solid mass.

If it should be necessary to hand rear a bird too young to feed itself, a good mixture which suits most species consists of whole meal bread, chewed up and well moistened with raw milk. A little sweet apple also chewed up and a little sweet grape juice may be added. Never on any account give sour fruit. A little yolk of raw egg may also be added to the mixture. Give the food warm, indeed almost hot. It can often be warmed by being placed in a cup put in a larger vessel of almost boiling water. The best implement for administering the food is a camel hair paintbrush. Put a little of the warm, semi-liquid mash on the brush and then place it gently against the side of the young bird's beak near the tip. When it is hungry it can, with a little patience, soon be induced to begin to feed and once it is feeding freely, meals administered every two or three hours during the day should enable the youngster to be reared successfully. Be careful not to let the young bird's plumage get sticky and messed up, wiping it clean, if need be, with cotton wool dipped in warm water. I have even known miniature bibs used with great success in the hand rearing of a family of young Turquoisines!

Birds which, like certain species of cockatoos, are inveterate wood-biters, sometimes need to have the whole of the outside of their nest box covered with strong-mesh wire netting to prevent them from destroying it.

A type of nest which often appeals to lovebirds and to some of the grass parrakeets has a kind of passage approach.

Birds which are rearing young should be very generously fed, especially in the case of the larger species. Rickets is the commonest trouble with young birds of the parrot family of many different species, and there is no more certain way of producing rickets than failing to make due allowance for the large appetites of a growing family. Species which normally should not be given too much hemp or sunflower seed may sometimes, when they are rearing young, safely be given rather more and it is a good plan at this time, not only to have dry seed in the shelter, but other seed in a clean receptacle in the flight so placed that rain can fall upon it. This naturally soaked seed should not, however, be left so long that it becomes stale and mouldy. Green food and fruit must also be supplied liberally, together with milk-sop made with whole meal bread and sweetened, which is especially useful for the larger species. When rearing young Amazon parrots successfully a friend of the writer's also offered the parent birds milk-pudding and even boiled white fish, not, of course, of a salty kind.

I have said before that there are certain species of parrot-like birds which do not follow the normal breeding habits of the majority of the members of the family. (Incidentally, it is generally the rule that if the male bird feeds the sitting hen he does not help to incubate the eggs, although he will assist in feeding the young. If, however, as is the case with some of the cockatoos, he takes his turn at incubating, he will not feed the sitting female.)

Most members of the lovebird family line their nest boxes with fine strips of bark, twigs, etc., carried to the nest in the beak in the case of some species, and among the feathers of the rump in the case of others. Liberal supplies of the fresh twigs of such trees as willow and poplar should therefore be provided throughout the breeding season. Lovebirds should also have plenty of spare boxes in their aviary which the young can use as dormitories after they have left the nest in which they have been hatched. It is said that hanging parrots also make use of some fine vegetable material to line their nests and the curious Palm Cockatoo is said to give the nest a lining of small branches and twigs. Even the common Roseate Cockatoo will sometimes go through a pretense of nest building, though this often does not get much further than waving a twig about at the entrance to the nest which is dropped before it is taken inside!

The only parakeet which builds a real nest is the South American Quaker. This relative of the conures should be provided with a large quantity of twigs and some kind of platform corresponding to the natural branches of trees on which the nest can be constructed. The Quaker, or Grey-breasted Parakeet, is an extremely dangerous bird in mixed company, but is does not object to the presence of its own kind, even when breeding.

The Cockatiel is amiable towards birds of other species, but breeding pairs should be kept separate from their own kind. All the parakeets of the Rosella family are dangerously spiteful when in breeding condition and, if a range of breeding aviaries should be put up, care must be taken to see that the partitions are double-wired. If this precaution be neglected the birds will bite off each other's beaks and toes when fighting through the wire. Even the much more gentle grass parrakeets must be kept apart from their own kind when breeding.

Some of the smallest lovebirds, such as the Nyassa and Black-cheeked will agree fairly well if allowed to breed on the colony system; but the larger species such as the Masked and Fischer's are best kept separate; and this is absolutely essential in the case of the Peach-faced, which is a most savage and pugnacious bird.

The Red-faced Lovebird, a very shy nester in captivity, should be tempted, in addition to ordinary nest boxes, by a large block of solid peat hung up in the aviary in which an artificial hole like a rathole is started.

The South American parrotlets are extremely pugnacious when in breeding condition and often at other times, and breeding pairs must always be kept separate. This sub-genus uses no nesting material.

Although cases to the contrary have been reported, Budgerigars will not, as a rule, feed nestlings which, when first hatched, are covered with long white down. They therefore make unreliable foster parents for young grass parrakeets which are better entrusted to the care of lovebirds if these do not suffer from the common vice of plucking their young.

The eggs of the tempermental and difficult Turquoisine can sometimes profitably be entrusted to the care of Elegants or Bourkes.

As a general rule avoid looking in the nests of parrot-like birds if you have reason to believe that all is well. Pileated parakeets and some lorikeets are especially likely to desert their young if they have reason to suspect that the nest box has been opened. Other species may be much more tolerant of interference, especially as the young get older, but members of the Ringneck family at any stage are best left very strictly alone.

If a case of egg-binding should occur, keep the hen at a temperature of at least eighty-five degrees Fahrenheit until the egg is laid and then allow her a long rest of several weeks before giving her the chance of going to nest again.

Occasionally, young birds leave the nest with only their flight and tail feathers, their bodies being almost completely bare. This is due to the fact that they have been plucked by their parent, or parents. Nearly always it is the hen who is the offender, but now and again the cock is also guilty. The cause and cure of this tiresome habit which sometimes, at any rate, seems to be hereditary are at present unknown. It appears most frequently among birds which have been improperly fed and kept short of exercise and amusement, but it can occur in even the best-managed aviaries where the inmates have a great amount of freedom and more or less natural conditions. I have known examples of the vice among broad-tailed parrakeets, Amazon parrots, lories, lovebirds and Budgerigars, but I have never yet come across a case among parakeets of the Ringneck family, cockatoo or grass parrakeets. Sometimes a young hen will pluck her first family and sometimes a hen will take to it later in life when she has reared several broods perfectly. The habit once started may be partially abandoned, but never, in my experience, completely so, and it usually tends to get worse rather than better. As a rule the plucking ceases when the young bird leaves the nest and occasionally a little while before it leaves, but I have known pileated parakeets, which are sometimes extremely bad pluckers, to continue the vice even after their young have flown. As a general rule, if the young birds escape a chill in their naked condition, they grow their plumage rapidly once they have left the nest and soon show no trace of the treatment to which they have been subjected.

Some young birds of the parrot family may leave the nest in a more or less rickety condition, either through some constitutional weakness in the parents, or through the failure of the owner to provide enough food of the right kind. Next to underfeeding, the commonest cause of rickets is putting the nest boxes in the aviary shelter and not in the flight.

I, myself, have found it quite impossible to breed healthy grass parrakeets, free from rickets, in indoor flight cages or aviaries, even when every comfort and delicacy in the way of varied green food has been supplied.

In the mildest form of rickets the young birds are unable to fly when they first leave the nest, but their feet and legs are quite strong and well-formed and they can walk and climb normally. Such birds can usually safely be left in the aviary for their parents to attend to and in a few days they will begin to fly, and before very long look perfect in every way, even though their breeding performance when they themselves are adult may not perhaps be all that is desired.

Incidentally, when a brood of young birds is expected to leave the nest, it is a very good plan to tie branches of trees all over both ends of the flight from ground level up to the top, and near the top it is well to provide some overhead and side shelter from wind and rain. The branches should be so shaped and fastened that they project at right-angles to the end of the flight so that they offer comfortable perching accommodation all the way up and an easy means of ascent. A flat branch, tightly tied against the end of the flight, like a fan, is very little use to the young birds. As many young parakeets are at first exceedingly wild and nervous and apt to injure themselves by crashing against the wire netting, it is very desirable to have some arrangement, like the one just described, which makes it possible to leave them in peace until they have grown accustomed to the use of their wings and to the sight of human beings. Nothing is more frightening and nerve-wracking than trying to drive a newly-fledged brood of parakeets, strong and very nervous, into the aviary shelter because the flight is so exposed that it is not safe to leave them there during the night.

Reverting to the problem of rickets, in more severe cases the young birds on first leaving the nest will be found, not only unable to fly, but also practically unable to walk. In this case, it is no use leaving them in the aviary, as the parents will soon give them up as hopeless and proceed to neglect them; and, if it should rain, they will be unable to find shelter and will become soaked and chilled. They should be placed in a roomy cage for which short turf, frequently changed, makes a good bottom and should be kept really warm. Appropriate seed and food of all kinds should not merely be placed in dishes but scattered over the floor of the cage as well. In most cases young birds will, before long, begin to feed themselves, but if they should show no signs of doing so after many hours have elapsed, hand feeding may have to be resorted to. In time, these rickety cases usually improve to an almost unbelievable degree so that they are quite suitable as pets, or even pleasingly ornamental in an aviary, even though they may never be any good for stock purposes. If the weather is very warm it is beneficial, once they have begun to feed freely, to put them out-of-doors in their cage for a few hours daily so that they can get the benefit of direct sunlight. They should not, however, be exposed to the full glare of the hot summer sun which nearly all parrots dislike intensely.

IV

Diseases of Parrots*

Disease problems in caged birds differ markedly among the various orders. Even among the parrots there is a difference between the larger parrots and parrakeets.

The large parrots, being quite long-lived, are subject to many degenerative diseases and long-standing, borderline nutritional deficiencies. Parrakeets, on the other hand, are very apt to suffer from obesity, tumors, mites (in breeding establishments), and a peculiar disease termed "French Molt." Infectious diseases (those caused by specific bacteria or viruses) or diseases from animal parasites are not often encountered in house pets because they are too isolated from contact with other birds to acquire the infection. In menageries, on the other hand, where large numbers of birds are kept in close contact and where introduction of new birds is occurring constantly, more infections and parasites are to be expected. Most deaths occur in newly acquired birds. Birds surviving more than a year become adapted to their new surroundings and usually live for long periods. An example of the type of disease expected in parrots in captivity may be had in the accompanying graphic summary from the records of the Philadelphia Zoological Society. These trends have been modified by recent changes in the diet.**

In all types of captive birds, nutritional deficiencies are prevalent. Most of these also used to occur in domestic chickens that were reared indoors, especially in battery brooders. However, now that the science of nutrition has solved most of the problems, scientifically compounded

* This work was carried on at the Angell Memorial Animal Hospital, Boston, Mass., and in the field in South America as part of a research program made possible by a bequest from Mrs. Marion L. Richards.

** Appreciation is expressed to Dr. Herbert Ratcliffe for advice in the preliminary planning of the program and for his permission to study the records of the Penrose Research Laboratory at the Philadelphia Zoological Society.

24

Incidence of Diseases in Parrots

No diagnosis 237
Injury 165
Malnutrition 41
Infectious Disease 215
Internal Parasites 119
Arteriovascular Disease 199
Gastrointestinal Disease 405
Diseases of the Liver 118
Diseases of Genito-Urinary System 108
Respiratory tract 52
Blood and blood-forming organs 16
Diseases of the skin 15
Bones, joints, and muscles 28
Nervous system 7
Eyes 1

1,726

(*NOTE*: *the records were accumulated over forty years. Recent improvements have modified the frequency of various ailments.*)

chicken feeds are highly successful in preventing these disorders. In parrots nutritional problems are somewhat different from chickens because very minute deficiencies will eventually show up because of the long life of the bird (chickens are rarely permitted to live more than a year or two), and because there are special substances needed for feather pigment in these many colored birds.

Examination of a sick bird

Unfortunately, regardless of the nature of the illness, sick birds look much the same. They sit in a dejected, hump-backed attitude with the feathers fluffed out and are disinclined to move. In parrots, failure to talk is often the first symptom. Other symptoms may be more specific, as for instance, diarrhea, shortness of breath, wheezing or gurgling respiratory sounds, or the presence of broken or incomplete plumage, overgrown beak and claws, or localized swelling or lumps on the exterior of the body.

Fluffing of the feathers is merely an indication that the bird feels cold and is erecting his feathers to increase the thickness of his insulating coat. This may be the result of fever or merely of devitalization resulting from nearly any disease process. Shortness of breath may either result from deficiency of the respiratory system; such as from infection in the air sacs, inflammation of the lungs (pneumonia), or edema and congestion of the lungs due to cardiac diseases with stasis of blood or simple edema of the lungs from protein deficiency.

Parrots are rather emotional birds and sometimes go into a depressed state with ruffled feathers and disinclination to talk, if they are roughly handled or rejected or if their favorite in the household is absent. Occasionally they will refuse to take food from a stranger for a few days.

Because of the fact that birds rarely show diagnostic symptoms, it is often difficult to specifically diagnose their complaints and treat them. Consequently, one must evaluate the diet, cleanliness, age, and handling of the bird very carefully in trying to arrive at a diagnosis. Frequently, a specific diagnosis is impossible and one must resort to generalities. In treatment, other than dietary complaints, few specific treatments are of value in birds. Those of value will be discussed under each disease below.

Common Diseases of Parrots
Air sac infection

This is a chronic disease in which there is an accumulation of cheeselike exudate in the air sacs (accessory respiratory organs of the bird). It sometimes spreads to the lungs or body cavities. The organism responsible is usually one of a group of mold or mold-like bacteria such as *Aspergillus, Nocardia* or *Actinomyces.* They are sometimes acid fast (retain fuchsin after decolorization), thus resembling the tubercle bacillus. True tuberculosis rarely attacks the air sacs. Symptoms are weakness, shortness of breath, and inappetence.

Egg-binding

Female parrots, even if not used as breeders, will occasionally lay eggs which sometimes become lodged in the oviduct. At such times the bird is likely to sit in a peculiar penguin-like attitude with its back-side on the floor of the cage. The condition can be alleviated by injection of oil into the oviduct, holding the vent over a gently steaming kettle, and manual manipulation. It is sometimes necessary to withdraw the content of the egg by syringe and needle, and then remove the shell and membrane by means of forceps.

Rarely due to anatomic abnormality, or because of spasm of the oviduct, and egg or egg yolk will spill into the body cavity. This condition is incurable, as it produces peritonitis due to a foreign body (the egg yolk).

Obstipation

Old, closely confined, poorly nourished birds are subject to impaction of the cloaca by fecal material and urates. This also occurs in cases of kidney disease in which urate material appears to be increased and in instances of weakness or paralysis of the cloaca. If the impaction is of simply a local nature, it can be alleviated by injections of oil or oil and water into the cloaca to soften the contents, then applying gentle manipulation. If, on the other hand, the impaction is merely a symptom of disease elsewhere, no permanent improvement can be expected.

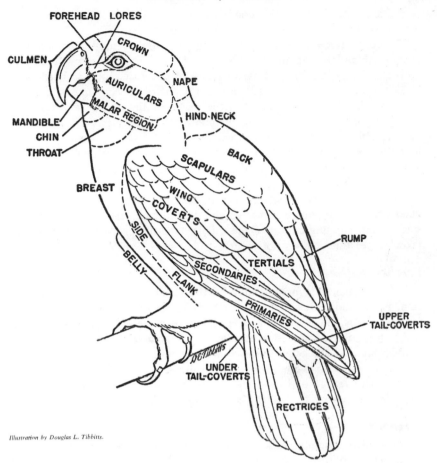

FOREHEAD LORES
CROWN
CULMEN
AURICULARS
NAPE
MANDIBLE
MALAR REGION
HIND-NECK
CHIN
THROAT
BACK
SCAPULARS
BREAST
WING COVERTS
SIDE
RUMP
BELLY
TERTIALS
FLANK
SECONDARIES
PRIMARIES
UPPER TAIL-COVERTS
UNDER TAIL-COVERTS
RECTRICES

Illustration by Douglas L. Tibbitts.

Topography of a representative member of the parrot family.

Overgrowth of horn of beak and claws

The horn of the beak and claws is analogous to our finger nails. It is not bone, although it overlies bone in part. It grows at a fairly uniform rate in any given individual and at fairly close to the same rate among individuals of the same species. Large parrots normally eat very hard nuts and fruits and it must grow rapidly to compensate for this. The shape of a bird's beak is in part governed by this constant growth and wear.

Overgrowth of horn is seen in parrots which do not have sufficient hard objects to gnaw on and that are forced to roost on perches of too small diameter to bring their claws into play. Inactivity due to malnourishment or sickness also leads to this condition, as the bird does not exercise his beak and claws sufficiently to wear them down.

There is some suggestion that malnourishment may predispose to overgrowth by altering the composition of the horn. Overgrowth may be prevented by giving the bird hard objects to chew on, such as hard wood blocks or a new branch of hard wood every day or so. Sometimes in severe cases, a large smooth pebble from the beach or the bed of a stream will supply a good object for the bird to chew on. When claws are overgrown they sometimes may be worn down by applying sand or emery powder to the bottom of the perch by means of dusting it on a fresh coat of shellac. This should not be placed on the top or side of the perch and only on the lowest perch in the cage.

In extreme cases, it is necessary to take the bird to a veterinarian or other experienced person and have him carefully clip the excess away with special claw-clipping cutters. Once this is done the proper steps should be taken to see that it does not recur.

Feather pulling

This pernicious condition may be the result of boredom, irritation of skin, nutritional deficiency or a combination of factors. In old confirmed feather pullers, no improvement is usually expected. In younger birds in which the habit is not long established, it sometimes can be cured by introducing toys and other forms of amusement and by feeding a nutritious diet high in vitamin B complex and the sulfur-containing amino acids, eggs, chick starter ration, and even meat together with a good nutritious green each day. Exposure to sunlight is sometimes helpful.

Screaming

Excessive screaming or loud raucous laughter can be very objectionable in the larger parrots and may be considered a vice. It is stimulated by boredom and by teasing. It is often set up by people, especially children, screaming at parrots in high, unnatural voices and otherwise exciting them.

Diseases of the cardiovascular system

The large parrots, together with other long-lived birds, are quite subject to arteriosclerosis (hardening of the arteries). This may progress to such an extent that the openings of the vessels are narrowed and diminished blood flow results, leading to weakness of the limbs or heart. Sometimes a small vessel in the covering of the brain may rupture, producing symptoms of vertigo and often sudden death (similar to apopleptic stroke in human beings). There is no treatment for arteriosclerosis. Unbalanced diets are thought by some to produce this condition, though there is no irrefutable proof of this belief.

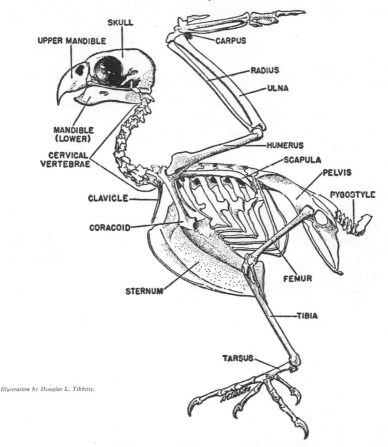

SKULL

UPPER MANDIBLE

CARPUS

RADIUS

ULNA

MANDIBLE (LOWER)

CERVICAL VERTEBRAE

HUMERUS

SCAPULA

PELVIS

PYGOSTYLE

CLAVICLE

CORACOID

FEMUR

STERNUM

TIBIA

TARSUS

Illustration by Douglas L. Tibbitts.

Skeletal structure of a typical parrot.

The lesions consist of hardening of the wall of the arteries, especially of the aorta and its larger branches, with plaque-like elevations in their internal surface. Cholesterol and other lipoids and calcium are deposited in these thickenings with the proliferations of fibrous tissue surrounding them. Both the internal layer of the vessels (intima) is involved — *athersclerosis* and the middle layer (media) *medial sclerosis* — in the process.

Arthritis

Arthritis (inflammation of the joints) or arthrosis (disease of the joints without inflammation) is seen in old parrots. There is good reason to believe that improper diets bring on this condition in pet birds. There appears to be no treatment other than prevention by adequate diets and exercise.

Abscesses

Abscesses may occur at any point on the skin surface of birds as firm swellings. The pus in such processes in birds is usually not fluid, as in mammals, but rather dry and cheese-like. They are frequently confused with tumors because of their firm character. Treatment consists of surgical removal of the contents or treatment by an appropriate antibiotic as in other animals.

Liver disease

Symptoms of liver disease may be nonspecific or consist of jaundice (yellowish discoloration of the skin and other tissues), edema of the lungs and air sacs, or sudden fatal hemorrhage from the gut.

Liver diseases are fairly frequent in parrots. The lesions may consist of multiple whitish or gray spots resulting from lodgement of bacteria from the blood stream (thromboembolic focal necrosis) in acute bacterial septicemias, such as Pasteurellosis or Salmonellosis. Larger foci or more diffuse lesions may occur as the result of localized infections of the bile ducts due to obstruction to the common bile duct. Swollen red livers are usually caused by passive congestion due to cardiac failure. Pale yellow, greasy livers are the result of fatty changes which may be due to phosphorous poisoning or more likely to dietary deficiency or pancreatitis. Diets deficient in the vitamin-like substance choline or of the sulfur-containing amino acid methionine or of another amino acid cystine are the dietary causes of this condition. Pancreatitis causes the condition because pancreatic enzyme is essential for the absorption of choline from the gut.

Fibrosis of the liver capsule is seen fairly frequently and relates to previous peritonitis.

Disease of the kidney

The symptoms of kidney disease may or may not be specific. Uremia or kidney failure frequently causes the bird to emit a sharp pungent odor. This is brought about not only by true kidney diseases but by many conditions causing dehydration or lowering of the blood pressure. No symptoms are diagnostic and no treatment is worthwhile in birds.

The excretion from the kidney of the bird is quite different from mammalian urine in physical appearance. The difference is due to the fact that most of the water is reabsorbed in the bird, the resulting urine being a semi-fluid suspension of whitish crystalline material, principally urates, which appears as the whitish portion of the droppings. Certain birds absorb more water than others, and the resulting excrement is more solid.

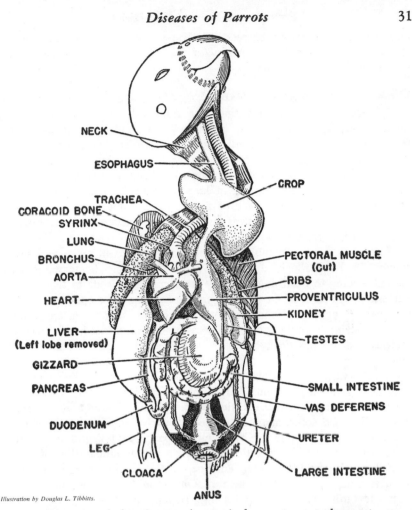

NECK

ESOPHAGUS

CROP

TRACHEA
CORACOID BONE
SYRINX
LUNG
BRONCHUS
AORTA
HEART

PECTORAL MUSCLE
(Cut)
RIBS
PROVENTRICULUS
KIDNEY

LIVER
(Left lobe removed)

TESTES

GIZZARD

PANCREAS

SMALL INTESTINE
VAS DEFERENS

DUODENUM

LEG

URETER

CLOACA

LARGE INTESTINE

ANUS

Illustration by Douglas L. Tibbitts.

Diagram of the viscera of a typical parrot, ventral aspect.

Budgerigars, for instance, have less watery excrement than canaries. When birds are inappetent the darker, fecal portion is reduced or absent and the excrement is white. If enteritis is present, blood or mucous is mixed with the urate material. When severe disease is present, catabolism (tissue wasting) is excellerated, the tissue proteins are broken down and excreted through the kidney, resulting in increased urate excrement. An example of this is the so-called white diarrhea or Pullorum disease of baby chickens. Birds subsisting on a high protein diet will excrete more urates and so will have more white in the stool. Fish-eating birds, such as herons or cormorants, are notorious for the amount of whitish stools they excrete. Parrakeets and large parrots usually excrete little water and thus have relatively dry stools. If they eat a large quantity of soft fruit and watery greens, the excrement is more fluid.

Diseases of the digestive tract

Diseases of the digestive tract are frequently the result of dietary irregularities, either nutritional deficiencies or sudden changes in the feeding schedule. They may consist of sore mouth from vitamin B complex deficiencies, ulceration or keratinization of the esophagus and crop from vitamin A deficiencies, or inflammation of the intestine from a variety of causes including sudden feeding of large amounts of laxative foods such as citrus fruits or greens. Lack of proper-sized grit also may predispose birds to digestive disturbances, as may too much excitement or stimulation in a recently purchased bird.

Infectious disease, notably *Salmonella* infection, will produce a severe mucous or hemorrhagic diarrhea. Sudden intractible hemorrhage from the gut leading to death is frequently the terminal episode in liver failure. Parasites, such as coccidia (minute protozoa of the class sporozoa), intestinal worms, or gizzard and proventricular worms sometimes are encountered in recently captured parrots. These should not persist in properly kept aviaries and are practically never encountered in single pets kept in the house.

Treatment for the various types of disease of the gastro-intestinal tract calls for a rational nutritious diet, withholding of greens or other fibrous material, and supplementation with vitamin A and B complex. Watery or mucoid diarrhea sometimes can be controlled by administration of small pieces of alopectose pills or by including pectin and kaolin in the diet. In the case of bacterial infection of the gut the administration of aureomycin or sulfasuxidine, sulfaguanadine or Sulmet in appropriate doses for a few days is sometimes helpful. One should never administer antibiotics to birds capriciously or for long periods, because of the danger of predisposing to mold infections of the intestinal tract.

French molt

This condition is manifested by the shedding of the primary tail and wing feathers (the long flight feathers) before they have matured of a more severe disease in which the feathers never grow normally and the bird never flies at all. Birds so affected are called a variety of terms, such as runners or crawlers. Usually not all of the birds in the nest are affected.

The disease has been attributed to many causes, such as the presence of feather mites, mold infection, dietary insufficiency, and overbreeding. It seems most probable that the disease results from an inherited predisposition complicated by malnutrition and weakness due to overbreeding.

Gout

Gout is an accumulation of waste material of other organic salts within the tissues of the bird as a crystaline precipitate. It is a rare condition and possibly relates to improper diet and inactivity. The affected birds have swollen, slightly warmer than normal feet. Sometimes the wings are affected as well. No cure appears worthwhile for this condition.

Going light

This term is sometimes used as a specific disease by bird fanciers. It merely denotes emaciation in a bird from any cause whatsoever.

Tumors

Tumors or cancers occur in nearly all species of mammals and birds. Parrots as an order are little more subject to tumors than other birds but Budgies appear peculiarly susceptible to them. They exist in many varieties. Some are local, not likely to cause death by invading tissue or by spread to other parts, and are called benign tumors. Others grow rapidly, invade normal tissue, and spread to distant parts of the body; these are malignant tumors or cancer. The most common benign tumors of parrots and especially Budgerigars are fatty tumors or lipomas which are rather soft, yellowish masses protruding from the skin surface. Skin carcinoma and various internal tumors also occur. Superficial tumors may oftentimes be successfully removed by veterinarians, but little can be done for deeply situated tumors.

Injuries

Due to their active habits and restricted space, caged birds are very subject to injuries. This is especially true when several are together in one cage or when new birds are added to the aviary or a young Budgie is permitted to fly about the house without clipping his wing feathers. The injury is usually to the head and produces symptoms of unsteadiness or paralysis. Frequently the birds are merely found dead. Such birds exhibit hemorrhage over the calvarium (bone of the top of the cranium) both on its external surface and internal surface, and bloody discoloration to the surface of the brain. Because of the likelihood of injury, the calvarium should always be skinned out when a bird is being autopsied. Osteomalacia appears to predispose to these head injuries, because of softening of the skull.

Infectious diseases

Infectious diseases (transmissible disease due to bacteria or viruses) are usually not a problem to the person possessing only a few birds in the home. However, when any considerable number of birds is possessed, and especially if new birds are being introduced from time to time, infectious disease is always a threat.

The symptoms are not specific and may consist of diarrhea, fever, ruffling of the feathers, inappetence and weakness. Sometimes one may find dead birds before any symptoms of disease are noted. Infectious disease is contracted from newly introduced birds; but may be caught from vermin such as rats, mice, domestic poultry, or wild birds which may be in contact in an outdoor aviary. One source of contact with poultry is brought about by feeding uncooked egg shells as a source of calcium (egg shells should be sterilized by boiling and allowed to dry before being used to supplement the diet). Several infectious diseases may occur. Most important are paratyphoid disease or Salmonellosis, fowl cholera or Pasteurellosis, tuberculosis, acid fast nontuberculus pneumonia, and psittacosis.

Salmonellosis is caused by bacteria of the genus *Salmonella* of several varieties. It is primarily a disease of the intestinal tract, producing diarrhea, but it soon spreads to the blood and is quickly fatal. It spreads easily from bird to bird via the droppings and contaminated feed and water. A few birds may survive and serve as carriers to spread the infection to the next generation. *Salmonella* infection frequently accompanies other disease, as for instance, psittacosis. The diagnosis is achieved by autopsy of a sick bird and the preparation of bacterial cultures from the organs. No treatment has proved to be of much value, but sulfa drugs and aureomycin may be beneficial. In breeding establishments, it should be combatted by isolation or destruction of the sick birds and rigid sanitary measures.

Pasteurellosis is perhaps the most sudden of all diseases of a bacterial nature. It is related to the black death or bubonic plague which decimated the human population in medieval Europe. The causative organism is *Pasteurella avicida,* which attacks all birds and can almost completely wipe out a poultry farm or a breeding aviary. Birds are usually found dead without symptoms, although a more chronic form exists in which there is swelling and watering of the eyes or swelling of the joints or feet. Such forms usually occur near the end of the outbreak and may serve as carriers of the infection. No treatment is of great value, although the measures recommended for *Salmonellosis* may somewhat reduce the number of deaths. Sanitary measures similar to the preceding must be instituted. Usually from 20 to 60% of the birds will die of this disease once it has gained entrance.

Bird pox is a disease in which there are blister-like vesicles and nodules about the base of the beak, eyes, in the mouth and throat, and sometimes around the vent and bare skin of the legs and feet. It is most commonly seen in chickens and pigeons but also occurs in canaries and has been seen occasionally in Budgerigars. It is caused by a virus which is similar to the one causing smallpox in persons. Vaccines are used to control this disease in chickens and pigeons but have not been successfully used in caged birds. Once birds recover they are immune and do not serve as carriers to spread the disease to others. There is no treatment for pox. It should be prevented by care in examination and isolation of new birds.

Mold disease (mycosis)

This sporadic infection is caused by organisms which belong to the groups higher than ordinary bacteria. They are characterized by long branching filaments and spore-like end organs. *Nocardia, Aspergillus, Actinomyces,* and other forms too numerous to mention, comprise this group. Sometimes the organisms are acid fast, thus resembling the tuberculosis bacillus. No treatment appears of value. This infection is a chronic, slowly progressing process with firm, cheese-like pus which may involve the air sacs, lungs, intestine or skin, or subcutaneous tissues.

Thrush occurs as a disease of the digestive tract with necrotic lesions which are overlaid by dense, corrugated pseudo-membranes in the mouth, throat crop or intestine. The diagnosis may be made by demonstrating oval yeast-like spores of *Monilia sp.,* the causitive agent, in scrapings from the lesions.

Tuberculosis

Tuberculosis is a rare disease of parrots, unless they are closely confined with other birds likely to spread the disease. Free-running pheasants, chickens, or waterfowl are sometimes the source by which other birds in a menagerie are infected. The symptoms are emaciation and anemia. The organs most affected are the liver, spleen, and lungs which have cheesy nodules which contain numerous acid-fast tubercle bacilli. Sometimes the intestine, kidneys, or superficial tissues are affected. Avian tuberculosis is rarely, if ever, transmissible to human beings. A few cases alleged to be tuberculosis of the human strain have been reported in superficial infections of parrots. Such reports should be critically reviewed, since birds are not usually susceptible to mammalian tuberculosis, and because the differentiation of the various strains of *Mycobacterium tuberculosis* and even other varieties of acid-fast organisms is not always successfully accomplished. It can be said that the parrot is no factor in the dissemination of tuberculosis to man.

Psittacosis or parrot fever

It is necessary to devote considerable space to this relatively rare infectious disease of birds, because of the popular misconception concerning it, the hysteria by which it is treated by certain disease-control people, and the equal hysteria by which its existence is denied by some commercial bird people.

Psittacosis is a real disease, not a myth. It is caused by an organism which is intermediate between the very small filterable viruses and the larger bacteria; and is placed in a class called the psittacosis-lympho-granuloma venerium group. It occurs naturally in many varieties of birds and is transmissable to mice and other mammals. In the early 1930's it was fairly prevalent among parrots, especially recent imports, and caused considerable disease and not a few deaths in persons coming in contact with them. Following this world-wide outbreak, when importation of parrots was prohibited by law in 1930, the disease persisted in domestic-ally reared Grass Parrakeets, pigeons, and other birds.

The disease was named psittacosis because it was first described in birds of the parrot order (psittaciformes). Soon afterward, however, it was discovered in birds of other orders. It now has been recognized in pigeons, egrets, turkeys, gulls, ducks, fulmars, many other birds, as well as domestic chickens. When the disease occurred in birds other than those of the parrot order, it was formerly called ornithosis. Now, however, it is realized that there is no valid distinction between the virus as isolated from parrots and other birds, and the term psittacosis is being used for the disease in all birds. The term psittacosis is retained because the disease was first described under that name (the nomenclature rule of priority). Since 1930, four hundred and fifty-eight cases of psittacosis have been discovered in human beings in the United States. Of this number, fourteen have been attributed to parrots and one hundred and seventy-two to par-rakeets. Other birds (principally pigeons and turkeys) have been incrimi-nated in one hundred and eighty-one cases. A number of persons have contracted the disease from patients who had originally been infected from avian sources, and it has been impossible to trace the source in a number of cases.

The natural history of psittacosis appears to be as follows. A few birds which have contracted the disease remain as apparently healthy carriers capable of spreading the disease to their nestlings, other birds, or persons should the virus become activated within them. Such a carrier state has been reported in a person by Meyer. The disease is frequently reactivated by poor nutrition, overcrowding, overfeeding, fatigue, or the occurrence of other disease. The nestlings develop severe disease and few or many may die, but a few survive to become harborers of the infection. It has been shown that psittacosis exists in wild birds in this manner. Wild Budgerigars are affected in Australia and the disease may serve as a population regulator to keep their numbers within bounds of the food supply. An awareness of the natural course of the disease should be helpful in preventing those practices which will introduce or perpetuate the disease in an aviary or disseminate it by the shipment of birds. It should also discourage those practices of bad sanitation, notably overcrowding and lack of isolation facilities, so prevalent in breeding aviaries.

In 1952, regulations governing interstate shipment of psittacine birds were relaxed upon the strength of the following facts. (1) certain antibiotics are thought to be beneficial in the treatment of psittacosis in human beings, (2) other birds are infected with and transmit psittacosis, thus it is not a problem peculiar to parrots, and (3) the expense of maintaining effective control did not appear warranted by the present danger to human health.

It is extremely important for those persons engaged commercially in rearing, selling, or traffic in birds to realize that this relaxation is a trial. If it is successful there probably will be further relaxation of the restrictive regulations. If it is unsuccessful, full regulations will be restored. Thus, it behooves the industry to put its house in order to keep psittacosis at a minimum. This is particularly true of raisers and sellers of Budgerigars which are notorious as disseminators of psittacosis. The following steps should be faithfully carried out.

Breeders
1. Prevention of overcrowding in the bird room.
2. Proper nutrition, especially when nestlings are being fed.
3. Isolation of all new imports for a period of weeks or months.
4. Prevention of contact with pigeons, or wild birds such as house sparrows or starlings.
5. Prevention of overbreeding and the elimination of "crawlers."

Bird Sellers
1. Provide proper nutrition for all birds when displayed for sale and during shipment.
2. Provide cages which are large enough for proper exercise.
3. Prevention of overcrowding, chilling, or suffocation during shipment.
4. Provide a separate room for holding sick birds until they may recover or be destroyed.
5. Cease lending support to illegal importation of parrots from outside the United States.

In addition to the above, I strongly recommend that a certificate showing the age, sex, and aviary where it was bred and additional aviaries where it was held, accompany each bird during shipment and be retained by the ultimate owner, so that in the event that psittacosis does originate from this bird the original focus may be promptly detected and eliminated. Such rules and regulations should be promulgated by the industry through consultation with public health authorities and followed as ethical business practice.

Diagnosis of Psittacosis

The specific diagnosis of psittacosis should not be attempted by those unacquainted with virologic methods and possessing a good knowledge of the disease because of the danger of human infection. While psittacosis is rather rarely encountered in house pets, a specific diagnosis should be made when the disease is suspicioned. Diagnosis can be achieved by three means: (1) a presumptive diagnosis can be made by the demonstration of the presence or absence of specific antibodies in the blood serum by the complement fixation test; (2) smears may be made from tissue at autopsy and stained to demonstrate the virus bodies; (3) a suspension of the tissue may be injected into mice or other susceptible animal in order to reproduce the disease.

These methods all have their place. When the first method is employed, the bird or birds may be kept alive until the report of the examination is rendered. This is useful when latent infection is suspected in valuable birds. It is more applicable to large parrots from which good blood samples may be obtained, than parrakeets which cannot usually give a large enough blood sample for the test. After the bird is bled, the serum should be freed from cells by centrifugation, preserved by the addition of merthiolate solution — one to one thousand at the ratio of one part to nine parts of blood, giving a final dilution of one to ten-thousand — or by placing serum in tubes containing dessicated sulfanilamide. This serum should be kept in the refrigerator and sent via air mail to the laboratory designated by the local public health authorities.

It is convenient to make smears from the surface of the pericardium and other places during the course of an autopsy, if psittacosis is suggested by the changes seen. These smears are stained by Macchiovello's technique or Giemsa stain and examined for evidence of the organisms. This is the quickest but least specific of the diagnostic methods.

When psittacosis is suspected and the bird is dead or may be destroyed, the third method above may be employed. This is the most accurate and specific test possible. It consists merely of wrapping the bird up in a phenol or merthiolate-treated cloth, packing in dry ice and shipping to the proper laboratory for diagnosis by animal inoculation. This method is specific and permits less chance of human exposure.

Parasites

Parrots that are kept as house pets are seldom troubled with parasites because of their isolation from other birds. However, birds newly acquired from the wild state may be troubled by lice and numerous internal parasites, most of which cause no harm whatever and eventually die and are not re-established in the captive bird.

Breeding aviaries may be troubled by mites and lice. Mites are tiny eight-legged creatures belonging to the order *Acarina.* They parasitize birds in two ways. Some live and breed in crevices about the cage and visit the birds only at night to feed. Other forms live continuously on the birds.

Red mites, *Dermanyssus sp.,* are small greyish mites which dwell in cracks in the cages and visit the birds at night to suck blood. After they are engorged with blood they are bright red in color — hence the name "red mite." They may be detected by handling the birds at night or by carefully examining the premises during the day by means of a magnifying glass.

Feather mites dwell on the birds continuously. Some, such as *Megninia sp.,* creep about the feathers; others, such as *Syringophilus sp.* burrow within the quills of the feathers and are termed quill mites. These mites are very difficult to detect. Freshly imported birds are often infested with other species of fatter mites which do not appear to persist in captivity.

Scaly-leg mite, *Cnemidocoptes sp.,* produces scaly legs and feet leading to severe inflammation and disfigurement. It is most apt to attack debilitated birds, but may then spread rather widely in the aviary.

Treatment of mite infestation

The best method of prevention or treatment of mite infestation (as is all forms of parasitism) is the establishment of measures to promote the health and vigor of the birds. This includes providing cages of adequate size for exercise and maintaining a diet high in protein, vitamins, and minerals. These measures, plus cleanliness of the cages and surroundings, will usually suffice to eliminate mites or keep them to a minimum.

Specific treatments must be attempted when the mites are causing disease and for the elimination of red mites from the premises. Control of red mites consists of extremely thorough cleansing of the quarters each day and frequent painting. The cages and other wooden portions of the premises may be painted with a bland, nontoxic light mineral oil containing *no* D.D.T. or other insecticide. One should examine for the presence of colonies of the mites around crevices in the cages and the edges of doors, nest boxes, etc. All surfaces should be thoroughly cleaned before applying the oil. During the course of treatment, the birds should be moved to other cages, which in turn should be cleansed. Allow the oil to soak into the wood or evaporate before returning the birds to the cages so that they will not soil their feathers or ingest an undue amount of it while chewing at the wood. Above all, practice good sanitation continuously, not heroic measures sporadically.

Control of feather mites should consist of health-promoting measures and sanitation as for red mites, plus treatment of the individual birds, if necessary. Measures used on chickens employing the newer, more effective insecticides can be tried cautiously on caged birds.

Dipping

Prepare the dipping solution as follows: two quarts warm water, one-half ounce laundry soap and one ounce of flowers of sulfur. Agitate this mixture and dip birds into it. Try to keep the solution around body temperature or slightly below ninety to one hundred degrees Fahrenheit. Be sure to keep birds in a warm room after dipping to prevent chilling.

A simpler but less effective method is to dust the bird with flowers of sulfur at frequent intervals, spreading the feathers so the sulfur gets in contact with the skin. Black-leaf-forty (nicotine sulfate) is an effective control measure for mites in chickens. This probably should be experimented with cautiously in small birds until its toxicity for small birds is ascertained.

Control of scaly-leg mites consists of measures to soften the scales plus application of a mite-killing oil. Possibly the best method for caged birds is as follows: soak the feet and shank in warm soapy water until the scales begin to soften. Allow to dry, apply a mixture of petroleum jelly, five parts, oil of caroway, one part.

Other parasites

Newly acquired wild birds may harbor tapeworms in the small intestine, filaria in the lining of the air sacs and around the proventricle. Gizzard worms (*Spirocerca*) may be found underneath the horny lining of the gizzard. Various other internal parasites also occur. These parasites are usually of interest to parasitologists but are usually not harmful, since they do not persist in captivity. Gizzard worms sometimes propagate in zoos (they require an intermediate host such as certain species of beetles) and create many deaths. Proper sanitation will remove the breeding sources for the intermediate host and prevent further trouble. Filaria worms produce larvae (microfilaria) which circulate in the blood and are seen in blood smears. These apparently do little or no harm since many wild birds possess them.

Bird Remedies

A great amount of lore concerning treatment of sick birds has been accumulated through the years. Many pet store operators and aviary keepers have favorite medicines for all varieties of ills. These include whisky, red pepper, niter, Epsom salts, aconite, borax, bromide, syrup of rhubarb, and others too numerous to mention. It is not the purpose of this article to detract from such treatment, and if a person honestly feels that he is getting results, he should of course continue. It has been my experience, however, that the diseases which they are alleged to cure are often nonexistent and many of the remedies themselves are carry-overs from medieval medicine and have been proven to have no value or have been replaced by more efficacious modern medicines. Furthermore, many of the diseases are the result of bad management and feeding practices, often fostered by the same persons attempting the treatment, which can respond only to proper nutrition, and all the pet nostrums in existence have no value whatever.

It is recommended that persons with a disease problem in a parrot or other bird or in an aviary solicit the services of a practicing veterinarian so that specialized training in nutrition and the use of modern drugs may be brought to bear on the problem. Since treatment of parrots or any other unusual pets is not common in most veterinarians' practices, it requires interest and patience on both the owner's and veterinarian's part to work out a therapeutic program. It is well to try to select a veterinarian who has some experience with such problems or is sufficiently interested to try to work out a therapeutic program for the bird.

Therapeutic methods suitable for parrots

Parrots are usually quite intractible and not amenable to examination and treatment by means customarily employed in cats and dogs. The following methods have proved of value during the course of this investigation:
1. Examination of the bird by inspection from a distance;
2. Meanwhile getting a history of the illness and of the diet and sanitation;
3. Closer inspection of the bird from the cage side (so to speak);
4. Inspection in the hand, if possible, to determine amount of flesh, presence of lumps, etc.

Drugs may be administered by putting them on a piece of bread or other solid food, mixing them with some favorite fluid which the parrot will drink, and giving by pouring into the mouth (only possible.with very sick or unusually tractible parrots), or by injection intramuscularly into the breast muscle when dispersed in an appropriate vehicle. Intravenous or subcutaneous injection is not ordinarily possible.

Since parrot diseases so frequently stem from nutritional dificiency, it is always a good idea to include dietary supplements during treatment. The dose must be estimated according to the size of the bird and calculated from the dog or cat dose. The rational for therapy is similar to other animals, but one must frequently experiment according to individual eccentricities of the patient.

The inappetent, depressed, weakened parrot with evidence of long-standing nutritional deficiency may be treated as follows: prepare a solution containing five to twenty-five per cent dextrose, protein hydrolysate and various vitamin supplements including B complex, A and D. This may be suspended in fluid of which the parrot is especially fond and the bird coaxed to drink it. If the bird will not take the fluid voluntarily, it may be administered as forced feedings, by restraining the bird and injecting small quantities into the mouth, waiting for him to swallow and injecting more until the whole amount is taken. Do not use a glass pipette, syringe, or eye dropper for this purpose, because of the danger of the parrot chewing off the tip and getting broken glass in the mouth. Use instead a metal syringe, or a glass syringe fitted with a long sixteen or fourteen gauge needle with the point ground off, or pour it from a teaspoon. Suspend the drugs in as small amount of fluid as possible to shorten the task. Avoid the use of oily medications for forced feeding, as inspiration into the lungs will cause pneumonia.

Intramuscular injections of vitamin preparations are practical and advisable at the beginning of treatment to establish a curative blood level at the outset. Merely restrain the bird on his back, part the feathers, wipe the skin with alcohol, and inject with a sterile twenty-two or twenty-five gauge needle and syringe deep into the side of the breast. Subcutaneous injections are impractical in birds because the skin is tightly bound to the flesh and intraperitoneal injections are not advised because of the danger of getting the material into an air sac with the production of chronic inflammation of the sac and possibly pneumonia.

When bacterial infection is suspected, specific antibacterial drugs may be employed. Birds tolerate the nonabsorbable sulfonamides which are useful in intestinal infections and may be given in combination with the supplement solution mentioned above. Penicillin may be injected into the breast muscle when systemic infections are suspected. Aureomycin may be given by mouth in a liquid vehicle.

Injuries

Because of their rugged skeletons, injuries are less frequently encountered in parrots and Budgies than in small passerine birds like canaries. These will consist of injury to the head, discussed previously, or fracture of the wing or leg. Unlike canaries and finches, parrots will sometimes not tolerate the presence of a splint but will chew it off with their beaks in short order. However, with patience one can often splint them long enough to get primary union. They sometimes heal without treatment if left alone in a small cage where they may remain quiet However, it is often most humane and practical to have such birds destroyed.

Hospital cages and isolation quarters

Each large aviary should be equipped with a separate room where newly arrived birds may be held for a few weeks to see if any signs of illness develop before admitting to the main bird room. This should be attended last so that no infection is likely to be carried from the new birds to the acclimatized ones. The larger the aviary the more important is this isolation procedure, since if several thousand birds are on the premises, it is fool-hardy to court chances of introducing some specific infectious disease, such as *Salmonellosis* or *psittacosis* which may sweep through a large percentage of the stock.

This isolation area, if not occupied by new imports or preferably another separate room, should be used as a hospital for sick birds. It is well to have a few cages well isolated and equipped with metal or glass sides well up from the bottom to prevent scattering of droppings, feed, etc., around the floor. The space should be warm, of fairly low humidity, and free from drafts. Sick birds, above all, should be kept warm. There is no need of a long list of remedies to be kept in such a room, for warmth, rest, and good nutrition will usually do as much for sick birds as the countless remedies frequently used, which have no rational value in the light of modern medical knowledge. From the practical standpoint, it is usually better for a breeder to sacrifice a gravely sick bird rather than trying to nurse it along, meanwhile possibly jeopardizing the health of other birds in the aviary.

Restraint of Parrots

The owner should get the parrot out of the cage and hold it for treatment by the veterinarian. However, if the owner does not wish to handle the bird, it may be up to the veterinarian or his assistant to catch and restrain it.

It is well to wear a heavy glove on one hand while handling strange parrots to prevent a painful bite. If the parrot is docile and one can gain his confidence, slowly approach with the gloved hand and encourage him to step to it. When he has done so, gently bring the hand and parrot from the cage. Gently examine the bird with the other hand. If the parrot is wild and aggressive, approach him slowly and try to get him to a corner of the cage, then quickly seize him forcibly but gently around the neck and base of the head. Secure the wings and feet with the other hand by grasping him around the lower abdomen so that the legs are directed backward and are held in the grasp together with the tail and wings. Parrots are very strong and require a fairly firm grip. *Never hold a bird by grasping it around its body because of the danger of suffocation.* A bird must have room for respiration. Now bring the bird from the cage, and transfer it to an assistant so that it may be examined. Most birds will remain relatively quiet when held with the ventral surface up. However, this does not apply to parrots which continue to struggle violently in whatever position they are held. Budgies and other small parrot-like birds may

44   *Parrots and Parrot-like Birds*

be held effectively in one hand, while examined with the other. Injections may be made in this fashion as well.

It is sometimes necessary to bleed parrots to obtain blood for the complement fixation test for psittacosis. This is a relatively heroic procedure, as the parrot will strongly resent it and struggle violently. Have the bird held as previously described, but with his back against the top of a table. Spread one wing and have an assistant hold it also fixed against the table top. Parrots struggle so that it is impractical to try to use a syringe and needle and perform a proper venepuncture; instead take a sharp pointed knife and nick the vein and catch the blood in a wide-mouthed vial as it wells from the puncture. See *Psittacosis* for methods of preserving the blood for shipment to the laboratory.

References

1. Feyerbend, Cessa; *Modern Feeding of Budgerigars*, All-Pets Books, Fond du Lac, Wis., 1951.

2. Feyerabend, Cessa; *Diseases of Budgerigars, with Special Reference to French Moult;* All-Pets Books, 1951.

3. Ratcliffe, H. L.; *Diets for a Zoological Garden: Some results during a Test Period of Five Years; Zoologica,* New York Zoological Society, 25, 4, 463-472, 1940.

4. Mayer, K. F. and Eddie B.; *Psittacosis, Past, Present and Future;* All-Pets Magazine, June and July, 1951.

5. Meyer, K. F.; *Psittacosis and Ornithosis, in Diseases of Poultry, 1952.* Third edition, edited by H. E. Beister and L. H. Shwarte, Iowa State College Press, Ames, Iowa. See also for general references for parasites and nutrition.

6. Fox, Herbert; *Diseases in Captive Wild Mammals and Birds; J. B.* Lippincott Company, Philadelphia, Pa., 1923.

7. Coffin, D. L.; *Manual of Veterinary Clinical Pathology;* Comstock Press, Ithaca, N. Y., third edition 1953.

8. Coffin, D. L.; *Psittacine Birds and Human Health,* Proceedings American Veterinary Medical Association Meetings, 1952.

9. Coffin, D. L.; *Parakeet and Parrot Booklet;* Angell Memorial Hospital, Boston, Mass. 1953.

V

African Parrots

African Gray Parrot
Psittacus erithacus

Distribution	Equatorial Africa.
Adult male	Ashy grey, paler on the rump and abdomen. Flight feathers dark grey. Tail and tail-coverts red. Bill blackish. Irises pale yellow. Length thirteen inches. Size about that of a pigeon.
Adult female	Similar to the male but smaller with a less massive head and beak. The bare skin at the back of the eye is said to be more rounded and less elliptical in shape.
Immature	Differs in having the tail dark red towards the tip and the under tail-coverts dark red, tinged with grey. Irises dark grey.

The Grey Parrot has been a well-known favourite for a great number of years, and many stories are told of its intelligence and linguistic powers. It is, par excellence, the bird for those who want a house pet to amuse them with its mimicry of the human voice. Not only does it adapt itself wonderfully to cage life, and with proper treatment survive for an immense number of years, but as a talker it has few rivals and no superior. Moreover, if some of its whistling cries are unpleasantly shrill, it never, unless terrified, can be properly said to screech. It is also of a more equable temperament than its noisier rival the Blue-fronted Amazon. Few Amazons can be trusted in moments of mischievous excitement to refrain from nipping the fingers of even their best friends, but a Grey is seldom treacherous. Once he has really given you his heart — and very often only one person is so honoured — he is always gentle except under great provocation, but anyone, especially a stranger, who is foolish enough to make advances that are not welcome, does so at his own peril and has no reason to complain if, as is extremely likely, he receives a severe bite.

The Grey Parrot should be fed on a seed mixture of two parts canary, one-half part hemp, one part sunflower, one part oats, with plenty of

45

fruit. Sweet, soft fruits like grapes are the most relished, as are ripe pears. Apples are eaten if of the best dessert kinds and in good condition, but a Grey has a very discriminating palate, and usually rejects this fruit if it is soft, sour, or ill-flavored. A very small bit of plain cake does no harm as a tit-bit, but tea, coffee, soaked bread, meat, bones, butter, and milk should never be given. According to one authority, the stupid habit of giving parrots bread and butter and milk is a common cause of the tuberculosis to which they often fall victims, it being claimed that they are susceptible to the bovine as well as to the avian form of the disease. Very young Grey Parrots will sometimes eat only boiled maize (corn), a food which must be prepared fresh daily, but they can usually soon be induced to take soaked seed and, in due course, dry seed. Sunflower soaked until the shell is quite soft is very attractive to young parrots, but the water in which seed is soaking must be changed daily or it will become very offensive.

Grey Parrots are not regular bathers, but appreciate an occasional spray or rain bath. The dry streaky plumage of the numerous unfortunate birds whose owners never allow them to bathe contrasts very unfavourably with the appearance of well-cared-for specimens.

A Grey Parrot should have a piece of wood to occupy its beak, but on no account should it be allowed to bite anything painted or varnished. Hen Grey Parrots in breeding condition spend a lot of time scratching up the sand at the bottom of the cage, as they would do when excavating a tree trunk hollow. If the litter on the floor is objected to, instead of preventing the poor bird from indulging its natural instinct by the insertion of a ridiculous grating, have a detachable sheet of zinc on each side of the cage of a depth sufficient to catch the flying sand and prevent it from passing through the bars. It is often asked whether or not parrots understand the meaning of what they say. In the majority of cases undoubtedly they do not, but it is almost equally certain that the more intelligent birds do so in some instances. A Grey Parrot is also quick to associate ideas by sight or sound. A hen bird in my possession imitates the blowing of a nose either on being shown a handkerchief or on hearing a sneeze. The pouring out of water also evokes from her a realistic gurgling noise which says more for her quickness of mind than for the table manners of her former associates. Very young parrots have grey irises but the colour soon changes to the pale yellow eye of the adult. There is not the slightest evidence that Grey Parrots, as is sometimes stated, take nearly twenty years to become sexually mature. In a wild state they almost undoubtedly begin to breed not later than their fourth year and possibly one or even two years sooner.

When newly imported, the species is apt to be delicate and sensitive to cold and may even, from overcrowding and neglect on the voyage, be found to be suffering from parrot fever (psittacosis), an infectious and always fatal complaint. Only complete scorching with a blowtorch will render a cage occupied by a diseased bird safe for a successor. When acclimatized, the Grey Parrot is perfectly hardy in climates similar to England's and can be wintered in an outdoor aviary without heat.

It has been bred both at liberty, in aviaries, and in close confinement, but only on rare occasions, not because there is any real difficulty in getting it to go to nest, but because few people give parrots any encouragement to do so and for some unknown reason a cock bird is extraordinarily difficult to get, the enormous majority being hens. A genuine male is usually a very big, rather gaunt-looking fellow, with, according to some authorities, the bare grey patch behind the eye less rounded and more elliptical in shape. If tame, he is generally a brilliant talker, though most hens also talk well, only a very few being unable to learn anything. If a true pair can be obtained, Grey Parrots are really easier to breed than some parakeets, for the cocks retain their fertility with very little wing exercise, and a good hollow log or barrel partly filled with decayed wood makes a satisfactory nursery for the young. A pair, when first introduced are very slow to make friends, but once mated, become savage and aggressive towards humans. If you want a parrot to be a pet, *don't* get it a partner! Single hen birds not infrequently lay and may die egg-bound if their owners do not give them relief by placing them in a very hot room when they show signs of illness.

The Grey Parrot is subject to colour variation. Birds with an abnormal quantity of pink feathers are not uncommon, also partial albinos; pure albinos with red tails occur, and, rarest of all, wholly white specimens and grey birds with white tails. I once had the transient pleasure of owning a red-tailed albino which a dealer transferred to me for a herioc figure. As the bird was very young and was suffering from parrot fever, its mortal remains soon graced a Scottish museum where I hope one day to see them — for I never set eyes on my expensive purchase, being away from home during its brief sojourn!

The Grey Parrot has been trained to stay at liberty. Birds that have been long caged are liable to need coaxing and watching until they regain their skill in flight, as they are apt to gain a lofty tree-top and then find great difficulty in flying down.

Old writers sometimes refer to the Grey Parrot as the Jaco.

Senegal Parrot
Poeocephalus senegalus

Distribution   Gambia.

Adult male   Green. Head dark greyish, paler on the cheeks. Lower breast and abdomen orange-yellow. Flights dusky with a green tinge on the outer webs. Tail short: greenish brown. Bill black. Length nine and one-half inches.

Adult female   Similar but with a much narrower and finer head.

A popular and well-known bird and probably one of the best of the small parrots for anyone who requires a cage pet. The Senegal becomes much attached to one person or to one sex and is lively and playful, learning to say a few words or short sentences. Its chief failings are a slate-pencil screech and a tendency to bite in moments of mischievous excitement, but not all individuals possess this vice.

The Senegal is said to have been wintered without heat, but little is known about any of the *Poeocephali* as aviary birds.

The Senegal Parrot usually behaves stupidly at liberty; even tame specimens quickly lose their way and are nervous and clumsy about flying down, dashing swiftly around their owner, only to take perch once more in the top of a high tree.

The food should consist of a seed mixture of two parts canary, two parts millet, one part sunflower and one part peanuts, with plenty of fruit if the bird's digestion remains in good order.

Senegals have laid eggs in captivity, but the cock of the pair killed the hen.

VI

Lovebirds

Nyassa Lovebird
Agapornis lillianae

Distribution	Nyassaland, Northern Rhodesia.
Adult male	Forepart of head orange-red, cheeks and throat slightly paler and merging into pink. Back of head yellow merging into green. Remainder of plumage green, slightly paler on the breast. Bill red. A white circle round the eye. Total length four inches. Size about that of a Budgerigar.
Adult female	Resembles the male. According to some authorities has a slightly broader beak.
Immature	Slightly less richly coloured than the adult.

Unknown to aviculture until recent times, this pretty little lovebird has now become one of the commonest of aviary birds in many parts of the world, threatening to rival even the Budgerigar in popularity. It is easily kept in any kind of aviary, birdroom or flight cage. The main occupation of its existence is the rearing of a numerous progeny, clutch after clutch of eggs being laid with only a pause of a few weeks for the moult. The only check on its fertility in captivity lies in the circumstance that the unhatched embryos are somewhat intolerant of a dry environment, while in cold weather a proportion of the hens are subject to egg-binding. Some aviculturists claim to have overcome the former difficulty, when breeding Nyassas under cover, by providing nest boxes with a false bottom filled with sponge or sphagnum moss kept soaking wet, and separated from the mass of twigs and bark composing the actual nest by a piece of wire gauze. One breeder even went so far, with successful results, as to soak the eggs daily in warm water from the tenth day of incubation, relying on the devotion to their eggs characteristic of lovebirds to keep the hen from deserting under the constant interference. Five eggs form the normal clutch, though larger numbers have been recorded. Lime and elm twigs make the best nesting material and the supply must be renewed even after the young are hatched. The cock Nyassa feeds his sitting mate and

49

spends a good deal of time with her in the nest. The difficulty of distinguishing the sexes by their appearance is largely made up for by the facility with which true pairs can be recognized by their behaviour. No self-respecting hen Nyassa dreams of delaying to go to nest at the earliest possible moment. If after the lapse of a few weeks, no eggs have appeared, you may be sure your birds are cocks, while double clutches of from eight to ten infertile eggs are equally certain proof that you have nothing but hens.

Nyassa Lovebirds are quite hardy, but their winter treatment in outdoor aviaries presents some difficulty owing to the egg-binding danger already mentioned, coupled with the fact that the removal of the nest logs in which they sleep is apt to be followed by an outbreak of chills. On the whole it is best to move the nests into the aviary shelter during the autumn and heat the shelter, resigning oneself to a proportion of useless clutches until the warm weather returns.

The Nyassa Lovebird is reputed to be fairly quiet in mixed company, but although it agrees well with its own kind, I should not care to trust it with valuable Budgerigars or finches, as some individuals can be very savage.

The food should consist of a mixture of two parts canary, two parts millet, one part oats, one part hemp, and one part sunflower. Green food may be offered, but they seldom eat much.

The species interbreeds freely with nearly allied lovebirds; the hybrid with the Black-cheek is rather pretty and perfectly fertile.

Fischer's Lovebird
Agapornis fischeri

Distribution   Uosure, Victoria Nyanza.

Adult male   General plumage green, paler on the breast. A band of bright orange-red across the forehead; the same colour in a paler shade on the cheeks and throat where it merges into rose colour and old-gold. Head and back of neck strongly washed with dull olive green. A patch of dark blue above the root of the tail. Tail feathers green, tipped with blue. Bill bright red. A white circle round the eye. Total length five and one-quarter inches. Somewhat larger than the Nyassa Lovebird.

Adult female   Similar to the male. Often appears larger and of a paler but brighter colour.

Immature   Resembles the adult, save that the olivaceous shade extends much further 'round the sides of the neck and down to the green mantle. Forehead slightly less richly coloured.

This lovebird, formerly to all intents and purposes unknown to aviculture, was in 1926 imported in large numbers and is now a well-known

Crimson Rosellas. Photo by Horst Mueller.

Top: Fischer's Love Bird. Bottom: Peach Face Love Bird. Drawing by R. A. Vowles.

aviary bird over a great part of the world. It seems a hardy and prolific species, some birds received by the writer in early autumn rearing their first brood in the open flight of an unheated aviary in the middle of winter. The weather at the time was exceptionally bad, and when the young birds were nearly ready to fly a raging blizzard covered the roof of the aviary with snow. A bitter hurricane blew for many days, during which it never stopped freezing and later there was a heavy fall of rain.

The nesting habits and requirements of Fischer's Lovebird resemble those of the Nyassa. It agrees fairly well with its own kind, though some pairs will kill their neighbour's young. A simple bird I introduced into an aviary of finches proved exceedingly spiteful, quickly murdering two of its companions.

Hardy as it is in the ordinary way, Fischer's Lovebird will not thrive outdoors in winter if its nesting logs be removed, even though it be driven into the aviary shelter at night. It is necessary, therefore, to allow it to go on breeding and if the hens should get egg-bound to warm the shelter and put the logs inside. If, as is likely, few young are reared in the over-dry atmosphere of the shelter, the logs can be hung in the open flight where the rain will fall on them as soon as the warm nights return. Strange to say, though so difficult to sex when adult, young birds just out of the nest show a decided difference in the size of the head and beak.

Young birds sometimes leave the nest fully fledged, but unable to fly. As no bird is more easily injured by a fall than a young lovebird it is prudent to lay a heap of fine resilient twigs beneath the entrance of the nest. The youngsters, when they emerge, should be picked up and put in a cage with clean blotting paper on the floor. Plenty of well-soaked millet and canary spray millet, crushed soaked hemp, shelled soaked sunflower, and stale brown bread crumbs should be sprinkled on the paper and renewed as they get dry or scratched into corners. Within forty-eight hours the young birds will begin to feed themselves if kept in a warm place. Care must be taken to provide both soaked millet and cracked hemp as some nestlings will starve sooner than begin on millet and vice versa. As soon as the young birds are feeding well, the seed can be put in a dish and sand can replace the paper on the floor of the cage, the size of which should be increased as the occupants learn to use their wings. After a fortnight, dry seed should be substituted for soaked, as they eat the latter so greedily that they may grow over-fat and die of apoplexy. This initial wing weakness in the young is most common when the parents are not fully recovered from the effects of the voyage. If it persists in later broods, tall, mould-filled boxes with no wooden bottoms may be substituted for whatever is in use. The mould should reach to within eighteen inches of the entrance hole and the interior must, of course, be climbable.

Fischer's Lovebirds should be fed on the same diet as Nyassas.

Masked Lovebird
Agapornis personata

Distribution	Tanganyike Territory, Nyassaland.
Adult male	Head blackish or blackish brown merging into the yellow of the neck and upper breast, the latter sometimes tinged with orange on the throat. Remainder of plumage green, paler on the abdomen. Lower rump tinged with dull, dark blue. Tail marked with black. Bill red. Large white circles 'round eye. Total length five and three-quarter inches.
Adult female	Resembles the male. Often larger.
Immature	Slightly less richly coloured than the adult.

This very striking-looking lovebird has become one of the commonest parrots on the bird market. It is among the hardiest of its tribe and among the readiest to go to nest; but it is also, next to the Peach-face, the most spiteful; although, to do it justice, less addicted to wholly unprovoked aggression than *A. roseicollis*. It will live well in an indoor or outdoor aviary, or in a flight cage, but it is cruel and stupid to confine it, or any other lovebird, in quarters so cramped that it cannot nest or freely use its wings.

The Masked Lovebird needs moisture in the nest for the successful development and hatching of the embryo chicks. For this reason the nest logs or boxes should be hung in the open flight where rain can fall on them. My own hens appear able to lay without trouble even in the coldest weather, but a friend of mine lost a hen from egg-binding, and if this ailment is feared, the only plan is to hang the nest logs in a heated shelter during the cold months and risk poor hatching results until spring returns.

The Masked Lovebird lines its nest with fine twigs and strips of bark and continues to add material after the young have hatched, so the nest must be a big one or the young will be cramped. Young birds which leave the nest in winter I catch up and treat as recommended in the article on Fischer's Lovebird.

The Masked Lovebird breeds continually, only stopping for the moult. Four eggs are the normal clutch, and the cock spends a good deal of time in the nest with his mate. The sexes are very hard to distinguish, but if you choose a specimen with a wide skull and one with a narrow one you will probably have a true pair. If you have not, you will soon be enlightened by the bird's behaviour, for hens always go to nest without delay.

As already stated, the Masked Lovebird has a fiery temper, but unlike most pugnacious birds, it is not aroused to evil deeds by prosperity and cowed by disturbance and misfortune, but vice versa. It is exceedingly risky to confine several adult birds in a cage or travelling box, as, exasperated by the discomfort of their cramped quarters, they are likely to emulate the exploits of the Kilkenny cats. I have had a bird torn to bits by its companions on a two hour's journey. On the other hand one aviculturist has found the species tolerably well-behaved in mixed company when not interfered with, and my own two pairs, though they have had a couple of shindies and removed the end of a few toes, have at least refrained from murdering each other's young in a twenty-four foot by eight foot by eight foot aviary. On the whole, however, to prevent accidents and mutilation that spoils the birds for show, I would certainly advise each pair being kept alone.

On first leaving the nest some young birds of the brood — apparently of the same sex — have the upper mandible streaked with black.

The London Zoological Gardens have a very interesting cock which is blue where the normal bird is green, and white where the normal one is yellow; the black head being retained. It is greatly to be hoped that a blue strain may be bred from it.

The Masked Lovebird has the squeaking, chittering cries of its near relations, but is not disagreeably noisy.

It should be fed like the Nyassa Lovebird and is fond of oats softened by soaking. The writer hand-reared a three parts grown nestling on porridge brown bread moistened by chewing in the mouth. The little bird was remarkably nervous, intelligent, wary and alert; and, as one would say of a child, in all respects strangely old for its age. It grew up to be a most cheery and amusing pet. A blue strain has been reported in Europe.

Peach-faced Lovebird
Agapornis roseicollis

Distribution   Southwestern Africa and possibly parts of Southeastern Africa.

Adult male   Dull green, paler on the breast. Forehead bright rose-red; cheeks and throat rosy pink with a greyish tinge at the edge of the cheeks. Rump brilliant blue. Tail short; blue-green with black and fiery pink markings. Bill coral-red. Total length six inches: about twice as large as a Budgerigar.

Adult female   Resembles the male; usually, but not invariably, duller in colour.

Immature   Has green areas of the plumage more brownish olive. Forehead brownish; cheeks and throat brownish pink. Base of bill dark. Adult plumage is assumed within a very few months.

Although, like all members of the lovebird family, the Peach-face is quite unsuited to life in a small cage; it will, if provided with a nest box to breed in and branches to nibble, readily adapt itself to life in any kind of aviary, birdroom, or even flight cage. There is, unfortunately, no absolutely certain way of distinguishing the sexes by their plumage. Since, however, the Peach-face belongs to that section of the lovebird family of which the main occupation is the reproduction of its species on every possible occasion, an aviculturist need never remain long in doubt as to whether he possesses a true pair. If the birds are not moulting, are in good condition and do not within a couple of months go to nest, they are males. If they both visit the logs and carry in building material on their backs, they are females. If only one carries building material and the other feeds it, they are all right. Peach-faces will make use of any kind of box or hollow log if it be sufficiently roomy to contain a good supply of fine strips of the bark of twigs of lime, elm, or poplar. Unlike some lovebirds their attempts at breeding are not easily rendered abortive by the fact that the nest is in a dry situation. The hen bird alone sits, but the cock joins her in the nest at night, and may also enter it in times of emergency, especially when the young are very small and danger appears to threaten.

The Peach-face is an exceedingly spiteful bird, which will neither agree with its own kind, nor tolerate neighbours of other species, even those considerably larger than itself. It has also an annoying predilection for biting toes. Sometimes the injury is inflicted in the ordinary course of combat with rivals, but in some cases it becomes an actual vice, parents maiming their young before they are independent and youngsters mutilating each other long before they are old enough to quarrel about mates or nesting places. There is no cure for the bad habit and birds addicted to it are best got rid of.

Some aviculturists have been successful in wintering the Peach-faced Lovebird in outdoor aviaries, but the writer has not found it completely hardy in very severe weather.

The species should be fed on canary, millet, and oats, but hemp and sunflower are liable to produce feather plucking; chickweed and other green food should be supplied to birds rearing young.

In addition to the chittering cries uttered by many members of the family, the Peach-face has a disagreeable penetrating shriek which has earned it a bad name with some aviculturists.

Although not every pair can be trusted to stay, Peach-faces can be bred at liberty during the summer months. Before being released they should be thoroughly accustomed in an aviary to the type of nest box they will find awaiting them in the garden; they do not take at all readily to natural holes in trees. If, as one observer states, the Peach-face in its native land breeds in the nest of the Sociable Weaver-bird, this reluctance is easily explained.

A hand-reared, talking Peach-face has been recorded, who after biting his owner, would say "Naughty Joey!"

Semi-lutinistic specimens have been reported.

VII

Asiatic Parrots

Red-sided Eclectus Parrot
Lorius pectoralis

Habitat
New Guinea and many neighbouring islands, North Queensland.

Adult male
General plumage brilliant green; bastard-wing, primary coverts, primary and secondary quills deep blue. Outer tail feathers deep blue. Under wing-coverts, auxillaries, and a large patch on the side of the body bright red. Upper mandible red with a yellowish tip; eyes brown. Total length fourteen inches. Size somewhat larger than a Blue-fronted Amazon.

Adult female
General plumage bright red, inclining to crimson on the back, wings, and base of the tail. A band of blue across the mantle, a narrow circle of blue 'round the eye; abdomen and sides of the body purplish blue; bastard-wing, primary coverts, outer portions of the primaries and tips of the secondaries deep blue. Tip of tail orange-red. Bill black.

The Eclectus Parrots have long been noted for the striking difference in the plumage of the sexes and some writers have mentioned them as a curious example of species where the female is more richly coloured than the male. Why a crimson bird should be considered more ornate than a brilliant green one is a little hard to understand.

When confined in parrot cages, Eclecti are usually melancholy and apathetic and seldom survive for more than two or three years. Occasionally, however, one meets with individuals — usually females — which have been carefully tamed and petted and allowed a good deal of liberty in the room, with the result that they have become docile and affectionate and have even learned to say a few words.

Of the Eclectus Parrot's voice, only one favourable thing can be said — that he does not make very free use of it. Indeed, if he be at all dispirited

55

and out of sorts he will not utter a sound of any kind. Let him be a little extra lively, however, or slightly alarmed, and the best efforts of an excited Lemon-crest or macaw are as music to the truly awful "Crrah!" he lets off. It goes through you like a knife, and I doubt if the whole realm of nature contains another sound so incredibly harsh.

Eclectus Parrots should be fed like Grey Parrots, fruit being an important item in their diet. They need plenty of warmth when newly imported, but when acclimatized can stand a fair amount of cold. Being exceedingly sensitive to septic fever infection, they must be kept in very clean surroundings. On the whole they do best in an aviary in summer and, if the aviary shelter be not well-warmed, they should be loose in a bird-room during the winter; or if that be not possible, in a large flight cage. When in breeding condition they are of a somewhat savage and uncertain temper, especially with their own species.

Pure Red-sided Eclectus do not appear to have been bred, but hybrids and nearly allied species have been reared in captivity. A hen Eclectus that laid in a cage was given a fowl's egg to sit on, which she hatched successfully. It is not recorded how she got on with her active foster child!

My efforts to induce Eclectus Parrots to stay at liberty were completely unsuccessful. I did not, however, experiment with the male of a breeding pair whose mate was confined in an aviary.

VIII

Hanging Parrots

Blue-crowned Hanging Parrot
Loriculus galgulus

Distribution   Malay Peninsula.

Adult male   Brilliant green, slightly darker on the wings. A dark blue patch on the crown and a gold or golden brown patch on the upper mantle. Upper rump yellow; lower rump and a large patch on the throat crimson. Tail short. Under surface of flights and tail pale blue. Bill black. Total length five and one-quarter inches.

Adult female   Differs from the male in being a much duller green, yellower on the breast. Only a slight trace of blue on the crown and gold on the mantle. Upper rump brownish green. No red throat patch.

Immature   Resemble the female but are even duller and greener. Adult plumage does not seem to be assumed for at least a year.

The Blue-crowned Hanging Parrot is the most commonly imported, as well as the most beautiful, member of an Asiatic genus of small nectar and fruit-eating parrots whose merits are not appreciated by aviculturists as they deserve. Certainly when he first comes over, usually in nestling feather, a small brownish green bird with a red back and soiled and sticky plumage, he gives little promise of ever being a great ornament to a collection. But once he has donned his adult dress of richest green, set off by the golden brown patch on the mantle, the rump and bib of flaming red, and the lovely blue spot on the crown, he is as dainty a little living jewel as ever left the tropics. He is, moreover, guiltless of making unpleasant noises, harmless to finches and not very destructive to growing plants.

Hanging parrots are easily fed and will not only do well on lory's food and fruit, but also on most of the foods recommended for lories (by no means the same thing). Mr. Farrar fed his birds on banana and

57

other ripe fruit and kept a narrow jar of honey at their disposal of a shape which permitted them to feed without soiling their plumage.

Like all nectar-feeding species, hanging parrots make a good deal of mess and the cage must be so arranged that every part can be easily washed. In unhealthy districts hanging parrots do not thrive very well, but in healthy ones they give no trouble if kept very warm on first arrival. They will not stand severe cold, but they have been wintered in an unheated birdroom with perfect success.

They perhaps do best loose in a birdroom, well provided with branches of different sizes, and they also thrive in a flight cage, but when caged their claws have a troublesome habit of growing too long and require regular cutting.

In outdoor aviaries they are not a great success as they are very apt to kill themselves flying against obstacles. Being short-winged, heavy-bodied birds, their flight, though swift, is not well controlled. If their claws have become long and they are thrown off their balance when taking off from the roof where they are hanging upside down after the odd custom of their race, they are very apt to hit something before they can stop themselves. Hanging parrots breathe in a curiously heavy manner, even when in perfect health, and this fact, together with their habit of ruffling their head feathers when at rest, makes it somewhat difficult to detect signs of incipient chill or other illness. The display of the cock is very pretty and amusing. He erects the flaming feathers of his rump and bib and makes short rushes along the perch, uttering a buzzing sound.

Blue-crowns agree tolerably well with their own kind, but breeding pairs are best kept separate. So far the species has not been bred, though fertile eggs are said to have been laid on several occasions. The hen is said to line her nest with grass, strips of leaves, and chips of wood carried tucked into the feathers of the rump or upper breast. When sitting she is fed by the cock.

The writer kept two cock birds at liberty during the course of a summer but the species does not stay too well.

Hanging parrots do best if rendered as tame and steady as possible.

Ceylon Hanging Parrot
Loriculus indicus

Distribution	Ceylon.
Adult	Green. Back of neck and mantle tinged with golden brown. Throat bluish. Crown and rump brickish red. Under surface of wings and tail pale blue. Bill light orange-red. Length five and three-quarter inches. About the size of the Blue-crowned.
Immature	Lacks the blue throat and nearly all red on the crown.

The Ceylon Hanging Parrot requires the same treatment in captivity as other members of the genus. The sexes are alike in colour, but the hen is said to have a shorter and more arched beak, broader at the base. When acclimatized they need only moderate heat in cold weather.

Golden-backed Hanging Parrot
Loriculus chrysonotus

Distribution   Cebu, Philippine Islands.

Adult male   Green. Forehead orange-red. Crown and back of neck golden yellow merging into the orange wash of the upper mantle. A large orange-red patch on the throat. Rump bright red. Tail dark green. Under surface of flights and tail bluish. Bill orange-red. Length six and one-quarter inches. Much larger than the Blue-crowned Hanging Parrot.

Adult female   Lacks the orange-red throat patch, the throat and cheeks having a bluish tinge. Crown and nape duller and darker gold.

This large and gorgeous hanging parrot has been exhibited at the zoos and appears to do well in captivity under the same conditions as the Blue-crowned.

IX

Amazons

Blue-fronted Amazon
Amazona aestiva

Distribution	Brazil, Paraguay, Argentina.
Adult male	Green with faint bluish reflections on the fore-neck and breast. Feathers of hind-neck and mantle barred with black. Forehead pale blue; crown, cheeks and throat yellow. Some birds have the crown all blue and others all yellow. Bend of wing yellow mixed with red. Outer web of primaries bluish. Secondaries show a large patch of red; also blue and green colouring. Tail feathers green with terminal portion paler golden-green. A red patch near the base of the outer ones. Bill blackish. Length fourteen to fifteen inches.
Adult female	Resembles the male but has a narrower skull. The bend of the wing is usually red.
Immature	Have the blue and yellow areas of the plumage reduced in size.

The Blue-fronted Amazon is the best known and most commonly imported of all the parrots, the numbers in captivity exceeding those even of the Grey. It takes well to cage life and usually makes an excellent talker and mimic. If not quite equal to the African bird in the number of words it can learn to repeat clearly, it surpasses its rival in its power of giving the general effect of a conversation, a song, or a person in tears; the mimicry being often exceedingly ludicrous. Some years ago my mother had a Pekingese dog of a very irascible disposition who particularly objected to the ministrations of the vet. An Amazon we had at the time learned to give a most realistic representation of a stormy interview between Che Foo and his medical adviser, the infuriated yells of the dog mingling with the soothing words wherewith his friends endeavoured to assuage his ill-humour.

The Blue-fronted Amazon has two failings. Like all its tribe it screams badly in moments of excitement and most, though not all, are liable to give an occasional nip even to their best friends, either when their jealousy is aroused by the presence of another parrot, or simply out of pure mischief. Covering the bird's cage as a punishment will sometimes teach it to control its desire to give vocal expression to its exuberant feelings, while if the bite is not inflicted from fear or active dislike, a gentle cuff, accompanied by a sharp word of reproof, will encourage better manners.

Being very common and easy to obtain, Blue-fronted Amazons suffer badly from the callousness and cupidity of dealers. Disgracefully cramped and over-crowded on the voyage, the poor birds arrive in a filthy condition, often suffering from incurable infectious enteritis, and in any case, in a state of health and plumage which renders them liable to chills on the slightest provocation. The advice given as to the general treatment of caged parrots is applicable to this Amazon. It is probably safe to say that nine-tenths of the Blue-fronted at the present time in captivity in this country are being kept in cages half the proper size, do not see a bath from one year's end to another, and get very little fruit. But lots of unwholesome milk and butter which may lead to tuberculosis, if not to digestive troubles and feather plucking, is given.

The Blue-fronted Amazon should be given a seed mixture of two parts canary, one part millet, one part oats, one part hemp, one part sunflower, and one part peanuts, with plenty of fruit. An Amazon will eat half an apple a day, or a whole one if the fruit be small.

Blue-fronted Amazons have been bred, but only rarely. This is not because the birds are in any way difficult to get into breeding condition, but simply because no one bothers to give proper breeding accommodation to such large and common birds. A hollow tree-trunk makes the best nest, but a box or barrel partly filled with decayed mould will also serve. The female must not be allowed to lay when the nights are cold. Paired Blue-fronts, like Greys, become excessively savage.

In suitable climates Amazons can be wintered in an outdoor aviary. In adverse climates they sometimes suffer from pneumonia and enteritis. An Amazon attacked by the latter complaint often passes a quantity of blood, but a very high temperature and a diet of bread and scalded milk for two or three days will usually effect a cure.

The Blue-fronted Amazon has been kept with success at liberty, though newly-released birds which have been long caged need watching in case they lose their bearings.

In the writer's collection is living a very beautiful lutino hen Blue-front. The areas which are blue in the ordinary form are in her case white; those which are green are the richest golden yellow; while the red is retained. Her eyes are red, her feet and beak are of a flesh colour. The crimson and white of her secondaries against the golden background of her body plumage are extraordinarily lovely. A similar bird is figured in Salvadori's old book on parrots together with another very beautiful lutino Amazon, each of whose yellow feathers is lightly edged wíth red, producing a scaly appearance. A blue specimen of this parrot is also on record.

Yellow-fronted Amazon
Chrysotis ochrocephala

Distribution	Brazil, Ecuador, Venezuela, Trinidad, Eastern Peru.
Adult	Green, paler on the head and yellower on the breast. Feathers of neck and mantle with dusky edges. Crown yellow. Flights blue and green with blackish webs. A red bar on the secondaries. A fiery-red patch near the base of the outer tail feathers. Bill blackish with flesh-coloured base. About the size of the Blue-front.
Immature	Appears to lack the yellow on the crown and the red on the wing.

The Yellow-fronted Amazon is not infrequently imported and makes an amusing talker and mimic. Dr. Butler mentions one that had entirely forgotten its own language and expressed all its emotions of rage, pleasure, fear, etc., as a child would, shouting and crying when startled or angry. It also appeared to understand the meaning of some of the sentences it used. If anyone dressed for a walk appeared in the room the parrot would say: "Are you going out?" "Are you going to the park?" "There's a cat in the park." "Good-bye!"

Mr. Brook had a specimen that was almost a pure lutino, showing only a slight trace of green. The female is said to have less yellow on the crown, a paler iris and a narrower beak.

Treatment is as for the Blue-front.

Levaillant's Amazon (often Double Yellow Head)
Amazona oratrix

Distribution	Mexico, Yucatan, and Honduras.
Adult	Green, paler and bluer on the breast. Head and neck golden yellow, paler on the crown. Mantle often flecked with yellow. Shoulder and bend of wing showing pinkish-red and yellow feathers. Wing-bar pinkish red, flights also showing blue, green and black colouring. Tail feathers with pale green tips. Outer pair with a blue edging. A patch of fiery red near the base. Bill whitish. Iris red with inner ring yellow. Total length fifteen inches. Size about that of the Blue-front.
Immature	Show less yellow and have green on cheeks and crown.

Levaillant's Amazon or the Double-fronted, as it is often called, is a rather striking-looking parrot with its yellow head, white beak and red eyes. It always gives the impression of being a colour variety rather than the typical representative of a species. It is, perhaps, scarcely as hardy as the Blue-front, needing more room and exercise and the best of feeding with plenty of fruit. Individuals vary greatly in disposition, some being amiable, others fierce or treacherous. Though noisy, Levaillant's Amazon often proves a brilliant talker. Canon Dutton had one which sang seven songs, did the French military exercises, said other things and swore volubly like a French sailor, and was always ready to perform at command. It was a gentle bird and bore its master no malice, though he had to hold it during a painful operation.

An old portrait by Marc Geerarts represents Lady Arabella Stuart with a Levaillant's Amazon, a Red and Green Macaw, and a pair of Red-faced Lovebirds. The date of the picture must be about 1590 and it is interesting to find that these birds were known to English aviculture at so early a date.

The female is said to be smaller and to have a shorter and broader beak. Levaillant's Amazon can be wintered out-of-doors.

Panama Parrot
Amazona panamensis

Habitat — Panama, Veraguas, Colombia.

Adult — Green with faint bluish reflections on the crown, cheeks, throat and breast. A patch of yellow on the forepart of the crown. A patch of red at the shoulder. Outer webs of primaries dark blue. Secondaries show the usual red patch found in nearly all Amazons. Bill yellowish. Length twelve to fourteen inches.

Immature — Entire head green.

A rare Amazon in captivity. Treatment as for the Yellow-shouldered.

Yellow-naped Amazon
Amazona auropalliata (*often miscalled "Panama Parrot"*)

Distribution — Western side of Central America.

Adult — Green, paler on the breast and much paler on the head. Feathers of the sides of the neck and upper breast faintly barred with dusky colour. Nape yellow; a few yellow feathers often present on the forehead. Flights green and blue with black inner webs, a pinkish red bar on the secondaries. Tail green with terminal half pale yellowish green. A patch of fiery red near the base of the outer tail feathers. Bill horn-grey with yellowish base. Total length fourteen inches. About the size of the Blue-front. (The male is often brighter and larger than the female with greater sheen to the feather.)

The Yellow-naped Amazon is a somewhat rare bird in captivity, but very abundant in a wild state. An observer, writing in the year 1896, comments on the large numbers that came to roost in the vicinity of the houses of the town. It is known to make an excellent talker.

The female is said to have a narrower beak, more arched, and with a shorter terminal hook. The treatment should be that of the Blue-front.

Yellow-shouldered Amazon
Amazona ochroptera, also Amazona barbadensis barbadensis

Distribution   Island of Aruba off Venezuela.

Adult   Green with bright bluish reflections on the lower cheeks and breast. Crown, throat, and feathers below the eye golden yellow, orange-salmon at the base. Forehead frosted with white. Feathers of neck, mantle, and rump barred at the tip with black; the barring being most pronounced on the lower part of the back of the neck. Bend of the wing yellow, or yellow and red. Thighs yellow. Tail feathers green with pale tips, the outer ones showing a patch of wine colour at the base. Flight feathers blue on the outer web, secondaries showing a large patch of red. Bill whitish horn. Iris orange. Total length thirteen to thirteen and one-half inches. Wings about eight and one-half inches. Slightly smaller than the Blue-fronted Amazon.

The Yellow-shouldered Amazon is a rarely imported bird. Like all the species smaller than the Blue-front, and many that are larger, it does much better in a flight cage, birdroom, or aviary than in a parrot cage. The food should be that of the Blue-fronted Amazon.

Old German aviculturists describe this parrot as very easily tamed but showing great individual variation in its powers of mimicry. Sounds were apt to be picked up more easily than words.

The female is said to have the region of the lower mandible, lower breast, and abdomen sky blue, and all the other colours duller.

Mealy Amazon
Amazona farinosa

Distribution   Guianas.

Adult   Green, brighter on the cheeks. Neck, mantle, and rump show a mealy tinge. Feathers of back of crown and back of neck tipped with blackish colour, the latter also showing a bluish lilac tint towards the ends. A spot or patch of yellow, or yellow and scarlet on the crown. Inner web of primaries black; secondaries show an area of red, dark blue, and green. A little red at the bend of the wing. Tail green at the base; yellowish-green for the terminal half. Bill light horn colour. Length fifteen inches. Larger than the Blue-fronted Amazon.

The Mealy Amazon does somewhat better in an aviary than a cage and can be wintered out-of-doors. Its treatment should be that of the Blue-front.

Canon Dutton had a specimen which was extremely talented, though its songs and conversations were in native dialect; it was also gentle and friendly but unfortunately noisy.

Guatemalan Amazon
Amazona guatemalae

Distribution   Mexico, Guatemala, Honduras.

Adult male   Green with a slight mealy tinge on the mantle and wings. Forepart of crown blue, merging into dull lilac towards the back of the head, and dull olive green tinged with lilac on the neck. From the centre of the crown to the base of the neck the feathers show a dark edging of an increasingly pronounced character. Tail feathers green with the lower half yellowish green. Tips of primaries black. Secondaries show a large area of pinkish red and dark blue. Bill bluish black; iris orange-red. Length about sixteen inches. Somewhat larger than the Blue-fronted Amazon.

A rarely imported bird not likely to differ from the better known Mealy Amazon in its character. The female is said to have a broader beak with a coarser terminal hook.

Plain-coloured Amazon
Amazona farinosa inornata

Distribution   Panama, Venezuela, Ecuador, Bolivia.

Adult   Green, brighter on the forehead, cheeks, and breast. Neck and mantle showing a mealy tinge. Feathers of back of crown and back of neck strongly marked with purplish black at the tip. Primaries blackish. Secondaries marked with red and dark blue, as well as green and black. A trace of red at the bend of the wing. Tail feathers green at the base and yellowish green for the terminal half.

Eye large. Bill light horn colour. Length fifteen inches. Larger than the Blue-fronted Amazon.

Not much appears to have been recorded of this big Amazon. A specimen in my collection proved amiable with other parrots and capable of wintering out-of-doors. It had a loud and unmusical voice and some talent for mimicry. It seemed amiable in mixed company.

Mercenary Amazon
Amazona mercenaria

Distribution   Peru, Ecuador, Bolivia.

Adult male   Green, brighter on the cheeks and paler on the breast. Back of neck and mantle with a mealy tinge. Feathers of crown, neck, and upper mantle tipped with purplish black, the marking being heavy on the neck and faint elsewhere. Primaries with green bases and blackish webs. Secondaries showing a large patch of red, as well as dark blue. Bend of wing shows a few red and yellow feathers. Tail tipped with greenish yellow, outer feathers with a large wine red patch in the middle. Bill dusky, yellowish near the base. Total length thirteen and one-half inches. Size about that of the Blue-front.

Immature   Said to lack the red wing-bar.

I have never seen a living specimen of this Amazon, so I am unable to say whether scientists are justified in ascribing to it a more mercenary nature than other parrots!

It is said to make a good talker in its own country and was exhibited at the Zoological Gardens in England in 1882.

Green-headed Amazon
Amazona virenticeps

Distribution   Costa Rica and Veraguas.

Adult   Green, yellower on the cheeks and breast. Crown of head tinged with blue at the front and lilac at the back, the same lilac tinge persisting at the back of the neck. Feathers of the hind part of the crown and neck edged with blackish colour. Mantle with a mealy tinge. Tail green at the base and yellowish green for the terminal half. A trace of dull orange near the base of the outer feathers. Flight feathers blackish on the webs. Secondaries showing a large patch of red; also dark blue and green. Bill bluish black. Total length about sixteen inches. Larger than the Blue-front.

This big Amazon is rare in captivity: it is really only a local race of the Guatemalan from which it is hardly distinguishable.

Fischer's Love Bird. The delicate beauty of Fischer's Love Bird, has made the species one of the most popular Love Birds in the United States. Photo by Horst Mueller.

Male Crimson Winged Parrakeet. Photo by Horst Mueller.

Chattering Lory. Photo by Horst Mueller.

Male (right) and female Crimson Winged Parrakeets. Drawing
by R. A. Vowles.

A pair of Australian King Parrakeets. The male is the upper
bird. Drawing by R. A. Vowles.

Festive Amazon
Amazona festiva

Distribution   Amazon Valley, up to Eastern Peru.

Adult   Green, brighter and sometimes bluer on the cheeks and mealy on the back. A narrow line across the forehead, and feathers between eye and beak wine red. Tips of feathers above and behind the eye blue and a trace of blue on the crown. A trace of dark edging to the feathers of the neck. Upper rump crimson. Bastard wing dark blue. Outer edge of primaries dark blue. Secondaries green with a tinge of dark blue. Tail green. Outer feathers with the merest trace of wine red near the base of the quill. Bill dusky. Total length fourteen and one-half inches. Size about that of the Blue-front.

The Festive Amazon is a handsome parrot and has the reputation of being much less noisy than most of its allies. Individuals vary greatly in docility and talent, but the best are said to be brilliant talkers with very clear pronunciation.

Canon Dutton had a yellow specimen for a short time, but it does not seem certain that it was a pure lutino. The natives of South America are credited with producing yellow feathers on green parrots by rubbing them with the poisonous secretion from the skin of a certain frog. Birds without the red eye and pale feet of the true lutino must therefore be viewed with some suspicion.

The female is said to have a shorter and fuller beak and to be smaller than the male.

The treatment should be that of the Blue-front.

Green-cheeked Amazon (often, Mexican Red Head)
Amazona viridigena

Distribution   Eastern Mexico.

Adult male   Green, very bright on the cheeks and paler on the breast. Cap and feathers in front of eye crimson. A strip of blue or lilac feathers extends over the area behind the eye. Feathers of hind-neck tipped with black. Primaries blue-black with faint pale tips. Secondaries with a large patch of red; also blue and green. Bill yellowish white, less short and curved than that of the Blue-fronted Amazon. Total length thirteen inches. Size about that of the Blue-front.

Immature   Said to have only the forehead and lores red, the crown being green.

The Green-cheeked is one of the most beautiful of the medium-sized Amazons. It does well in captivity but is somewhat rare and there appears to be little recorded of its character and habits. It should be fed like the Blue-fronted Amazon.

The female is said to have less red on the crown and a smaller beak.

Yellow-cheeked Amazon
Amazona autumnalis

Distribution   Eastern Mexico and Central America.

Adult   Green, paler on the breast. Forehead and forepart of the crown red. Feathers at the back of the crown tipped with lilac; those of the neck with lilac edged with black. Area below the eye yellow or red and yellow. A few red feathers under the chin. Wing-bar red, secondaries showing some green; blue and black also. Tail with yellowish green tips. Bill light horn. Length thirteen and one-half inches. Size about that of the Blue-front.

Immature   Little yellow on cheeks.

A rare Amazon which has been exhibited at the zoos. The female is said to be smaller than the male; to have a narrower red frontal band, less scarlet and more yellow on the cheeks; and a much shorter and lighter beak.

Spectacled Amazon
Amazona albifrons

Distribution   Western Mexico, Yucatan, Guatemala, Nicaragua, and Costa Rica.

Adult   Green, brighter on the cheeks and breast and faintly barred with black on the neck. Forepart of crown white; rear part blue. Feathers round the eye and between eye and beak, red. Some bright red on the lower edge of the wing. Flight feathers rich dark blue and green with blackish inner webs. A patch of wine red near the base of the outer tail feathers. Bill light yellow. Total length ten and one-half inches. Much smaller than the Blue-front. (Female has less white on the crown, and is smaller and duller than the male.)

Immature   Has less red on the wing, and probably less white and more blue on the crown.

This very small and rather striking-looking Amazon is extremely rare in captivity. It does badly in a parrot cage, but will live well in a flight cage, birdroom, or aviary. Little is known of its ability to stand cold and it would be unwise to expose it to a low temperature without great caution. The few birds the writer has known have been unfriendly and inclined to bite. The food should be that of the Blue-fronted Amazon, without hemp.

Finsch's Amazon
Amazona finschi (*also called lilac-crowned parrot*)

Distribution	Western Mexico.
Adult male	Green, paler and brighter on the cheeks. Forehead and area between eye and beak dull red. Crown and outer edge of cheeks lilac with a few green feathers interspersed. Feathers of neck and breast edged with black. A pinkish red bar on the wing, flights also showing blue and green areas. Outer tail feathers with paler tips and a yellowish patch on the inner webs. Bill dirty white. Total length thirteen inches. A little smaller than the Blue-front.

In a wild state this parrot is said to fly in large flocks and to be very active and graceful on the wing.

It is uncommon in captivity.

The female is said to have a broader and shorter beak, and is smaller and duller than the male.

Jamaica, All-green, or Active Amazon
Amazona agilis

Distribution	Jamaica.
Adult	Green, darker on the crown and paler on the breast. A scarlet patch on the lower edge of the wing. Flights blue and green, with black inner webs. Bill greyish-black. Total length ten and one-half inches. Much smaller than the Blue-front.
Immature	Has no red in the wing, and the flights are a duller blue.

A very rare parrot which has been exhibited at the Zoological Gardens in England. Unless bred in captivity it will become extinct.

The female is said to have a shorter and broader beak with a shorter terminal hook.

Red-throated or Jamaican Amazon
Amazona collaria

Distribution	Jamaica.
Adult	Green, very bright on the breast and yellowish on the tail coverts. Forehead white; more rarely pink. Crown dark bluish with black edgings to the feathers. Feathers of the neck edged with black and a trace of the same marking on the mantle. Throat deep pink. Outer web of

flight feathers slate blue. Tail yellowish green, outer feathers with a deep pink patch near the base. Bill whitish. Length about twelve inches. Smaller than the Blue-front. The Jamaican or Red-throated Amazon is rare in captivity. It has the reputation of being affectionate, but noisy and a poor talker. Like most of the smaller Amazons it needs more exercise than permanent confinement in a parrot cage permits. It should be fed like the Blue-front.

Yellow-lored Amazon
Chrysotis xantholora

Distribution   Yucatan, Cozumel Island, British Honduras.

Adult   Dark green, paler and yellower on the tail-coverts. Feathers edged with black most heavily on the neck, mantle, and upper breast. Forepart of crown white with rear edge dark blue. Feathers above, below, and at the back of eye bright red. Feathers between beak and eye and a small spot under the lower mandible yellow. Flights green and dark blue with blackish inner webs. A patch of scarlet on the lower edge of the wing. A patch of wine red near the base of the outer tail feathers. Bill yellow. Total length ten and one-half inches. Much smaller than the Blue-fronted Amazon.

Immature   Appears to have the crown mainly blue and less red 'round the eye and on the wing.

This curious little Amazon is extremely rare in captivity. It is really a local race of the Spectacled Amazon and should be treated in the same way. It requires more care than its larger relatives.

White-fronted or Cuban Amazon
Amazona leucocephala

Distribution   Cuba, Island of Pines.

Adult   Green, yellowish on the tail coverts. Forehead white, sometimes tinged with rose. Cheeks and an irregular patch on the throat rose red or rose pink. Feathers of the forepart of the body edged with black, the marking being heaviest on the head and neck. Feathers of abdomen show a considerable amount of wine colour. Outer web of flights slate blue. Tail yellowish green, outer feathers with a large red or wine red patch near the base. Bill whitish. Total length twelve to thirteen inches. Slightly smaller than the Blue-front.

The Cuban is the most frequently imported of the group of dark green Amazons with pink or white on the face and throat. It is a very beautiful bird but is noisy and an indifferent talker and does better in an aviary, birdroom, or flight cage than in very close confinement.

Newly imported Cubans sometimes suffer from infectious maladies contracted while they are overcrowded on the voyage. I remember a lot of twenty birds which seemed in the best of health for two or three weeks after arrival and then began to drop off until not a single one was left.

This Amazon is not a particularly reliable stayer at liberty, but I once had a female which spent the winter free in the garden and paired with a young cock Adelaide Parakeet. Strange to say the latter was bred at liberty and had never known confinement and it is extraordinary that when less than twelve months old he should have deserted the company of his own kind for that of the parrot. When spring came 'round the Adelaide was most attentive in feeding his strange partner and the pair set up house in a hollow oak, but just when the breeding of remarkable hybrids seemed possible the Amazon unfortunately died.

A hybrid Cuban X Blue-fronted Amazon has been bred on the Continent.

X

The Smaller South American Parrots

Blue-headed or Red-vented Parrot
Pionus menstruus

Distribution	Costa Rica, Colombia, Trinidad, Guiana, Peru, Amazon Valley, Ecuador.
Adult	Green; wings strongly tinged with yellowish bronze. Head, neck, and upper breast rich, dark blue. A blackish patch behind the eye and a trace of red on the throat. Tail-feathers rich blue mingling with green; a patch of fiery red near the base. Under tail-coverts fiery red with a little blue and green. Bill blackish with a red patch near the base. Length about eleven inches. Between a Senegal and a Blue-fronted Amazon in size.
Immature	Said to be greener on the head, neck, and upper breast and sometimes to show a pinkish band mixed with blue on the forehead.

The Blue-headed Parrot does tolerably well in a parrot cage, but far better in a flight cage or birdroom. If kept in very close confinement, it should be tamed, so that it can be let out daily for exercise. It is a very pretty bird, not noisy, and makes an affectionate pet. It is not a brilliant talker, but may learn to say a few words, and it is said to be amiable in mixed company.

There appears to be no information as to its hardiness or behaviour in an aviary, but it is said to have bred in Yorkshire, England, many years ago.

The species is fairly often imported and is common on the show bench.

The food should consist of a mixture of two parts canary, one part millet, one part oats, one part sunflower, one part peanuts with plenty of fruit and green food.

The natural cries are a cooing note, a whistle, and sound like "kike-kike!"

The female is said to have a smaller and narrower beak.

72

Dusky or Violet Parrot
Pionus fuscus

Distribution   Guiana and Lower Amazons.

Adult   Crown and cheeks very dark, dull blue; a few minute red feathers 'round the nostrils A blackish patch behind the eye, surrounded by brownish feathers showing a lot of pale buff, the general effect being strangely falcon-like. Feathers of mantle and rump dark brown with pale vinous pink and buff edges. Breast wine red. Flight feathers violet with a faint greenish tinge on the last pairs of secondaries. Tail violet with a fiery red patch at the base of the feathers. Bill greyish black with a yellowish mark near the base. Total legth ten and one-half inches. A little larger than the Senegal Parrot.

Immature   Said to show more green on the wing.

This pretty and unusually coloured little parrot is imported at not very infrequent intervals. In disposition and needs it resembles the Blue-headed Parrot.

A lady who kept one as a pet found that it possessed an unpleasant voice, of which, however, it did not make very free use. It was usually good-tempered but would bite sharply if frightened or jealous. It would not perch on its mistress's finger or wrist, but preferred to squat in her hands. It appeared by no means dull nor lacking in intelligence, though it did not learn to talk.

An experienced aviculturist found that very young birds of the species, like very young macaws, benefit by bread and milk, but this food should never be given to adults. There appears to be no information as to the Violet Parrot's behaviour in mixed company nor as to its ability to stand cold.

The species has not been bred.

The female is said to be smaller than the male with a beak smaller and broader and with a shorter terminal hook.

XI

Caiques

Black-headed Caique
Pionites melanocephala

Distribution	Guiana and Upper Amazon.
Adult	Crown black. Wings, rump, tail, and a spot below the eye green. Collar yellowish salmon. Cheeks and throat gold. Breast buffish or silvery white. Thighs, under tail-coverts, and flanks orange. Bill horn-black. Length nine and one-quarter inches. Tail short.
Immature	Said to have brown and green feathers on the crown.

The Caiques are a small group of short-tailed South American parrots which resemble the Conures in many of their habits. They are intelligent, playful, amusing and, when tamed, most affectionate pets, nor is a companion of their own species and of the opposite sex so likely to spoil their amiability towards human friends as in the case of most other parrots. They possess the drawback of being rather noisy and very sensitive to cold, needing plenty of warmth and care when newly imported. Of their disposition in mixed company, little appears to have been recorded, but most birds of their character and disposition are as savage to their psittacine companions as they are affectionate towards their mates or human friends.

The owner of a tame Caique describes his pet as follows: "Jot's chief amusement is to climb up the window cord, sailor fashion, or to hop upstairs and have a good chuckle at the top, after which he will creep into my pocket and there go to sleep; and when I was ill in bed he would lay his little head confidingly on the pillow and cuddle under the blankets. Eminently sociable, he will go to any stranger and very gently pinch an ear or finger to test his power of endurance. If they show signs of fear, he has a hearty laugh at their expense. For vice he has none, and he never means to hurt them. He plays with balls and reels of cotton and will drive an imaginary wheelbarrow across the table with his beak. He is a good

74

dancer and loves to display his talent whenever a tune is whistled, preferably 'Old Kent Road.' "

Caiques should be fed on a seed mixture consisting of two parts canary, two parts millet, one part oats, one part sunflower, and one part peanuts, with plenty of fruit.

They appreciate a box to roost in.

They pair readily in confinement, but do not appear to have been bred. The female is said to have a longer and narrower beak.

Caiques require plenty of exercise and should not be permanently confined in parrot cages.

White-breasted Caique
Pionites leucogaster

Distribution	Lower Amazons.
Adult	Head and back of neck yellowish salmon-colour. Cheeks, throat and under tail-coverts, yellow. Breast buffish or silvery white. Wings, rump, tail, and thighs green. Flights dusky with blue-green outer webs. Bill whitish. Length nine and one-half inches.

Often imported. Does not differ from the Black-headed Caique in character and requirements.

Yellow-thighed Caique
Pionites xanthomera

Distribution	Upper Amazons.
Adult	Crown yellowish salmon-colour. Cheeks, throat, a spot at the end of the wing, thighs, and under tail-coverts yellow. Breast buffish or silvery white. Wings green; flights bluish on the outer webs, blackish on the inner. Tail green; short. Bill white. Length nine and one-half inches.

Fairly frequently imported of recent years. Exactly like the Black-headed Caique in disposition and needs.

Hawk-headed Parrot (often, Red Fan)
Deroptyius accipitrinus

Distribution	Guiana, Amazon Valley.
Adult male	Wings, rump, under tail-coverts and central tail feathers green. Flight feathers blackish with some green and dark blue on the outer webs. Breast dark red with blue tips to the feathers. Head and cheeks brown streaked with pale buff. Nape with an erectile ruff of red feathers tipped with blue. Outer tail feathers dark blue shading into green

and chocolate; a red spot near the base. Bill black. Length fourteen inches. About the size of a Blue-fronted Amazon.

Adult female   Resembles the male but is thought to lack the red spot at the base of the tail feathers.

The Hawk-headed Parrot has long been famous for its intelligence, playfulness, and, when its temper has not been spoiled by teasing, amiability. It is, however, somewhat noisy and it is very sensitive to cold. It does best in a flight cage or birdroom; if kept in a parrot cage it must be let out daily for exercise, as it does not thrive in permanent close confinement. The food should consist of a seed mixture of two parts canary, one part millet, one part oats, one part peanuts, and one-half part sunflower, with plenty of fruit, especially sweet grapes. Hemp is bad and likely to induce feather-plucking. When excited or angry the bird has the power of erecting the curious ruff of feathers 'round the neck.

A Hawk-head in the possession of Mr. W. T. Greene learned to address people by the right name and to make his remaks on the right occasion. When given a piece of food he appreciated, he used to say "Ta," and kept on repeating his thanks as he ate it. But if the taste displeased him, he threw the morsel away with a disgusted "Huah!" and began to scream. The same bird had a trick of revolving rapidly 'round his perch and would do so at command, finishing up the performance by erecting his ruff and exclaiming "There!" in a tone of great satisfaction.

Hawk-heads have been known to lay in captivity, but the species has not been bred.

When desiring to intimidate another parrot, the Hawk-head makes a hissing noise.

The female is said to be smaller than the male and to have a smaller beak.

XII

Parrotlets

Blue-winged Parrotlet
Forpus vividus vividus or passerinus

Distribution   Southern Brazil, Paraguay.

Adult male   Bright green, darker on the back and wings. Secondaries, under wing-coverts, and rump deep blue. Bill whitish horn. Length about five inches. A little smaller than a Budgerigar.

Adult female   Similar to the male but is of a duller green and shows a yellowish tinge on the face and breast. Blue entirely lacking.

Immature   Males in first plumage have the blue areas of the plumage present but much reduced in extent.

This rather pretty little short-tailed parrot is imported in large numbers and is sometimes sold under the name of "Blue-winged Lovebird." On first arrival it needs warmth and care, but when acclimatized it can be safely wintered in an outdoor aviary. It does badly in very close confinement but will breed in an indoor aviary or even in a flight cage. It has a weak, chirruping cry and is quite good-tempered with other birds, but it fights most savagely with its own kind and does so from pure love of fighting. It is of a rather nervous disposition, hiding in a corner of its cage when closely approached, or swaying itself to and fro in an attitude of defiance.

It is a free breeder, but the young are rather troublesome to manage, as they need artificial heat during their first winter, yet do badly in cages and, once they have reached maturity, quarrel when several pairs are associated in more roomy quarters.

Where owls are not too numerous Blue-wings may be kept and bred at liberty during the summer months. Pairs can be released together once they are used to their surroundings and care must be taken not to catch up the old birds in autumn when they have young still in the nest. Blue-wings will breed in any small nest box and require no building material. They should be fed on millet, canary, and hemp, with apple, pear, and any green food they will take, especially plantain heads. They are often

77

fond of a turf of short grass and also of stale bread dipped in water and squeezed almost dry.

Blue-winged Parrotlets are stupid about finding their way into an aviary shelter through a small opening and care must be taken that they do not get chilled or starved in a flight where the way back to food and warmth is not very obvious. It has been stated that parent birds sometimes carry seed for the young to eat in the nest.

Guiana Parrotlet
Forpus passerinus passerinus

Habitat	Guiana(?), Venezuela, Trinidad, Colombia.
Adult male	Green; hind-neck with a greyish tinge. Rump emerald green. Some dark and pale blue feathers at the bend and along the lower edge of the wing. Under the wing-coverts and a patch of feathers over the ribs, brilliant dark blue. Bill whitish horn. Total length five and one-half inches.
Adult female	Green; rump brighter; forehead, sides of head, and lower parts more pronouncedly yellowish green than in the female Blue-wing.

The Guiana Parrotlet does not differ in disposition and needs from the Blue-wing. The writer has kept and bred it at liberty and with almost complete success in a flight cage. It has also been bred at Brighton.

Turquoise-rumped Parrotlet
Forpus cyanopygia

Distribution	Western Mexico, Tres Marias Islands.
Adult male	Green, paler on the breast and cheeks. Rump, lower edge of the wing, and some of the under wing-coverts pale turquoise blue. A bluish tinge on the secondaries. Total length about five inches.
Adult female	Green; lower back, rump, and upper tail-coverts lighter but brighter; forehead, sides of head, and underparts yellowish green; quills darker green than the coverts.
Immature	The young male in first plumage has the blue areas reduced in extent.

This rather rarely imported parrotlet has been bred by a lady at Swindon. It would not appear to differ from the Blue-wing in character and needs.

XIII

Macaws

Red and Yellow Macaw
Ara macao

Distribution	Mexico and Central America.
Adult	Scarlet; feathers of the central part of the wing showing a mixture of red, green, and yellow. Flights and lower edge of the wing blue. Rump pale blue. Some greenish blue and olive feathers at the sides of the rump and on the thighs. Central tail feathers of great length; scarlet with a purplish blue tinge at the base and tips. Outer tail feathers blue; some reddish chocolate near the base. Upper mandible whitish. Length thirty-six inches.
Immature	Greener on the wings.

The large macaws, of which this gigantic and gaudy bird is a typical example, are easily tamed and have a fair capacity for learning to talk. They are perfectly hardy, can be wintered out-of-doors, and they are usually fairly safe in mixed company. Among their chief failings are voices in proportion to their size and beaks which only the strongest aviary can resist. It is customary to keep them chained by one leg to a perch, but this is not fair or humane treatment for creatures that are active, playful, and intelligent. There are really only three tolerable ways of keeping macaws — in aviaries, at complete liberty, and with cut wings in enclosures from which they cannot escape by climbing.

The Red and Yellow Macaw is usually gentle with a person to whom he is attached, but it is extremely risky to make advances to a strange macaw unless he be of one of the all-blue species. It is recorded that an untamed and savage Red and Yellow actually killed a bull terrier after a Homeric combat in which both its wings were broken.

Undoubtedly the Red and Yellow Macaw shows to best advantage as a liberty bird. In a state of freedom it is said to be far less noisy and destructive than might be expected and tame single birds, or pairs —

one member of which is tame — are reputed not to leave the neighbourhood of their homes.

Macaws should be fed on a mixture one-half of which consists of peanuts, while canary, hemp, sunflower, oats, and wheat make up the remainder. Plenty of fruit is a necessity. Very young birds benefit by a diet of bread and milk or milk pudding.

The female Red and Yellow Macaw is said to have a shorter, broader, and more arched beak.

Hybrids with the Blue and Yellow Macaw have been bred. A very large barrel partly filled with decayed wood, or a hollow tree trunk, makes the best nest.

Red and Blue Macaw
Ara chloroptera

Distribution   Guatemala to Guiana.

Adult   Crimson. Mantle crimson mixed with olive green. Wings olive green mixed with slate blue. Flights blue. Under wing-coverts red. Rump pale blue. Feathers at the sides of the rump tinged with olive. Central tail feathers dark red with blue tips. Outer tail feathers maroon at the base; blue at the tips. Bill horny-white. Total length thirty-four inches.

A well-known bird, imported as early as the end of the sixteenth century. It is as hardy as other macaws and has the same disposition and needs

The female is said to be smaller, with a shorter beak. It has hybridized with the Military Macaw.

Blue and Yellow Macaw
Ara ararauna

Distribution   Tropical America from Panama to Guiana.

Adult   Blue, darker on the flights and tail. Sides of neck, entire breast, and under wing-coverts yellow. Throat blackish with an outer edging of greyish olive or greenish feathers. Some black feathers on the naked skin of the cheeks. Bill black. Total length thirty-one inches.

A freely imported and well-known bird which is the best talker of the genus, some specimens being very talented. It usually becomes attached to one person or one sex, being inclined to bite strangers. It is perfectly hardy and a good stayer at liberty, with the possible exception of very shy individuals with equally untamed mates. Like many macaws it is capable of blushing when excited, the bare skin of the face becoming suffused with pink.

Early in the last century a pair of these macaws bred freely in France, laying sixty-two eggs and rearing fifteen young which spent three months in the nest.

The female is said to be smaller, with a shorter and narrower beak.

Military Macaw
Ara militaris

Distribution   Mexico, Central and South America.

Adult   Olive green, more golden brown on the wings and brighter and bluer on the head. Forehead red. Rump pale blue. Flights and lower edge of the wing blue. Central tail feathers wine red at the base; blue at the tip. Outer tail feathers mainly blue. Bill blackish. Length twenty-seven inches.

Fairly often imported and likely to make a good talker. Treatment as for other large macaws. Hybrids between this species and the Red and Blue have been known.

The female is said to be smaller, with a shorter and more arched beak.

Glaucous Macaw
Anodorhyncus glaucus

Distribution   Paraguay, Uruguay, and Southern Brazil.

Adult   Slate blue, brighter on the rump and very dull on the head, neck and upper breast. A patch of naked yellow skin on the cheek. Bill black. Total length twenty-nine inches.

A rarely imported bird resembling other large all-blue macaws in disposition and hardiness.

Lear's Macaw
Anodorhyncus leari

Distribution   Brazil.

Adult   Hyacinth blue. Head and neck paler and more slate coloured. Breast feathers with paler tips. Bill black. A patch of naked yellow skin on the cheek. Length twenty-eight and one-half inches.

Lear's Macaw differs from its close ally, the Hyacinthine, it its slightly smaller size and less richly coloured head and breast. Unmated birds are gentle, friendly creatures and, though they can certainly make themselves heard, they screech somewhat less raucously than their parti-coloured relatives, their voices, as Mr. Astley noted, having something of the carrion crow timbre about them.

The species is excessively hardy. A bird in my possession, when in rough importation plumage, flew into the top of a bare oak tree and stayed there for more than forty-eight hours during a spell of raw January weather. When at length he decided to come down he was not a penny the worse for his long fast and exposure.

Lear's, like Hyacinthines, are bad stayers at liberty. After a lot of trouble I did manage to induce a couple to settle down for some months, but both eventually strayed and were shot. The hen used to gratify her taste for society by flying daily to a town three miles distant where she amused herself by pulling out the pegs of people's clothes lines and playing with the dogs. She was sometimes bitten, but such an embarassing occurrence did not make her any less fond of her canine companions.

Hyacinthine Macaw
Anodorhyncus hyacinthinus

Distribution   Central Brazil.

Adult   Deep hyacinth blue. A patch of bare yellow skin at the base of the beak. Bill black and very large. Total length thirty-four inches.

The Hyacinthine Macaw is certainly one of the most remarkable of living birds. Its great size, immense curved beak, and wonderful garb of uniform: deep, hyacinth blue make it, if not one of the most elegant of its family, at least the most imposing. Single birds are very gentle and affectionate, though, as with other macaws and indeed most parrots, the presence of a female companion will often make a cock Hyacinthine somewhat unfriendly towards humanity. The species is extremely hardy and, provided it escapes the miserable fate of being chained permanently by one leg to a perch, will live for a great number of years, showing itself wholly indifferent to cold in an outdoor aviary. It is unfortunately a bad stayer at liberty, even tame birds going straight off and flying for miles, being usually shot in mistake for a hawk.

The Hyacinthine should be fed like other macaws, and when very young benefits by being given bread and milk.

Severe Macaw
Ara severa

Distribution   Brazil, Amazon Valley, Guiana, Colombia, Panama.

Adult   Dark green, a bluish tinge on the crown and lower edge of the wing. A dark brown band across the forehead and some dark greenish brown feathers on the edge of the cheeks. Outer webs of flights slate-blue. Under wing-coverts mainly red. Tail reddish brown at the base and on the under surface; remainder blue-green. Bill black. Total length twenty inches.

The smaller macaws have the reputation of being intelligent and affec-

Ivory Conures, very similar to Petz' Conure. Photo by Horst Mueller.

A pair of Manycolor Parrakeets, male at left. Photo by Horst Mueller.

Red-Fronted Parrakeet.
Photo by Horst Mueller.

Stanley Rosella, male. Photo
by Horst Mueller.

tionate pets with some talent for talking and no worse proclivity for screaming than Amazons. They do quite well in cages if let out for daily exercise. As to their ability to stand cold there seems to be little information. They should be fed like Blue-fronted Amazons. A Severe Macaw in Miss Knobel's possession was devoted to his mistress and liked climbing about her and lying in her lap. He talked a good deal, but with indistinct articulation.

Illiger's Macaw
Ara maracana

Distribution	Brazil and Paraguay.
Adult male	Dark green. Forehead red. Crown and cheeks bluish; also lower edge of wing. Flights bluish slate. Some red feathers in the centre of the abdomen and on the upper rump. Tail brown and olive at the base; blue-green at the tip. Bill horny black. Total length sixteen and three-quarters inches. Smaller than the Severe Macaw.
Adult female	Said to have less red on the forehead.
Immature	Said to have less red on the forehead and the red patches on the body replaced by yellowish colour; upper parts spotted with pale grey-brown.

Illiger's Macaw is said to make a very affectionate pet and a fair talker. One in Miss Knobel's collection was most playful and amusing and loved emptying the waste paper basket and distributing the contents over the floor. His one failing was a fondness for nipping his mistress's ankles, a form of practical joking to which many parrots are addicted. He bathed freely and talked in an amusing way.

A pair on the Continent hatched a young one, but did not rear it. The cock fed the hen while she was sitting and the pair were very spiteful to other birds. Like the larger macaws, the small species, when young, should be given bread and milk.

XIV

Conures

Red-masked Conure
Aratinga rubrolarvata

Distribution	West Ecuador.
Adult	Green. Crown and face red. Some spots of red on the neck. Shoulders, under wing-coverts, thighs, and bend of wing red. Bill yellowish white. Length thirteen and one-half inches.
Immature	Much less red.

The Red-headed Conure is a typical member of a large group of South American parakeets which have a strong family resemblance in character and habits. They make affectionate, intelligent, and playful pets, but are too active to be suited to permanent confinement in a parrot cage, and if caged must be let out daily for exercise in spite of their fondness for chewing up wood and other relatively soft substances. Most species are hardy and can be wintered in outdoor aviaries. The chief fault of the genus is their excessive noisiness and spitefulness towards parakeets of other families. Like lorikeets they are a little less intolerant of their own kind and also of non-psittacine birds.

They nest fairly freely in captivity and are usually double brooded. In their domestic arrangements they closely resemble lorikeets, and they will use a hollow log or tree trunk in aviary shelter or flight.

They appreciate logs to roost in, but a careful watch must be kept in case a hen tries to lay in cold weather and gets egg-bound. Where this danger has arisen the log must be put in a heated shelter and the birds driven in at night. It may be added that it is a great mistake to leave nests in the aviary out of the breeding season where species are kept which do *not* use them as dormitories. Conures should be fed on a seed mixture of two parts canary, one part millet, one part oats, and one part peanuts with plenty of fruit. Hemp is liable to cause liver disease and feather plucking. The sexes are always much alike.

The Red-headed Conure makes a fair talker.

84

Mexican Conure
Aratinga holochlora

Distribution Mexico and Guatemala.
Adult   Green; paler and yellower on the breast. Sometimes a
              fleck of red on the cheeks. Bill yellowish flesh-colour.
              Length twelve and one-half inches.
A rarely imported species of no great beauty.

Green Conure
Aratinga leucophthalma

Distribution Guiana, Trinidad, Colombia, Peru, Boliva, Brazil.
Adult male   Green. Sometimes with speck of red on the head or neck,
              or a tinge of wine red on the breast. Bend of wing and
              under wing-coverts orange-red, the latter merging into
              yellow. Bill yellowish flesh-colour. Naked skin 'round eye,
              ashy flesh-colour. Length thirteen and one-half inches.
Immature   Bend of wing yellowish.
    A rarely imported species, which, like other large conures, atones for
its harsh voice and not particularly beautiful plumage, by unusual intelligence and docility and talent for talking.
    The female is said to have a broader beak.

Queen of Bavaria's Conure
Aratinga guarouba

Distribution Para, Northeast Brazil.
Adult male   General plumage rich golden yellow; flight feathers dark
              green. Bill pinkish horn; feet flesh-colour. Total length
              fourteen inches. Size about that of a woodpigeon.
Adult female Similar to the male but smaller and with a less massive
              head and beak.
Immature   Nestling plumage shows more green. At a certain stage
              has cheeks and upper wing-coverts with scattered green
              feathers.
    The Queen of Bavaria's Conure has long been famous for its great
rarity; its docility when tamed, and its marvellous golden plumage. I have
never been what the late Mr. Jamrach used to call "a strong buyer of
conures," but the Queen of Bavaria was, when it arrived, a welcome
addition to my collection. Certainly though not graceful in form, and
endowed with a voice as disagreeable as that of any of his noisy congeners,
Conurus guarouba has a barbaric splendour that cannot fail to attract.
He *looks* South American! Although my Queen of Bavarias are not tame,
I can well believe that the accounts of their good qualities as pets are not
over-rated, for they are continually caressing each other, and play together

in the most amusing fashion, shoving and mauling like puppies, yet never evoking a protest by too hard a nip. They are typical conures in all their habits, ruffling their feathers, doing all kinds of gymnastics, and assaulting any parakeet of another family that approaches them, for although single birds are harmless enough in mixed company, pairs are decidedly aggressive.

When newly imported this conure requires warmth and care; afterwards it becomes tolerably hardy, though my birds make a good deal of use of their warmed shelter during cold weather.

Unfortunately, no parakeet in existence is more addicted to the vice of feather plucking. Even the plainest diet combined with plenty of exercise in a large outdoor aviary and a companion of the opposite sex will not prevent some birds from disfiguring themselves.

The Queen of Bavaria's Conure should be fed on sunflower and canary seed with an unlimited supply of apple and other fruit.

When tamed, the species is said to make a good talker, and my hen bird mimics the Barabands with which she lives.

Golden-crowned Conure
Eupsittula aurea

Distribution Guiana, Amazons, Bolivia, Brazil, Paraguay.
Adult Green: forepart of crown and feathers 'round the eye orange-salmon. Rear of crown bluish. Throat, cheeks, and upper breast olive, the cheeks with a faint bluish tinge. Lower breast pale yellowish green. Flights blue-green. Tail tip tinged with blue. Bill blackish. Total length ten and three-quarter inches.

The Golden-crowned Conure has been bred several times on the Continent, but in England only hybrids with the Jendaya appear to have been reared. The species is easily tamed and becomes docile and affectionate, but breeding pairs are spiteful with other birds.

The Golden-crowned Conure can be wintered out-of-doors.

The female is said to have a shorter and broader beak.

Lesser Patagonian Conure
Cyanolyseus patagonus

Distribution La Plata and Patagonia.
Adult Dark, brownish olive, paler and more bronze on the wing, and less olive on the upper breast. A little whitish colour on the upper breast. Abdomen yellow with a large orange-red patch on the centre. Rump pale golden-bronze. Flights slate colour. Bill horn black. Length seventeen and one-half inches.

The Patagonian Conure, though not a gaudy bird, is decidedly handsome in its unusual garb of brown and yellow. Like other big conures it is very intelligent, a good talker and mimic, and an amusing and playful companion. It is recorded of one that he was quiet and well-behaved in respectable company, but raised a great uproar on the appearance of tramps.

The species is quite indifferent to cold, and, it breeds in colonies in burrows in the face of cliffs, is probably tolerant of the presence of other conures.

The female is said to be smaller, with a smaller, shorter and broader back.

Petz' Conure (occasionally, Half Moon)
Eupsittula canicularis

Distribution   Mexico and Central America.

Adult   Glittering olive green. Abdomen bright yellow-green. Throat and upper breast pale yellowish olive brown. Forepart of crown salmon colour. Rear of crown slate blue. Flights blue-green. Bill fleshy-white. Length nine and one-half inches.

Immature   Much less salmon on the forehead.

This little conure is not very often imported, but is said to make a nice pet.

In a wild state it feeds largely on the fruit of the tree Pileus conica and, strange to relate, soils its plumage badly with the sticky juice. This circumstance is not a little remarkable when one recollects how strongly healthy birds object, as a rule, to dirt on their feathers; but I have seen skins of wild Amazon parrots badly disfigured from the same cause.

It is said that Petz' Conure is difficult to distinguish from the fruit on which it feasts so greedily and is apparently aware of the protective resemblance, as it remains quiet and motionless when a hawk surprises it on a "Parrot fruit" tree, but takes to noisy flight if approached by its enemy elsewhere.

Aztec Conure
Eupsittula astec

Distribution   Southern Mexico, Guatemala, Honduras, Nicaragua, and Costa Rica.

Adult   Green. Throat and upper breast brown. Lower breast yellowish olive brown. Flights tinged with bluish slate. Bill brown horn colour. Length nine and one-half inches.

The Aztec Conure is not very often imported. It has been bred in a flight cage in Jamaica. As with most small conures, more than one brood is produced in a year. The normal clutch consists of four or five eggs.

The female is said to have a broader beak.

Cuban Conure
Eupsitulla euops
Distribution   Cuba.

Adult male   Green: cheeks, crown and bend of wing flecked with scarlet. Under wing-coverts scarlet. Bill whitish flesh-colour. Length ten and one-half inches.

A rarely-imported bird, said to be intelligent and amusing.

Brown-eared Conure
Eupsittula ocularis
Distribution   Veraguas and Panama.

Adult   Green, paler and yellower on the breast. Crown slightly tinged with bluish slate colour. Cheeks, throat and upper breast brown. Some orange feathers below the eye and sometimes a slight tinge of orange on the abdomen. Bill horn-brown. Length nine and three-quarter inches.

The Brown-eared Conure was bred in captivity and found to be quiet with non-psittacine birds and not destructive to shrubs. If teased, the pair performed very quaint antics, but did not bite. Nesting operations lasted nine weeks.

Cactus Conure
Eupsittula cactorum
Distribution   Southeastern Brazil.

Adult   Green. Head tinged with brown and faint slate colour. Flights and tip of tail tinged with slate blue. Throat and upper breast brown. Lower breast yellowish buff. Bill whitish. Length ten and one-quarter inches.

Immature   Crown plain green. Throat and breast olive.

This rather pretty little conure does well in confinement and has been wintered out-of-doors. It has the family failing of noisiness, but is said to agree fairly well with other members of the genus. It becomes very tame and amusing, single birds, and even pairs, showing a lively interest in their owner, running to meet him fluttering and jabbering in a sort of ectasy. The species has been bred in captivity. Treatment as for other conures.

The female is said to be smaller and to have a shorter beak.

Jendaya Conure
Eupsittula jendaya
Distribution   Brazil.

Adult   Head and neck orange-yellow. Breast and under wing-coverts orange-red tinged with olive. Thighs olive and tinged with rust red. Upper rump orange-red; lower rump green. Mantle and wings green: lower edge of wing and flights partly blue. Tail bronze-green at the base, dark blue at the tip. Bill dusky horn colour. Length twelve inches.

The Jendaya, or Yellow-headed Conure, is a freely imported species, which does well in an aviary and is reputed to be peaceable with other birds. It has been bred in England, nesting operations taking about three months from start to finish. The species has some talent for mimicry, but the usual conure failing of a harsh voice and a mischievous beak.

Black-headed or Nanday Conure
Nandayus nanday

Distribution Paraguay.

Adult Bright green. Crown brownish black merging into chestnut at the rear edge. Front of cheeks marked with black or black and chestnut. A pale bluish tinge on the upper breast. Thighs rust red. Flights lower edge of wing and tail blue and green. Bill horn-brown. Length twelve inches. Female with a smaller head and more sharply curved beak.

Immature Duller.

This rather handsome conure is well-known in confinement and has bred on several occasions. It is noisy, but can be wintered out-of-doors and is said to agree fairly well with other members of the genus. Food and treatment as for other conures.

Thick-billed Parakeet
Rhyncopsitta pachyrhyncha

Distribution Mexico.

Adult Green, brighter on the cheeks. Forepart of crown, feathers above and behind eye, shoulders, and a touch on the thighs and lower edge of the wing, red. Lower part of under-coverts yellow. Bill black. Length seventeen inches.

Immature Less red; bill horn-whitish.

This large conure-like parakeet is extremely rare in captivity. The reason may perhaps be found in the answer of a Mexican trapper to a question put by an American friend of mine as to why he did not catch Thick-bills. "Señor, they no good. Bite like hell. Perhaps catch three, four pair; no can use hands for weeks. Lady no buy; gentleman no buy; and damn bird no good to eat. What de hell de use?"

Nevertheless, according to Karl Plath, the species has some virtues to offset its harsh voice and powerful beak, a tame bird in his collection showing great affection for his little son and following him about with a queer shuffling gait, shaking its tail from side to side.

The species would no doubt thrive on the treatment of a conure.

Quaker or Grey-breasted Parakeet
Myopsittacus monachus

Distribution	Bolivia, Paraguay, Argentine, Uruguay.
Adult male	Green, brighter on the rump and belly. Forehead and lower part of cheeks grey with pale edges to the feathers; lower breast greyish olive. Flights and bastard-wing bluish. Tail long and narrow, green slightly tinged with blue. Bill reddish white. Total length eleven and one-half inches. Size about that of a Ringneck.
Adult female	Said to be more bulky and with a much longer and more powerful beak. (Did the observer mistake the cock for the hen?)

The Quaker Parakeet has the distinction of being the only parrot which is known to build an actual nest. It is an excessively hardy bird and the only thing that will kill it is permanent confinement in a parrot cage. It is highly gregarious in a wild state, even during the breeding season, and the old nests are repaired and re-occupied until they reach a great size. When not employed for the rearing of a brood they are kept in good condition for a dormitory. A species of Teal, *B. monachus,* often lays its eggs in the Quakers' nests and appears to live on quite good terms with the rightful owners. The nest itself is entirely composed of sticks and consists of two chambers, an inner and an outer one. As the young brood increase in size the parents sometimes reconstruct and enlarge the nursery. From four to six eggs are usually laid and the period of incubation is thirty-one days.

The Quaker is a noisy bird, continually uttering its "Quak, Quaki, quak-wi, quak-wi, quak-wi, quarr! quarr! quarr!" Some people find its vocal efforts distressing, but in justice it must be admitted that while the Quaker talks far, far too much, he just fails to reach the unendurable pitch in all his remarks. Pet birds are intelligent and amusing. An aviculturist had one which was an excellent talker, its longest sentence being "Merrily danced the Quaker's wife with all her bairns about her." It would do tricks to order. At the command "Act daft!" it would ruffle its feathers put up one leg, open its beak, and nod its head. At the command "Act proud!" it would turn its beak against its breast and draw up its head. It showed great affection for its owners, but would attack visitors and strange dogs and cats and pull off the maids' caps. It was never shut up in the daytime. It bathed freely and was so indifferent to cold that it would dry itself on the crack between two window sashes through which a keen northeaster was blowing.

The Quaker will flourish in an outdoor aviary and care nothing for the cold. It requires netting of cockatoo strength to confine it, as it can bite through ordinary wire.

For breeding, a large heap of twigs and sticks must be provided and a framework or platform as a foundation for the nest. Both sexes share in the work of building. The Quaker agrees well with its own kind but is very savage with all other birds, a pair delivering a joint attack after the manner of lorikeets.

The Quaker should be fed on canary, millet, oats, and sunflower with peanuts and plenty of fruit. The species has bred at liberty both in England and on the Continent, a pair in Saxony producing a flock of forty birds. Notwithstanding these successes, it cannot be considered an ideal liberty subject. The great majority stay only for a time and then wander away after a few months or even a year. They are also fearfully destructive in the garden, sheering off innumerable branches and committing havoc in the orchard. They are fond of feeding on the araucaria, or monkey-puzzle tree, eating the base of the leaves as we eat the base of the sepals of an artichoke.

Brown-throated Conure (often Chocolate-face)
Eupsittula pertinax aeruginosa

Distribution   Colombia, Venezuela, Brazil.

Adult   Green; crown with a slate bluish tinge. Cheeks, throat, and upper breast brown, sometimes some orange feathers round the eye. Flights tinged with slate blue. Lower breast yellowish green tinged with more or less orange. Bill whitish. Length ten and one-quarter inches.

Immature   Said to have a greener crown and an olive throat and breast.

The Brown-throated Conure is freely imported and is an amusing, if noisy, little bird. Single specimens become very tame and playful and can be taught to talk.

The species was bred by Mrs. Williams, who describes the young as having a whitish ring round the eye.

Birds in the writer's collection needed artificial heat in winter.

The female is said to have a longer and more slender beak.

XV

Brotogerys and Lineolated Parakeets

Tovi Parakeet (often, Bee Bee's)
Brotogerys jugularis

Distribution   Southern Mexico, Central America, Colombia.

Adult male   General plumage green of various shades. A bluish tinge on the rump and abdomen; an olive tinge on the mantle and a yellowish tinge on the upper breast. A conspicuous brownish bar on the wing and a small orange patch on the chin. Under wing-coverts yellowish. Some trace of blue on the lower edge of the wing. Specimens from Colombia may show a quantity of rich, dark blue on the wings. Tail pointed and of medium length. Bill pale horn flesh colour and unusually long and narrow. Total length seven and one-half inches.

The Tovi Parakeet resembles other members of the genus in being noisy, lively, playful, and easily tamed and capable of learning a few words. It is rather spiteful in mixed company and is sensitive to cold, an unheated room being the limit of what it can safely endure.

The species has often bred in Germany, but not, it would seem, in England. It will use an ordinary nest box or hollow log.

The food should consist of millet, canary, and oats with plenty of fruit. The Tovi does best in a flight cage, birdroom or aviary. If kept in a parrot cage it must be let out for daily exercise. Mr. Philipps had a pair that were very bold and savage and assaulted him without mercy. Not only did they bite like bulldogs, but the cock would dash violently against his master's forehead, striking him with almost the stunning force of a cricket ball.

The female is said to have a narrower, shorter and more arched beak. She is generally duller and much smaller.

Lineolated Parakeet
Bolborhyncus lineolatus

Distribution   Southern Mexico.

Adult male   Green of various shades, paler on the breast, brighter on the forehead and more yellowish olive on the back, rump, and flanks. The plumage with the exception of the centre of the breast and abdomen, is curiously barred with blackish colouring, the barring being heaviest on the back. There are some black and black-tipped feathers on the wing and the feathers of the lower rump are tipped with black spots. The tail feathers are pointed, green with blackish tips and are of no great length. Bill horn-yellowish white. Total length six and three-quarter inches.

Adult female   Said to be stouter in build with the green areas of the plumage more olive and less brilliant, the tail wholly green and the marking less distinct.

Immature   Paler than the adult.

This gentle and beautiful little parakeet has only one failing — that of being sensitive to cold. It should never be exposed to a lower temperature than sixty degrees Fahrenheit. It does well in a flight cage, birdroom, or, in summer, in an outdoor aviary. The food should consist of canary, millet and oats, with plenty of fruit.

The Lineolated Parakeet has bred on the Continent and a young one lived to leave the nest in England, but was killed by an accident. Breeding birds have been observed to line their nest with bark and the cock spends a lot of time in the log with the hen.

The Lineolated Parakeet is easily tamed and a talking specimen is on record.

XVI

Cockatoos and Cockatiel

Palm or Great Black Cockatoo
Microglossus aterrimus

Distribution   Papuan Islands and North Australia.

Adult male   Black, the races from the New Guinea region with a slate grey tinge. A patch of naked pink skin at the base of the beak. Bill of great size and black in colour. Upper mandible notched. Eye large and dark. A long crest of hair-like feathers. Total length twenty-nine inches.

Adult female   Smaller and more slender, with a much smaller head and beak.

This extraordinary-looking cockatoo was rare in aviculture until recent years, when a number — mostly males — were imported, both the New Guinea race and the smaller subspecies being represented.

In a wild state the Palm Cockatoo is said to subsist on nuts and on the green centre of the palm cabbage. Its eggs are laid in a hollow tree on a bed of green twigs.

In captivity it has the reputation, when tamed, of being a very gentle bird, not biting even when annoyed, but merely scratching with the tip of its upper mandible. Unlike the *Caltyptorhynci,* it is said to enjoy being petted and there are records of specimens which said a word or two in a very small voice. The curious bare pink skin on the face is capable of changing colour and becomes bluish when the bird is cold or ill.

The Palm Cockatoo's natural calls consist of whistles, screams, and croaks, and when hurt or terrified it utters a loud grating screech.

Palm Cockatoos should be fed on hemp, sunflower, peanuts, and any other nuts or grain that they fancy. They will sometimes also eat apple and green food and milk-sop should be offered to birds with young.

The courtship of the Palm Cockatoo is the quaintest and most ludicrous of any member of the parrot family and perhaps of any bird in the world. Blushing bright red with excitement, the male erects his weird crest, spreads his wings, stamps with his feet, and utters the most incredible assortment of whoops, shreiks and strange clicking noises. At frequent intervals he ducks his head sharply and turning it on one side gazes up adoringly into the face of his beloved.

Male Palm Cockatoos resemble Banksians in that they feed their mates but do not caress them and take no part in the incubation of the eggs. A large natural tree trunk makes the best nest and the birds should be plentifully supplied with leafy branches as they are said to line their nests profusely, no doubt as a precaution against their being filled by tropical rain.

When acclimatized, this species can stand a fair amount of cold.

Banksian Cockatoo
Calyptorhyncus banksii

Distribution	Australia.
Adult male	Black with a dull gloss on the wings and a faint greyish tinge on the breast. A long scarlet bar across the outer tail feathers. Bill greyish black. Length twenty-seven inches.
Adult female	Black, feathers of head, neck, and mantle with dull, pale yellow spots. Breast barred with dull, pale yellow. Under tail-coverts pale yellow and orange-red with black bars and freckling. Tip of tail black: basal portion pale yellow merging into orange-red, with transverse black bars and black freckling.
Immature	In first plumage much resembles the female. With the first moult young males become less spotted and show more red on the tail than females of the same age. With the second moult they become entirely black with scarlet tail bars freckled with black. With the third, adult plumage is assumed in the fourth year.

The Banksian Cockatoo is a variable species of which three or four races exist, differing considerably in size and to some extent in the plumage of the females and the dimensions of the beak.

The typical *C. banksii* is a big race. The female has the head well-spotted and the breast well-barred, the tail feathers showing pale yellow and orange-red colour. The voice of the male when in flight is deep, melancholy, and sonorous.

The Great-billed Banksian Cockatoo is about as large as the typical form and has a larger beak, while the female has scarcely any orange-red in her tail, pale yellow colouring predominating. The Western Black Cockatoo *C. stellatus* is about a third smaller than the two forms already mentioned. The voice of the male is pitched in a higher key and the female is very profusely spotted and barred, her tail being like that of a female *C. banksii* in colouring. This race, of recent years, has been the most frequently imported of the three.

In my collection at the present time I have a female Banksian Cockatoo which is no larger than a *C. stellatus,* but has hardly any spotting on the head or barring on the breast, while her crest is less rounded than that of a typical Western bird.

In a wild state the Banksian Cockatoo occurs in fairly large flocks, although it seems to be diminishing under persecution for its feathers and flesh, as well as with the settlement of the country. A party of Banksians have a habit, not uncommon among parrots, of refusing to leave a wounded companion, their concern exposing them to still further casualties from a person armed with a gun.

In their nesting habits they resemble the broadtailed parakeets, and differ from most other cockatoos, the cock feeding his sitting mate, but making no attempt to incubate the eggs. The normal clutch consists of two, but single eggs are common.

Banksian Cockatoos are seldom seen in captivity and command very high prices. Presumably the nests are inaccessible and the young troublesome to rear, while adults usually refuse food and die when deprived of their liberty. Birds well on seed are, however, as easy to keep as their commoner white brethren and will survive for a long period either in cage or aviary. A female in my collection must have been at least twenty years in captivity and is still a magnificent specimen showing not a sign of age.

By reason of their great size, their powerful beaks, and their loud and strident cries, Banksians are certainly not everybody's birds, but they have a dignity and charm about them which endears them to the aviculturist who has proper accommodation to place at their disposal. The males become exceedingly tame; so tame, in fact, that it is almost impossible to find one that is of any use for breeding; their affections and interest become so centered in humanity that they have no time for the females of their own kind. No animal will give his master a more disinterested devotion than a Banksian Cockatoo. Unlike most cockatoos they dislike being touched and having their heads scratched, and at most tolerate rather than enjoy such familiarities; they have also little fondness for tit-bits. All that they ask is to be with their master or mistress, and a few kind words and a little flattery will evoke from them a transport of excitement and delight. They throw up their crests into the shape of a Roman helmet, spread their tails and go off into their peculiar love-song, "Kooi, kooi, kooi, kooi." A very tame male who lived for, alas! but a short two years in my collection, was one of the most interesting and delightful birds I have ever kept. With some little difficulty I trained him to fly at liberty and a wonderful sight he was in the air. We have no English bird which in the least resembles *C. banksii* when in flight. The wings and tail of a Black Cockatoo are of great length and give a strangely aeroplane-like appearance. Indeed, my birds used to get wildly excited at the spectacle of an aeroplane in the sky, apparently taking it for a rather odd-looking member of their own species! The flight, though not rapid, is extraordinarily buoyant, the bird having the appearance of a great leaf wafted about by gusts of air. All the time it is on the wing it keeps uttering its strange cry, which in the case of a cock of the large races is wild and melancholy as that of a lost soul. The call of females is harsher and more strident. At first my cock "Teddy" gave us some little trouble. Like many big parrots that have been long confined he was afraid to fly *down* from a height; also, if people went indoors, he was inclined to become anxious and restless and opening his great wings would betake himself, wailing, to fields and pastures new. He was never a fool, however, for, on finding that he had lost his way, he would, like any other traveller, betake himself to the nearest inn and wait there until his friends came to fetch him home! He was amiable with everyone and ready to perch on an arm or shoulder; or, if such close company were not desired, to sit quietly by you without making himself a nuisance. His particular chum was one of the gardeners. To this man he became so much attached that he would follow his bicycle as he rode home in the evening to the town three miles away and, having seen him safely to his house, he would return long after dusk had fallen. I have often, on a summer evening, sat on the top of the hill near my old home when flocks of wild fowl were feeding on the grass below. Then faint and far away I would hear Teddy's approaching voice, followed by a roar of wings as company after company of ducks feld in unnecessary consternation and a great dark shadow would drift over my head on noiseless wings as Teddy betook himself to his accustomed perch on the ledge of the stable window. That the ducks should be frightened by Teddy was, perhaps, not unnatural; but strange to say his appearance in the air at first filled my Australian parakeets with as much consternation as if he had been an eagle. As a matter of fact with other birds he was the gentlest and most timid thing imaginable, giving way before the smallest parakeet that approached him closely.

Teddy had a peculiar habit of flying on moonlight nights, and I would often hear him on the wing at house when one would expect only an Owl Parrot to be active.

Poor fellow! He was one of the first Banksians I ever had and I did not know that, while they can stand dry cold and rain, cold fog and snow are most injurious. I allowed him to roost out one foggy night in late October and he caught a chill, only a very slight chill it seemed, but he just would not feed. I put him in a room at about seventy degrees Fahrenheit (had it been eighty-five degrees I should probably have saved him) but it was no good. Day after day he grew slowly weaker and at length after nearly a fortnight of complete fasting I lost what was in many ways the nicest bird I ever kept.

Banksian Cockatoos should be fed on hemp, sunflower, and peanuts, with a few Brazil nuts. They seldom touch fruit or green food, but occasionally when in an aviary eat a little grass or oats softened in the rain and about to sprout. In a wild state they live largely on grubs, but in captivity they reject mealworms, gentles, and wasp larvae and the larvae of wood-boring beetles. They are, however, exceedingly fond of the little white grubs found inside oak apples and a few will eat smooth caterpillars from rose and apple trees. In collecting oak apples for Banksians look carefully to see that there is no little round hole in the gall, as this means that the insect has made its exit and the "apple" is empty. Banksians are very conservative in their diet and if accustomed to a particular kind of seed will sometimes starve sooner than touch an unfamiliar one. They are also very sensitive birds and even a tame one will refuse food for some days after arriving at a strange place. As, however, their powers of fasting are considerable no undue anxiety need be felt. A timid bird, which seems very nervous and unhappy, can sometimes be induced to start feeding if turned into an aviary with a companion already used to the place. Banksian Cockatoos are difficult birds to mate up; for not only will the cocks persist in getting too tame and reserving all their affection for human beings; but the hens, unless actually in breeding condition, are snappy and discouraging to their potential suitors. It is only when two birds have been flying together for many months that a good understanding may be hoped for when the hen comes into breeding condition. If the cock is master and bullies his companion, the outlook is hopeless and he can only be tried with a more determined lady who keeps him in his place. Although not great fighters, Banksians do not agree well with their own kind. The hens are jealous of others of their sex and the cocks, especially if tame, are also exceedingly jealous of one another.

With other birds these cockatoos are very inoffensive and if they do make a hostile demonstration it is as much from nervousness as real anger. A cock Crimson-winged Parakeet I once kept with some Banksians bullied them so badly that I had to remove him.

Banksians may nest at any time of year but the majority lay in autumn and winter. They will use a large, hollow, mould-filled tree trunk and sometimes a barrel. One hen I had insisted on sitting on the ground in a corner of the aviary, like a chicken. All three hens in my collection have laid and two have incubated, but the eggs have never been fertile. I think pairing has not taken place, the cocks never troubling to do more than feed their partners and more usually neglecting them entirely!

Black Cockatoos usually moult in spring, but the moult is not a very thorough one, only a portion of the feathers being cast each year. A hen

Gold Mantled Rosella.
Photo by Horst Mueller.

Albino Cockatiel. Photo by
Horst Mueller.

Australian King Parrakeet.
Photo by Horst Mueller.

A pair of Stanley, or Western, Rosellas. The male is at right. Photo by Horst Mueller.

Male Blossom Head, or Plum Head, Parrakeet. Photo by Horst Mueller.

Blue variety of Alexander Ringneck Parrakeet. Photo by Horst Mueller.

Indian Ringneck Parrakeets. Blue variety above, lutino
variety below. Drawing by R. A. Vowles.

Banksian, like a Grey Parrot, may lay within a day or two of dropping some feathers. Tame Banksians can be trained to fly at liberty, but they need constant watching and shepherding for several days until they have learned their way about, discovered their feeding place and overcome their fear of flying down from a height. Untamed birds are a very risky proposition and if turned out at all really need to be first released with cut wings.

Banksians are rather sensitive to tuberculosis. Many years ago the writer foolishly placed a very old and decrepit Roseate Cockatoo in the Banksians' aviary. After a time it fell ill and died, and proved to be badly infected with the disease. A little while later three Banksians went wrong, and one died and also proved to be tubercular. The others I fully expected to lose as well, for they went as thin as rails. However, I caged them in a very warm room and fed them on rich food with quantities of oak-apple grubs. The older hen seemed in great pain. She constantly vomited, became very cross and irritable and continually tore up large quantities of rotten wood with which I provided her. Gradually, however, the symptoms abated and to my intense astonishment both she and her companion began to improve and eventually made a complete recovery. The old hen is still alive twelve years after her illness and recently laid eggs. The younger hen also lived some time and had grown into a magnificent bird when she was lost by an accident.

Female Banksians are harder to tame than males and are less good-tempered when their fear is overcome. But, while they threaten and snap when there are cage bars or aviary wire between them and their visitor, they seldom do much if he goes inside with them. When I was able to keep her at liberty, I often carried my old hen "Timmie" on my shoulder, and though I had anxious forebodings that she might take a piece out of my cheek or ear, I am thankful to say that she never abused my confidence.

Banksians are not talkers. I have only heard of one, who said "Cocky" in a very small voice quite out of proportion to his size.

As already indicated Banksian Cockatoos are not absolutely hardy and need a little artificial heat during periods of snow or cold fog when they should not be allowed in the open.

Funereal Cockatoo
Zanda funerea

Distribution	South Queensland, New South Wales, Victoria, Tasmania, South Australia.
Adult male	General colour above blackish brown with smoke-brown edges to the feathers of the neck, back, and wings. Crown blackish brown; under surface dark brown with pale yellowish tips to the feathers. A lemon yellow patch in the region of the ear. The lateral tail feathers have a large

patch of pale yellow freckled with brown. Bill whitish. Length twenty-four and three-quarter inches.

Adult female   Said to resemble the male but to be smaller and to have the yellow edgings to the feathers more pronounced.

Immature   Said to resemble the female in having the yellow edgings to the feathers very pronounced.

The Funereal Cockatoo is common in a wild state but extremely rare in confinement, where it appears to be more delicate than the Banksian. I have a photograph of a tame bird which belonged to a resident in Tasmania and was said to be a great pet and much beloved by its owner. A pinioned female in my own possession only survived a few months. She was subject to severe attacks of vomiting, one of which ultimately proved fatal. Rightly or wrongly I attributed her malady to the bad and musty quality of the seed (she was imported during World War I.) Had we been giving her the wrong diet altogether she would presumably have got worse and worse as long as the same seed mixture was continued, but in point of fact she would recover and live for weeks in perfect health on hemp, sunflower, and peanuts before getting another attack. In disposition she was snappy and unfriendly.

In a wild state the Funereal Cockatoo lives largely on the grubs of woodboring beetles, as well as on seeds. It is said to have a harsh, grating cry sounding like a guttural "Keow."

Gang-gang Cockatoo
Callocorydon fimbriatus

Distribution   New South Wales, Victoria, Tasmania.

Adult male   General colour dusky slate with lighter margins to the feathers. Some of the feathers on the lower abdomen barred with white and orange-red. Flights and tail dark grey. Head scarlet with short erectile crest of soft, loose, curly feathers. Bill horn-grey. Length fourteen and one-eighth inches. Size about that of a pigeon.

Adult female   Upper surface more boldly marked than in the male. Breast and abdomen barred with dull orange and greenish white. Head grey.

Immature   The cock in first plumage has only the red crest and a few small red feathers on the head.

The Gang-gang Cockatoo will sometimes live in a cage, becoming fond of its owner and sometimes learning to say a few words, but most caged birds become feather-pluckers and it is too noisy to be a pleasant companion in a room. As an aviary bird it is one of the most desirable of the cockatoos, for, though it is less beautifully coloured than the Leadbeater and Salmon-crest, it is irresistibly quaint and amusing. The red-headed cock and his grey mate are the most comical Darby and Joan imaginable, with their chubby faces and quizzical brown eyes. They are much attached to each other and indulge in a continual flow of small talk in a minor key, which occasionally develops into a duet of a more audible and by no means harmonious description. When on the wing they continually utter a loud screeching "Ky-or-ark!" Their flight bears a very close resemblance to that of the Short-eared Owl. They have the same long, round tipped wings, the same method of alighting and the same complete noiselessness. When acclimatized they are indifferent to cold and will breed readily in a suitable aviary.

Both sexes incubate, the cock sitting on the eggs quite as much as his partner. When rearing young, they should be supplied with whole wheat, rye, or other dark bread moistened with milk.

Toward other cockatoos the Gang-gang is rather savage and aggressive, particularly when kept in pairs.

The food should consist of a seed mixture of one part canary, two parts sunflower, and one part oats. Unlike most cockatoos, they are fond of apple. A fresh turf is also appreciated. The species is very prone to feather plucking and a constant supply of branches *must* be kept in the aviary for the birds to bite up the entire day.

The Gang-gang Cockatoo does well at liberty, and a pair will often stay and nest in the vicinity of their owner's home if care be taken to allow the cock to be loose for several months before his mate is allowed to join him. If an additional precaution is desired, male and female can be let out alternately, each for some months at a time, before they are allowed their freedom together. Gang-gangs range to some distance from their feeding place and they are exceedingly fond of the seeds of thuja and cypress, and are apt to subject these trees to a rather severe pruning in the process of obtaining their favourite delicacy. Consequently, it is inadvisable to keep this species at liberty when you have near neighbours who are particular about their ornamental evergreens, or, it may be added, about their apples and walnuts.

A pair at my old home nested in an oak tree in the garden, but as the cock had only one leg the eggs were infertile. It may be observed that a male parrot, unlike a male finch, is always useless for breeding if his leg or foot be severely damaged. Even a hen so mutilated is of little value.

White-tailed Black Cockatoo
Zanda baudini

Distribution	Southwestern Australia.
Adult	Brownish black, feathers tipped with pale buff. A whitish patch in the region of the ear. An incomplete white bar across the tail. Bill lead colour. Length twenty-three inches.

Young birds of this species were imported by Mr. Frostick many years ago, and fed by hand on sponge cake and hard-boiled egg. He had difficulty in inducing them to take to seed and they unfortunately succumbed to fits, no doubt by reason of the too-stimulating properties of the egg. He describes them as charmingly tame and intelligent, but even at an early age tremendous wood-biters. Possibly, sterner measures would have forced the birds to adopt a more wholesome diet. The Black Cockatoos have tremendous powers of fasting and a hunger-strike of a few days does them no harm whatever.

Roseate Cockatoo
Eolophus roseicapillus

Distribution	Widely distributed over the interior of the Australian Continent.
Adult male	Back, wings, and tail hoary grey, paler on the lower back, rump, and upper tail-coverts. Flight feathers darker grey; crown of head and hind neck pinkish white; throat, sides of face, breast, abdomen, and under wing-coverts rich rose-pink, deepening considerably, without a moult, at the approach of the breeding season. Feet and legs mealy black. Bill greyish white. Iris so dark in colour as to appear black. Length fourteen and three-quarter inches. Size roughly that of a wood-pigeon. Both sexes have a short erectile crest.
Adult female	Similar to the male but slightly more slender in build. Iris hazel or reddish, providing an easy indication of sex.
Immature	In first plumage have the pink of the breast paler and considerably tinged with grey. Adult plumage is assumed with the first complete moult which in English-bred birds begins in the spring following the year of their birth. I am inclined to think that the sexual distinction in the colour of the eye is slight or absent in birds under a year old.

The Roseate Cockatoo is exceedingly abundant in its native land and is also the best known member of its genus in Europe, hundreds being imported annually and sold at a low price — some being offered (usually at a higher price!) as "Australian Grey Parrots."

Many writers have described the beauty of a large flock of "Galahs" in a wild state. "Usually when the weather is broken and unsettled, though, often on a windy winter morning, or in thundery weather in March or April, against the grey masses of cloud which bank up, forming a sombre background, it would seem as if all the Galahs in the vicinity had gathered in one flock, shrieking and screaming as they circle high in the air, all beating their wings in perfect unison. So, as it were at a given signal, the delicate rose-coloured breasts are all turned the one way, making a beautiful glow of colour as the birds veer 'round; then, with one beat the flock seems almost to have disappeared, just a glimpse of silvery grey flashing as they turn their backs; then a mere speck where each bird is flying, so small that one would hardly believe it to be a bird, so almost invisible does the grey become; then a flash of silvery light before the glow of their breasts flashes into view again."

From the avicultural point of view the Roseate Cockatoo possesses a good many virtues and some failings. As a talker it has seldom much merit, though a hand-reared bird may learn to say a few words. Like nearly all cockatoos, it can, when excited, yell distractingly and if kept in an aviary no unprotected woodwork will long survive the attacks of its beak. On the other hand, it is easily tamed and becomes devotedly attached to its owner, females being often so gentle as to allow even strangers to handle them with impunity. It is intelligent and playful, and, although one cannot help feeling some regret at keeping in close confinement a bird which takes such an evident joy in flight, it will take quite kindly to cage life.

The Roseate Cockatoo should be fed on a seed mixture consisting of two parts canary, one part hemp, one part oats, one part sunflower, and one part peanuts. Raw carrot or any kind of wholesome green food may be offered and a fresh turf of grass is usually much appreciated. Fruit may be given, but is seldom much relished. A small log of wood, preferably with the bark on, will provide the bird with much amusement and exercise for its beak. On no account should a Roseate Cockatoo or any other parrot of similar size be kept in so small a cage that it has not room to flap its extended wings. How many unhappy birds are immured for life in miserable little bell-shaped cages where they have hardly room to turn around! Would that I could confine their owners in similar prisons! Pet Roseates can often be allowed greater liberty if the flight feathers of one wing are kept cut. They love walking about a lawn, eating roots and digging in the turf and will even breed thus under favourable conditions. Many years ago I successfully reared two young from a cut-winged pair that had the run of a grass quadrangle in the centre of the house.

Roseates love a rain bath and should have regular opportunities for indulging in it. In warm weather they may be stood out in a shower or in winter sprayed with tepid water. If a cockatoo or parrot feels the need of a bath it will ruffle its feathers and spread its wings as the drops begin to fall on it, and the bath may be safely continued as long as the bird shows its desire for further wetting; when it seems to have had enough it should be put in a fairly warm place until dry. If, however, the bird shows from the first a persistent desire to escape from the moisture, the bath should not be forced upon it or a chill may result. Parrots are generally very wise in the matter of their ablutions, seldom bathing to their own hurt, or refusing a bath when their health and plumage need it.

Few people are willing to provide so common a bird as the Rose-breasted Cockatoo with aviary accommodation, especially as the need for covering every bit of woodwork with strong one-half inch mesh wire netting makes the initial cost of the aviary rather high. On the other hand, there are few foreign birds which nest more readily with suitable encouragement. In a twenty-four foot by eight foot aviary I have bred Roseates without the least trouble. They lose no time about settling down and a rough-plumaged wild hen imported in mid-winter will be rearing young the following July. They are not particular about their nesting site, using either a barrel or a natural tree trunk. In a wild state the birds are said to lay four or five eggs and to line their nest with green leaves. In captivity two or three eggs are the usual clutch. The hen does most of the sitting but her mate relieves her when she comes off to feed. Incubation lasts about four weeks and the young are a considerable time in the nest. When first hatched they are naked and hideous little objects. Their parents feed them on regurgitated food, holding their beaks and administering the nourishment with a rapid jerking motion quite different from the action of a feeding parakeet. When hungry the babies keep up a hoarse grumbling whine which changes to a rapid "Ek-ek-ek-ek-ek" as soon as they are receiving parental attention. Like most of the larger parrots they are dependent on their father and mother for some weeks after leaving the nest. Roseate Cockatoos have an amusing habit of correcting their offspring with a peck should they keep on nagging for food without reasonable excuse. Very few birds discipline their brood in this way; either they submit to any amount of badgering without retaliation, or else they get completely tired of them and send them packing for good and all. Dark bread soaked in milk should be provided for birds with young.

A male and female Roseate are a very devoted couple throughout the year and even when the breeding season is over it is a pretty sight to see the hen walk up to her mate, lean across his breast and gently preen the further side of his neck while he lovingly fondles that part of her person which happens to be within most convenient reach. Faithful as they are to one another during life the partners are not, however, unreasonably slow in consoling themselves should death remove male or female. The survivor, on being introduced to a new mate, will make a few conversational remarks, sidle up fairly close and start to preen his feathers. The stranger will do the same. At intervals, as the toilet proceeds they drift a step or two nearer until finally, when they are almost touching, one or other will cautiously nibble the head beside him and if the salute is well received the simple courtship is ended. Few foreign birds present a more charming spectacle at liberty than a pair of Roseate Cockatoos. Their flight, though not particularly rapid, is very buoyant and when in a playful mood, as they often are, they indulge in a most fascinating display of aerial gymnastics, swooping and twisting and shrieking with excitement and *joie de vivre*. The adults also possess the recommendation of being too big for owls to tackle; absolutely indifferent to cold; and practically harmless to growing fruit. Unfortunately, however, the Roseate Cockatoo has certain failings as a liberty bird which somewhat discount its good points. Pairs are decidedly difficult to induce to stay, while at the best of times they range far from home so that it is necessary to warn neighbours in order that they may not be accidentally shot. Hens, if left at liberty throughout the year, usually try to breed in cold weather and succumb to egg-laying troubles.

Lastly, young birds are delicate during the first twelve months of their lives. If bred at liberty they often die shortly after leaving the nest and in any case they are unable to survive the first winter without artificial heat. To get the best results it is desirable to obtain an adult pair and turn them into a movable aviary. It should be possible to shut the birds into the shelter so that later the young may get the benefit of the warmth of a portable heating apparatus during the cold season. If all goes well, the first autumn should see you with a couple of youngsters of your own breeding. As soon as these are able to feed themselves the old cock can be turned loose. He will never stray so long as his mate in confined, but should she die or fall ill and have to be taken indoors, he should be caught up at once or you may lose him. The young birds can be left with their mother until the cock is put back in April, unless she begins to show signs of being spiteful with them sooner, in which case they must be removed immediately. In favourable climates one youngster can be given his liberty at the end of May, but in places where birds thrive indifferently it is better to wait until he has completed his first moult. The second young bird should not be let out before the old cock is again released at the close of the second breeding season. If the first year's young survive the winter and prove a true pair the owner can please himself whether he will let them breed at liberty their third summer or catch them up in order to make sure of the brood surviving. In any case, it will be unwise to allow the hen to winter out, once she has become mature, for the reason already given. Cock Roseates, whose mates are confined, have an annoying habit of destroying the woodwork of aviaries in close proximity to their wives' abodes. For this reason it is necessary to place the hens' aviaries not less than fifty yards from any vulnerable woodwork and to make sure that they are completely wired outside as well as inside.

Tame Roseate Cockatoos when kept at liberty sometimes develop an odd fondness for mechanical travel. A hen bird, the property of a butcher on Hayling Island, was for some years quite a well-known figure by reason of her fondness for riding on motor cars. She would settle on the back of a car and, after enjoying a spin of a mile or two, would fly back to her home. Another hen which I gave to a gentleman in France repaired to the local railway station and spent her time riding on the engines until her plumage was blackened with smoke!

Hybrids have been produced between the Roseate Cockatoo and the Greater and Lesser Sulphur-crests.

Far more amazing is the production of fertile eggs as the result of a mating between a hen Roseate and a cock Rosella Parakeet. Unfortunately the Cockatoo sat unsteadily (no doubt expecting the Rosella to take his turn on the eggs after the manner of gentlemen of her own race), and she fell ill and died before the period of incubation was completed. Had young been reared it would indeed have been interesting to see how nature solved the puzzle of fusing two birds so totally different in form, voice and, most of all, colour!

In mixed company the Roseate is a fairly peaceful bird when not breeding, but it become decidedly aggressive when it has young to defend.

A very pretty variety is occasionally seen in which the grey areas of the normal plumage are replaced by white, the pink being retained. A pair of these albinistic birds are at present living in my collection.

Greater Sulphur-crested Cockatoo
Kakatoe galerita

Distribution   Widely distributed over Australia.

Adult male   White, with sulphur yellow crest, under surface of tail and inner webs of primary and secondary quills. Bill black. Iris almost black. Total length twenty inches.

Adult female   Resembles the male, but is said to have a slightly paler iris, though this is doubtful.

Immature   Said to resemble the adults.

The Sulphur-crested Cockatoo is a very common bird in Australia, congregating in large flocks and laying its two white eggs, either in hollow trees or in holes excavated in the face of a cliff. One observer writes, "They are found all year along the (Murray) river and a great distance back. They congregate in great numbers at nesting time and take possession of the holes worn by the weather into the high cliffs rising several hundreds of feet out of the water; here they lay their eggs upon the bare sand and hatch out their young. It is a very interesting sight to see many hundreds of these birds half out of their nesting holes or sitting upon the ledges of rock near their nests; depressing and raising their beautiful yellow crests. They are very noisy birds and keep up a continual screeching call."

The Sulphur-crested Cockatoo is very destructive to growing crops and is much hated by the farmers, who kill them wholesale either by scattering poisoned grain, or by putting poison into drinking places. While appreciating the point of view of the settlers whose livelihood is threatened, this terribly cruel method of destruction is much to be regretted, as not only are the chief offenders killed, but numbers of rare, beautiful, and sometimes harmless birds perish with them. It is particularly hard that the Australian authorities should place every obstacle in the way of the export of so many kinds of birds, even under humane conditions and for the purposes of legitimate aviculture, when every year thousands are poisoned and the bodies left to rot on the ground.

As a cage bird the Sulphur-crested Cockatoo is hardy and enduring and there are records of individuals living to a stupendous age — over one hundred years in a few cases. The bird becomes very tame and much attached to its owner, sometimes allowing even strangers to handle it with impunity. It also makes a fair talker, but, like all its tribe, is given in moments of excitement to yelling in the most appalling fashion.

The Sulphur-crest is perfectly hardy in an outdoor aviary, though needing the strongest material to resist its powerful beak. When suitably housed it is quite ready to go to nest. I am a little uncertain as to whether the colour of the iris is a reliable guide as to sex in this species. Mr. Whitley, who owns a breeding pair, informs me that his hen has a slightly paler eye than her mate, but I have only once seen a Sulphur-crest with an eye that did not look boot-button black, so if the light iris is always characteristic of the female, the number of hens must be exceedingly small.

In disposition the Sulphur-crest is inclined to be somewhat aggressive to other parrot-like birds of large size.

At liberty this species has been kept with some measure of success and young have been reared. Although a handsome and imposing bird on the wing it is decidedly destructive to trees and is inclined to range some distance from home. Cock and hen should be released alternately for some months before they are allowed free together.

At Lilford, hybrids between this species and the Roseate Cockatoo were produced at liberty.

The Sulphur-crested Cockatoo should be given a seed mixture of one part canary, one part oats, one part hemp, one part sunflower, and one part peanuts, with any raw vegetables it will eat, except potatoes. Fruit may be offered, though it is seldom greatly relished. Tea, coffee, meat, and butter should never be given. This cockatoo must have made its first appearance in England a surprisingly long time ago, as a portrait by Simon Verelot, painted about the middle of the seventeenth century, shows a little girl with a pet bird unmistakably belonging to this species.

Blue-eyed Cockatoo
Kakatoe ophthalmica

Distribution   New Britain.

Adult   White. Part of crest lemon yellow. A faint yellow tinge on the inner webs of some of the flights and tail feathers. Naked skin round eyes blue. Bill black. Total length nineteen inches.

A rarely imported bird. Its disposition and needs are the same as the Sulphur-crest's.

Lesser Sulphur-crested Cockatoo
Kakatoe sulphurea

Distribution   Celebes, Buton and Togian Islands.

Adult male   White with a faint yellow tinge on the breast and a more pronounced one on the under surface of the quills and tail. Crest long, pointed and lemon yellow. A yellow patch on the cheeks. Iris practically black. Bill black. Length thirteen inches.

Adult female   Has a red iris.

The Lesser Sulphur-crest does not do very well in a cage, but is hardy and enduring in an outdoor aviary, or at liberty. It is very noisy and seldom a good talker, but, like all white cockatoos, is easily tamed. The food should be that of the Greater Sulphur-crest: green peas and green wheat are much appreciated.

Both sexes sit, the cock quite as much as, if not more than, the hen. The period of incubation is twenty-four days. The species has been bred in captivity and hybrids with the Roseate have also been reared.

Leadbeater's Cockatoo
Loppochroa leadbeateri

Distribution   New South Wales, Victoria, South Australia, Southwest and Northwest Australia.

Adult male   Back, wings, and tail white. Inner webs of primary and secondary quills and inner tail-feathers red. Sides of face, hind-neck, chin, breast, sides of body, and under wing-coverts salmon-pink. Base of forehead dull rose-red. The long crest is red at the base, then yellow, then red, and then white. Bill whitish. Iris practically black. Total length fifteen inches.

Adult female   Resembles the male, but has the iris hazel or reddish.

Immature   Said to resemble the adult.

An observer writing of this very lovely cockatoo in a wild state says, "As far as I know only the flamingo exhibits such a beautiful rosy flush, contrasting with snowy white. The birds seem quite aware of their beauty and spend much of their time showing off to one another. By opening their wings partially, they exhibit the pink colour underneath, at the same time spreading the magnificent crest with its bands of yellow and scarlet until it forms a perfect semi-circle. If I had not seen it done repeatedly I could not have believed that the crest could be spread so far forward, the front feathers seeming almost to touch the beak." Another naturalist found a layer of pebbles four or five inches deep in the nests of these birds, immediately below the debris of leaves and wood in which the two eggs lay.

Leadbeater's Cockatoo will live quite well in a cage, but although tame individuals which say a word or two are by no means rare, it has the reputation of being less easy to demonstrate than its near allies. Its voice is exceedingly unpleasant, a loud, quavering scream uttered in a harassed tone, and when frightened or angry it emits a truly hideous din.

As an aviary bird it is exceedingly hardy and a free breeder. I knew a pair which lived for many years in a small ramshackle fowl run in Scotland. They nested each season and on the first occasion nearly reared their young which were killed by rats when almost ready to fly. In subsequent years the chicks were weakly and did not survive long, doubtless owing to the parents' loss of stamina through cramped quarters and lack of fresh ground.

Both sexes incubate the eggs, the male sitting quite as much as, and indeed more than, his mate. The young when being fed make a noise like young Roseates.

The species is spiteful in mixed company.

Leadbeater's Cockatoo has been kept and bred at liberty and its management should be the same as that of the Sulphur-crest. Where natural hollow tree-trunks are not available barrels should be put up for the birds to occupy.

A bird of this species has been known to live wild throughout a whole winter in the comparatively wet and bleak climate of Galloway in Scotland.

Citron-crested Cockatoo
Kakatoe citrino-cristata

Distribution   Sumba.

Adult male   White; a long, pointed orange crest. A yellowish patch on the cheek. Under-surface of quills and tail tinged with pale yellow. Bill black. Iris practically black. Total length fourteen inches.

Adult female   Differs from the male in having a red iris.

The Citron-crested Cockatoo is imported at somewhat infrequent intervals. It does not differ from its allies either in disposition or requirements. The food should be that of the Sulphur-crest. It does better in an aviary than a cage.

Rose or Salmon-crested Cockatoo
Kakatoe moluccensis

Distribution   Ceram and Amboyna.

Adult male   White tinged with salmon-pink, especially on the breast. A long, broad crest with some of the central feathers hairy and deep salmon colour. Under-surface of quills and tail suffused with a yellowish salmon tint. Bill black. Iris practically black. Total length twenty inches.

Adult female   Very similar.

The Salmon-crest is one of the most beautifully coloured of the cockatoos. It has a quaint, solemn appearance and is rather slow in its movements, but it becomes very tame and affectionate and sometimes makes an excellent talker. It is perfectly hardy and can be wintered out-of-doors and it is said to be a good stayer at liberty, though probably destructive to trees. It has nested in a California aviary, but the eggs were destroyed by an accident.

The Salmon-crest's failings consist of a terrific voice, a very powerful and destructive beak, and a rather spiteful disposition towards other birds. It will live quite well in a cage if the cage is very large and plenty of wood is provided for the bird's amusement. The food should consist of a mixture of canary, wheat, oats, and sunflower. Fruit and raw vegetables should be offered.

White-crested Cockatoo
Kakatoe alba

Distribution   Halmahera group of islands.

Adult   White. Crest long and broad. Inner surface of inner webs of flights and tail tinged with pale yellow. Bill black. Length eighteen inches.

The White-crested Cockatoo is in every respect an exact counterpart of its near relative the Salmon-crested. Its virtues and vices are identical and it requires the same treatment and the same precautions to prevent feather-plucking. It has produced hybrids with the Leadbeater when kept at liberty in Norfolk.

Slender-billed Cockatoo
Licmetis teniurostris

Distribution   North and Southwest Australia, South Australia, Victoria, New South Wales.

Adult male   General colour white, tinged with sulphur yellow, especially on the under surface of the tail. Base of feathers on head, throat, neck, and all 'round the breast pink. Base of forehead and a large patch in front of the eye red. Bill whitish horn and upper mandible very long and slender. Eyes dark. Total length seventeen and seven-eighths inches.

Adult female   Said to resemble the male.

Immature   Said to resemble the adults.

An observer, writing of this bird, says: *"Licmetis nasica* lives almost exclusively on a small yam which it digs up with its long bill. Of course, such a vast amount of digging must wear the upper mandible very rapidly, but this is compensated for by the rapidity of its growth. An old pet bird tried to lever a brick out of a drain with its bill and split the upper portion from near the point to the base. I mended the break and in three weeks the split portion had grown down to the point and before the end of the following week no trace of the injury was visible."

The Slender-billed Cockatoo compensates for its somewhat grotesque appearance and unmusical voice by an absurd amiability when tamed and a fair capacity for learning to talk. It should be fed on a seed mixture of canary, millet, and oats with as many peanuts as it likes to eat, and any raw vegetables that it cares for with the exception of potato and parsley. A good-sized turf should be kept in the cage to provide the bird with amusement and exercise for its digging propensities. The Slender-billed Cockatoo is perfectly hardy in an aviary and would probably breed if given the encouragement to do so. The sexes appear hard to distinguish and as I have never seen a bird with a light Iris, I conclude that the Slender-bill is one of those cockatoos in which the colour of the eye is of no assistance in telling the male from the female.

A pair of these birds I released without special precautions only stayed for a few weeks, but it is possible that they would have become more attached to their home had I first let out male and female, alternately, for some months.

The Western race of the Slender-bill, sometimes known as the Dampier Cockatoo (*Licmetis pastinator*), has been exhibited at the Palace.

Bloodstained Cockatoo
Ducorpsius sanguineus

Distribution   Australia.

Adult male   White; bases of the feathers of head and neck, pink. Some pink in front of and below the eye. Crest short. Inner webs of flights and under surface of tail pale yellow. Bill bluish white. Length sixteen and nine-tenths inches.

Adult female   Smaller than the male.

The Bloodstained Cockatoo, unlike some of its near relatives, appears to be in part, at any rate, a beneficial bird in a wild state, living on the fruit of a creeping, noxious plant called Double-gees whose seeds seriously lame sheep. Certain districts passed laws protecting the birds, but a wise-acre visiting the district (whose opinions we trust were not heeded) pointed out that the protection was a mistake because whole seeds would probably be voided by the Cockatoos and the range of the plant extended. Anybody possessing the most elementary knowledge of a parrot's feeding habits and digestive system would know that the chances of an undigested seed passing through the bird's body are practically nil. Moreover, one would have thought that the thousands of seeds actually assimilated by the cockatoos would, if they had not been eaten, have been a far more likely means of spreading the plant than the one or two supposed to escape destruction! Among birds it is not *seed* eaters which are seed distributors, but *berry* eaters.

Three eggs are usually laid, and the nest is situated in a hollow in a tree, cliff-face, or large termite mound. In captivity the Bloodstained Cockatoo makes a docile and affectionate pet and a good talker. It can be wintered out-of-doors, but, like all its family, it is addicted to screaming.

It should be fed like the Gang-gang Cockatoo. Hemp is absolute poison to it and must never be given. Before the writer discovered this fact he killed two remarkably fine birds in a very short space of time, simply by the free use of hemp and sunflower.

Two birds which I released stayed well, but were so fearfully destructive to trees that I had to get rid of them. They were spiteful with other parrots and with their own species.

Wild birds have been known to evict sitting Roseate Cockatoos, add their own eggs to the clutch, and hatch and rear a mixed brood.

Bare-eyed Cockatoo
Ducorpsius gymnopis

Distribution   South Australia.

Adult male   White. Bases of feathers of head and neck and feathers below and in front of eye, pink. Inner webs of flights and under surface of tail pale yellow. Bill bluish white. Length seventeen inches.

Adult female   Similar but smaller.

The Bare-eyed Cockatoo is in every respect an exact counterpart of the Bloodstained, from which it differs in having a large area of naked blue skin below the eye, whereas the blue skin round the Bloodstained Cockatoo's eye is of equal width above and below. In captivity it makes an exceptionally good-tempered, playful and amusing pet, with, however, the family weakness for screaming. It does best when not permanently confined in a parrot cage.

It should be fed on canary, oats, sunflower, and peanuts with any fruit, green food, and raw vegetables that it will eat. Hemp is extremely injurious and causes liver disease in a remarkably short space of time unless the bird has complete freedom.

The Bare-eyed Cockatoo has been bred at the Zoological Gardens in England, and also by an aviculturist in Holland. The young birds remain nine weeks in the nest. Unlike some cockatoos, the sexes of this species do not differ in the colour of the iris, the eyes of both male and female being almost black.

The Bare-eyed Cockatoo is spiteful in mixed company. It can be wintered out-of-doors and will stay at liberty, but is terribly destructive to trees.

Cockatiel
Leptolophus hollandicus

Distribution	Widely distributed over the interior of the Australian Continent.
Adult male	General colour above and below dusky brown, more greyish brown on the under surface and blackish on the shoulders and under wing-coverts. Hind neck, mantle, and upper back, smoke brown. Large whitish patch on the wing. Forepart of head, sides of face, throat, and crest lemon yellow, the tips of the crest feathers becoming brown. Ear-coverts bright orange; sides of crown white. Tail fairly long and blackish brown, central feathers projecting beyond the rest. Bill dark horn, eyes brown. Total length thirteen and one-eighth inches. Size roughly that of a thrush, but tail much longer.
Adult female	Bears considerable resemblance to the male, but her wing patch is smaller and of less pure a white, her thighs are barred with pale yellow, her tail is freckled and barred with dark grey and the outer feathers are yellowish. Orange cheek patch present, but lemon and white areas practically absent from the head.
Immature	Much resemble the female, but young males are said to be distinguishable from the time of leaving the nest by a perceptible shade of yellow on the head and face.

Although one of the most soberly coloured members of the parrot family, the Cockatiel has long been popular among aviculturists by reason of its hardiness, prolificacy, and gentle disposition. As pets hens have not much to recommend them, but a hand-reared male will often learn to talk and whistle a little and become much attached to his owner. He is not exactly a silent bird, but there are many worse noises than his shrill "Curryou! Creeou!" If kept in a cage he should always, when sufficiently tamed, be allowed to take daily flying exercise in a room.

The Cockatiel should be fed on canary, millet, hemp, and oats, together with green food.

As aviary birds Cockatiels have much to recommend them. Healthy, unrelated pairs are very free breeders, often rearing two or three broods of six or seven. If permitted to do so, they will go on nesting far into the winter, but in the English climate it is very desirable to restrict breeding to the warmer months of the year, so the nest logs should be removed in October and not put back before April is well advanced. It is not wise to keep more than one pair of Cockatiels in the same aviary while breeding is going on, as they squabble a good bit among themselves. With other species of birds they are usually safe, but their restless habits are sometimes disturbing to the peace of mind of small finches.

As with some of the cockatoos, the male Cockatiel assists his mate in the duties of incubation. No nesting material is needed, a little earth or moist decayed wood being all that the eggs require to rest on. The log should be roomy, as the Cockatiel has no fondness for cramped quarters.

Unfortunately, while healthy Cockatiels are hardy and prolific, there are often on the market a number of birds inbred or badly reared that are a source of trouble to their purchasers, the cocks proving sterile and the hens getting egg-bound or indulging in some physical or mental vagaries that effectually prevent the propagation of their kind. It is to be hoped that some day breeders of foreign birds will begin to observe the elementary rules of hygiene and management that no one engaged in rearing domestic animals would think of neglecting.

As a liberty bird the Cockatiel is one of the most unpromising subjects I have tried. A migrant and wanderer in his own land, his attachment to his home is remarkably small. The only way to enjoy his very beautiful and extremely powerful flight is to train one cock of a breeding pair as a day-liberty bird. The hen's aviary must be placed in a conspicuous position near tall trees with the roosting and feeding aviary alongside. The cock's first release should take place on a calm winter morning when the trees are bare, as a Cockatiel has a rooted objection to settling on any branch that has leaves on it. He should also be turned out before he has had his breakfast and his general training and management should be the same as that of a Barraband — not forgetting the danger of allowing him to be loose in a snowstorm. As long as he is the only one of his kind at liberty and his wife remains in the aviary as a decoy he may stay and behave himself, but allow him even one companion in freedom — and that a male — and the chances are you will see him no more.

Yellow Fronted Amazon Parrot. Photo by Horst Mueller.

Mexican Double Yellow Head Amazon Parrot, also known as
Levaillant's Amazon. Drawing by R. A. Vowles.

Some years ago I had a cut-winged pair of Cockatiels which nested in the grass quadrangle where Roseate Cockatoos reared young. Unfortunately the hen was taken by an owl and the cock soon afterwards deserted the eggs.

In Australia the Cockatiel is sometimes known as "Cockatoo-parrot" and "Quarrion."

XVII

Asiatic Parakeets

Indian Ringnecked Parakeet
Psittacula torquata

Distribution	India, Ceylon, Indo-Burma.
Adult male	Green; back of head tinged with blue. A black bar on the lower part of the cheek running from the base of the lower mandible up 'round the neck, forming an incomplete collar. Another incomplete collar of fiery pink running 'round the back of the neck. Tail bluish green. The colour of the face is brighter than the rest of the body and that of the wings darker. Bill red with a blackish tip. Total length sixteen to seventeen inches. Size about that of a small pigeon. Tail very long and narrow. Iris partly grey and partly pale yellow.
Adult female	Differs from the male in being entirely green with a slightly more yellowish tinge. Iris pale yellow.
Immature	Resembles the female but the difference in the colour of the iris is fairly soon apparent on close inspection. Adult plumage is not attained until the second complete moult when the bird is about three years old. The plumage change of most, if not all, the other parakeets of the same family, is similarly delayed.

The Indian Ringneck has been known in captivity from the very early times and was often kept as a pet by the Romans. One Roman writer informs us that this parakeet was taught to talk by striking it on the head with an iron rod, its skull being so thick that no milder method of discipline was sufficient to compel its attention to its lessons! Needless to say the modern Ringneck does not possess such remarkable cranial development, and its owner will do well to adopt the more normal plan of repeating constantly in its hearing the words it is desired that it should learn, particularly at times when the bird is resting quietly with its mind unoccupied in other directions. The Ringnecked Parakeet stands cage life well, though

116

its cry is too shrill and too often repeated to make it a pleasant companion for a person with sensitive ears. Cocks become much attached to their owners, and although they do not particularly like being stroked, will perch freely on the hand and show their pleasure at being noticed by many amusing gestures. They often become good talkers and some can be taught to perform tricks. A bird in the possession of a friend is marvellously talented. He will thread beads on a bit of cotton with his beak; retrieve small objects with a "cleanness" that few sporting dogs could rival; ring a miniature bell; and twirl a rod 'round his head after the manner of an acrobat. The most wonderful of all his tricks is done with six or eight cards. His owner gives the cards to the visitor and asks him to choose any one that he likes, mentioning his choice to him. The cards are then placed face downwards on the table and the parakeet walks along from one end of the row to the other, lifting each card as he comes to it and letting it fall again, until he reaches the card the visitor has named, when he carries it up to his master, nor is he ever wrong in his choice, whatever the position of the selected card in the row. The secret of this uncanny performance lies in the fact that the bird's master keeps his hands on the table and when the Ringneck reaches the right card he gives his thumb a slight twitch which the intelligent parakeet recognizes as the signal to retrieve that particular card and no other. This bird was trained by an Indian who kept him rather short of food and rewarded him with a grain of rice when he did what was required of him; but he goes through his tricks for his present owner simply for the inducement of flattery and praise. Indeed, almost the prettiest part of the whole performance is his evident demand for an abundant supply of commendation, his pleasure when he receives it, and the little airs and graces which accompany the exhibition of his talents. Hen Ringnecks vary greatly in temperament. A few make docile pets and fair talkers, but the majority are untalented; and even if tamed, snappy and ill-tempered, except when in breeding condition.

When acclimatized, the Ringneck is perfectly hardy and will live in any sort of indoor or outdoor aviary. Neither it nor the Alexandrine Parakeet should, however, be exposed to really intense frost or their feet will suffer from frostbite. It will also attempt to breed, but the cocks are usually infertile in very cramped quarters. If you wish to rear young which are themselves to be of any use for stock purposes on reaching maturity, a fair-sized aviary is an absolute necessity. Cock birds reared in small, fixed aviaries are sterile. Hen Ringnecks when not actually in breeding condition are often very spiteful with a strange cock and unless there is plenty of room for the gentleman to keep out of the way, it is prudent to defer the introduction until March, when his appearance is likely to be more welcome. Once she has paired with a particular male, a hen will usually tolerate his presence throughout the year, though her conduct may be shrewish and unloving out of the breeding season. I once had a very amorous cock who was given to boring his partner with unseasonable attentions. Pairs of Ringnecks when on extra friendly terms have a pretty habit of sharing a piece of food, the bird which first secures it holding it out for the other to break off a portion. On one occasion during the moult the hen of the pair just mentioned was eating a peanut. The cock, from sentimentality rather than greed, kept trying to coax her to share it in lover's fashion. She repulsed him irritably until the nut was finished and then fairly shoved the empty shell into his beak, the action saying as plain as words, "There, take it, stupid, and much good may it do you!"

The same hen, when I first had her with different mates, used to lead them a dog's life for half the year. Finally, however, the rather short-tempered cock she was with at the time, after enduring her oppressions for many months, one day turned upon her and would have killed her if the aviary attendant had not rescued her only just in time. From that day onwards her treatment of her husbands showed a marked and lasting improvement!

The courtship of the Ringneck is very amusing. The cock slightly spreads his wings, draws his plumage close and hops and bows 'round the hen; or he may sit by her side and rock himself backwards and forwards, letting go the perch with one foot and pawing the air, and at regular intervals imprinting an impassioned kiss on the back of her neck. If the tender interview be the first he has had with his sweetheart, he accompanies the performance with a rhythmical and not unpleasant kind of song. When feeding the hen, even after the young have hatched, the cock strikes a gallant attitude for her benefit between each mouthful he gives her.

While the male Ringneck certainly knows how to look his best and show off the good points of his elegant figure, the same cannot be said of the hen. When much smitten with the tender passion she crouches on the perch and turns her head right back until her beak points straight to the sky; at the same time she rolls her head from side to side as though she were drunk, or recovering from a fit of apoplexy!

The female Ringneck alone sits, being fed by her mate, who also assists in rearing the young. Three or four eggs are the usual number laid in confinement and only one brood is produced. Ringnecks come into breeding condition very early in the year, but it is usually prudent not to put in the nests until March, as egg-binding is not an unknown trouble with this species. The nests should be placed in the open flight, as the young do badly in an aviary shelter. A perpendicular hollow tree trunk or a bottomless wooden box six feet high with the interior filled to within eighteen inches of the entrance with mould and decayed wood makes the best breeding place. Young Ringnecks will breed while still in immature plumage when two years or even twelve months old, but the eggs laid

are few and often infertile until they are fully adult. Even when in immature
plumage, the hen's eyes show a little more yellow.

Ringnecks are decidedly subject to colour variation. Lutinos, through
lack of blue colouring, are a beautiful golden yellow with whitish flights
and tail, just like a clear canary. They have dark red eyes and are generally, though not invariably, females. Green birds marked with yellow also
occur, as do those of a greenish yellow and yellowish buff colour; while
a blue variety, the color of a Blue Masked Lovebird, is being bred by
the writer. There is no doubt that these rare colors can be propagated in
captivity by anyone who was willing to provide aviaries of sufficient size.
The young bred from a lutino and a green are always green, but a pair
of lutino-bred greens in my collection laid three eggs and reared a green
and a lutino young one. In mixed company the majority of Ringnecks
are fairly peaceable, but individuals of a spiteful disposition are not
uncommon. One hen in my collection had a special hatred of Barrabands.
If a Barraband alighted on her aviary she rushed to attack him, at the
same time imitating his call, apparently in derision; even when no Barraband was in sight she would sometimes imitate their cry and, as she did
so, every now and then make a vicious lunge at the perch, just to show
what she would like to do to a Barraband if she could get hold of one.
The performance was one of the strangest and most comical I have ever
witnessed. The Barrabands seemed rather amused by her hatred and
enjoyed teasing her. I once saw a cock at liberty alight on her aviary
and when he was assaulted by the Ringneck and her mate, he tore 'round
and 'round them in a mock display and then flew away, leaving them giddy
and furious. He acted from pure devilment, as he had a mate of his own
and did not care a pin about Ringnecks. When he had left the outraged
couple, the hen began doing the Barraband call and turning her head
'round in the middle of the performance, she seized the end of her own
tail and nearly severed it with a savage nip!

As liberty birds, Ringnecks are rather uncertain, some staying perfectly; others staying for a time and then leaving; and others going clean
away on the day of their release. The best plan is to let the cock out first
for a few weeks during the breeding season when his affection for his
mate is at its strongest, for at other times of the year, unlike a cock
broadtail, he has no scruples about deserting his partner. When he has
got used to the place in spring he may stay in winter also.

Ringnecks are not difficult to breed at liberty, and are less particular
about nesting sites than broadtailed parakeets, but it is seldom possible
to allow them to do so as they are terribly destructive to apples, beginning
to attack the fruit in June long before it is ripe. They are not, however,
bud eaters, and can safely be left out from October to May. They are
attractive flying loose, becoming very lively towards dusk, though their

flight does not approach that of the polyteline parakeets in speed and grace. I have had African Ringnecks killed by owls, but a big Indian bird can generally defend himself. One winter night, a few years ago, a dismal screeching in my garden told all too plainly that one of my cock Ringnecks had been seized by an owl. I gave him up for dead, but next morning he appeared with the mark of the owl's claws on his wing, but otherwise uninjured. Evidently he got hold of the aggressor's leg and taught him that although a Ringneck and a Barraband may look much alike, there is a considerable difference in the power of their beaks!

There must be quite a number of escaped Ringnecks living wild in England. Two have inhabited the neighbourhood of Portsmouth for some time, while a few years ago a bird of this species resided for several seasons in Kensington Gardens, where he became quite a well-known favourite and was fed by visitors. Eventually I got him a mate, but he died soon afterwards and she only survived him about a year.

The Ringnecked Parakeet should be fed on a seed mixture of two parts canary, one part millet, one part oats, one part hemp, one part sunflower, and one part peanuts, with an abundant supply of fruit. Green peas are also relished.

In an aviary no unprotected woodwork is safe from a Ringneck's beak.

An account of this bird may fitly close with the quotation of Mr. Frank Finn's charming little poem:

> The Hindu Love-god's steed am I,
> Fast as his strong-sped arrows fly
> I bear him through the tropic sky
> Beneath the fierce sun's fire:
> And in return he grants to me
> Ever to wear spring's livery,
> And take my toll of field and tree
> Of grain and fruit and spicery,
> To all my heart's desire.

African Ringneck
Psittacula Krameri

Distribution	Tropical Africa north of the Equator from Abyssinia to Senegambia.
Adult male	Green, very bright on the cheeks, crown and forehead. Rear portion of the head tinged with lilac. A black edging to the lower cheeks forming a slight collar. Behind it a narrow incomplete collar of fiery pink. Tail blue-green. Bill blackish red or blackish, much darker than in the Indian bird. Size usually somewhat less than the Indian Ringneck.

Adult female Green; no collar, cheek marking, nor lilac tinge to head. Tail feathers greener.

Immature Resemble the female. Adult plumage assumed with the second complete moult.

The Rose-ringed Parakeet, or African Ringneck, does not differ in any respect from the larger Indian race with which it has inter-bred. The writer had a fine lutino female some years ago, but she was killed by an accident before she left any descendants. In South Africa the Indian Ringneck is said to have been introduced.

Alexandrine Parakeet
Psittacula nipalensis

Distribution North and Central India.

Adult male Green, brighter on the forepart of the crown and darker on the wings. Mantle, cheeks and breast tinged with mealy buff. A bluish tinge at the back of the head. A salmon-pink nuchal collar. Lower edge of the cheek broadly edged with black which runs up the sides of the neck. A dull maroon-red patch on the wing. Tail pale blue-green and very long. Bill red. Length twenty inches.

Adult female Lacks the black and pink on the head and neck.

Immature Duller than the female. Crown with a bluish tinge. Wing-bar dull and broken by green feathers. Young males presumably attain a plumage like the adult female with the first complete moult and adult plumage with the second complete moult.

The Alexandrine Parakeet stands cage life well and the cocks, especially, become much attached to their owners, and may show a fair talent for talking. Like their smaller relative, the Ringneck, they possess, however, a loud and unpleasant cry.

They are excessively hardy birds, and with the minimum of reasonable care on first arrival will live in any kind of aviary and stand the most severe cold. Indeed, though I have kept Alexandrines for many years, I have never yet seen either a sick or a dead one. In mixed company they are usually trustworthy, the males, in particular, being most easy-going and good-natured. Their chief drawback is their destructiveness to perches and woodwork; while they will bite their way out of an aviary which is not stoutly wired.

They go to nest readily, but are not very easy to breed, as the cocks are often sterile when kept short of wing exercise, and being such big birds they require a very large aviary to permit much flying.

When courting, the cock sits by his partner and keeps turning his head sharply from side to side, making confidential murmuring noises and occasionally giving his wings a shivering shake. The hen, meanwhile, crouches on the perch in much the same unbecoming attitude as is assumed by an amorous hen Ringneck.

In confinement two eggs form the normal clutch, and in breeding habits and in its needs in the matter of food and nesting accommodation the Alexandrine resembles the Ringneck.

As a liberty bird this species is somewhat uncertain in its behaviour. Some stay in exemplary fashion; some stay for a time and then stray; some go off on the day of their release, and some depart, return, and again depart for good. The safest plan is to give the cock his first taste of liberty when he is in breeding condition and most attached to his mate.

The Alexandrine is a striking and handsome bird on the wing, but he is as destructive to apples, ripe or unripe, as his smaller cousin, and cannot be trusted within reach of an orchard from June until the end of October. Occasionally, also, an Alexandrine at liberty will do a certain amount of tree pruning, but to do him justice he usually selects those specimens which are large and of no special value. A liberty bird is likely to range for two or three miles 'round his home.

Naturally this species is in no danger from owls.

Lutino varieties of this parakeet occasionally occur. In these the pink wing-bar is retained and forms a very attractive contrast to the yellow background of the rest of the plumage. Mr. Ezra also possessed a magnificent blue cock with a white collar and wing bar. The Alexandrine is sometimes called the "Indian Rock Parrot," possibly because it sometimes breeds in cliffs and ruined buildings as well as in hollow trees.

Banded or Moustache Parakeet
Psittacula fasciata

Distribution	Eastern Bengal and Himalayas, Amoy, Andamans, Indo-Burma, Cochin China.
Adult male	Green, very bright on the nape. Head, cheeks, and throat lilac. A greenish tinge 'round the eye. A line from eye to beak and a broad strip on the lower cheek black. Upper breast deep lilac. Abdomen tinged with pale blue. A yellowish patch on the wing. Tail blue-green. Bill red. Length fifteen inches.
Adult female	Has a black beak; no lilac on the throat and very little blue on the abdomen. Breast and a patch at the side of the neck pinkish brick colour.
Immature	Green with the black bar on the lower cheek and a patch of yellowish green on the wing.

A commonly imported and hardy species, which, however, does not seem to have been bred. It does well in an aviary and can be wintered out-of-doors, but its voice is harsh and its temper uncertain.

It makes a good liberty bird, though, like the Ringneck, it is a bad neighbour to an orchard. A pair in the writer's collection nested in the garden, but were disturbed by a pair of lorikeets, who killed the male. The hen laid several infertile clutches during her widowhood.

Treatment as for the Ringneck.

Plumheaded Parakeet
Psittacula cyanocephala

Distribution	Ceylon, southern, central, and northern India.
Adult male	Yellowish green, very bright on the breast. Rump, neck and centre of the wing with a bluish tinge. Head plum colour, redder on the cheeks and forehead. Throat and a narrow collar black. Under wing-coverts pale bluish green. A maroon-red spot on the wing. Central tail feathers very long, blue with white tips. Outer tail feathers green and yellowish. Bill orange-yellow. Total length fourteen inches.
Adult female	Smaller; tail shorter, head lavender-grey, cheeks duller. A yellower collar 'round the neck. No red wing spot.
Immature	In first plumage the head is mainly green with a faint brownish tinge on the forehead and cheeks. After the first moult the young male assumes a plumage like the female and comes into full colour when in his third year, with the second complete moult.

This lovely little parakeet, certainly the most beautiful of the seed-eating species of the Northern Hemisphere, shares with the peacock the fate of being somewhat despised simply because it is so common. If the Plumhead were as seldom imported as the Princess of Wales what fabulous sums would not be paid for it and how many aviculturists who never keep it now would vie with each other for its possession!

The Plumheaded Parakeet does well in confinement and birds of either sex become attached to their owners and may learn to say a few words. Unlike the rest of the genus their cry is comparatively feeble and is not offensive to the ear.

Although rather delicate when newly imported and requiring warmth and care until through their first moult, Plumheads are quite hardy when acclimatized and can be wintered out-of-doors. In adverse climates, however, they require watching during late summer and autumn, and young birds should have a warmed shelter during their first winter.

Plumheads are not difficult to breed if the hens are restrained from indulging their fondness for laying before the nights are warm. Unfortunately, for some unknown reason, females are extraordinarily scarce in the bird trade. It is not only because the brightly coloured adult males are more usually selected by native catchers, for even with a consignment of immature birds the advent of the third moult will produce an unwelcome majority of plum coloured heads and possibly not even a single grey one.

When courting, the Plumheaded Parakeet runs up and down the perch in a consequential manner uttering a kind of song and occasionally gives a quick bow. The nesting habits and requirements are the same as those of the Ringneck. Some hens are inclined to bully their husbands out of the breeding season.

Lutino varieties of the Plumhead occur and are of great beauty, the head being pink and the body plumage a glorious golden yellow. A cock in the writer's possession was first green pied with yellow; then for a few moults a pure lutino, and then he once more reverted to pied plumage. A typical lutino, however, retains its colour from the first to last. A blue variety is also known.

The Plumhead is usually inoffensive in mixed company and not very destructive to shrubs. It should be fed like the Ringneck.

The species is almost hopeless at liberty and the worst of stayers. Possibly something could be done with the male of a pair in breeding condition in a district free from owls; or he might be trained for day liberty.

Blossom-headed Parakeet
Psittacula rosa

Distribution	Sikkim, Dacca, Eastern Bengal, Assam, Burma, Cochin China.
Adult male	Green, with a slight yellowish tinge on the breast and mantle. Forehead and cheeks rose-pink merging into pale plum colour on the crown and edges of the cheeks. Black feathers form a broad edging to the lower part of the cheeks and a slight collar. Central tail feathers blue with yellowish white tips. A small maroon-red patch on the wing. Bill pale yellowish. Total length thirteen inches.
Adult female	Differs from the male in having a greyish head and a very faint trace of a yellowish collar. Reddish wing patch present as in the male.
Immature	Green with a faint greyish tinge on cheeks, forehead and front part of crown. Tail bluish green. No wing-bar. After the first moult a plumage like that of the female appears to be assumed and adult plumage with the second complete moult when the bird is three years old.

The Blossom, or Rose-headed Parakeet does not differ in any important respect from its ally the Plumhead. It is scarcely as pretty as the latter and is more rarely imported.

It has bred in captivity.

XVIII

The Larger Australian
Broadtailed Parakeets

Rosella Parakeet
Platycercus eximius

Distribution   Queensland, New South Wales, Victoria, Tasmania.

Adult male   Head, neck, bib, and under tail-coverts red, the red of the bib sometimes running in a streak some way down the centre of the breast; cheek-patches white; black pale green; feathers of the mantle black with broad pale yellowish green edges, tending to pure yellow near the neck. Lower breast and abdomen yellow merging into light green near the thighs. Inner, lesser, and median upper wing-coverts black; outer wing-coverts and those 'round the bend of the wing Wedgwood blue; outer edges of flight feathers dark blue. Middle tail feathers bluish green. Lateral one various shades of blue merging into white. Bill bluish white. Total length thirteen inches. Size about that of a Barbary Dove.

Adult female   Bears a general resemblance to the male but is slightly smaller and usually less brilliant, and the edging of the red bib is more ragged. At the back of the eye there are a few small brownish green feathers which are always absent in the adult male. There is usually a strip of green running from the nape to the back of the crown and some of the secondary flight feathers have a white spot on the inner webs.

Immature   Bears a general resemblance to the adult but the colours are duller, the markings much fainter, the red areas smaller, and the plumage permeated with a faint greenish wash. On first leaving the nest the bill is of a yellowish white colour but quickly darkens. Young males are from the first brighter than their sisters in the same nest. About three months after leaving the nest the young birds moult

126

a number of body feathers and assume a brighter colouration. Full adult plumage is gained with the first complete moult which begins when the birds are just over a year old.

In Australia the Rosella frequents the open park-like country and out of the breeding season is said to occur in flocks, a sociable habit due probably more to necessity than to inclination. I have kept and bred most of the broadtails at liberty in England and have never noticed the least tendency to flock at any time of year. Each adult pair goes its own way and should pairs meet, for instance, near the feeding place, it is at best an armed neutrality always liable to end in open warfare. Even birds of the year split up into pairs before the autumn is very far advanced. For cage life this beautiful parakeet is utterly unsuited and the cruelty of keeping any broadtail permanently in a parrot cage cannot be too strongly emphasized. For one that will survive for a decent period in close confinement, a score will pine away within two or three years. The Rosella and its allies also lack the disposition which makes an ideal pet and companion. Although their natural cries are usually musical and seldom unpleasant, they rarely learn to talk and then only repeat a word or two in a faint, husky tone. They show no affection for their owners, but are excitable and aggressive, and once they lose their fear of human beings, are ever on the lookout to inflict a painful bite. Anyone who wishes to remain on the best terms that circumstances permit with a tame Rosella should remember that he is a gentleman who above all things appreciates modesty, humility, and self-control in his associates. Offer him dainties quietly and then leave him alone to enjoy them. Don't try to play with him or scratch his head; don't poke your fingers at him or address him in loud and familiar tones. If he cannot be induced to tolerate you, even by respect for his prejudices, and if he flies at your head the moment you come within reach and tries to remove a section from your ear or nose, coaxing and kindness are of no avail and stern measures must be resorted to. Covering the vulnerable parts of your person and arming yourself with some large, soft weapon that cannot hurt him, go into the aviary prepared for battle and knock him about until he is forced to admit defeat. Any recurrence of "sauce" must be quelled by a repetition, or threatened repetition, of the punishment. Although quite unfitted for very close confinement, the Rosella will live well enough in a flight cage three or four yards long and may even go to nest, though infertile eggs and weakly young will be the rule rather than the exception.

The Rosella makes an excellent aviary bird and in good climates is perfectly hardy and can be wintered in the open when acclimatized. Newly imported birds should not, of course, be turned out-of-doors except when the nights, as well as the days, are really warm and likely to remain so.

Even new arrivals, however, are not unduly sensitive to cold and if robust and lively, can, after a few days rest and a bath in fairly warm quarters, often be transferred to a cool, or even an unheated room, provided it is free from draughts. As all broadtails are not likely to avail themselves in bad weather of the protection provided for them, it is a good plan, out of the breeding season, to drive them into the aviary shelter at night.

When a cock Rosella is introduced to a hen, if he be at all in good condition, it is a case of love or hate at first sight. If he displays to her, all is well, though she must have room to keep out of his way in case he suspects her of lack of modesty; for if there is one thing a cock broadtail resents and will instantly punish, it is any suggestion of forwardness in his sweetheart. He has no use whatever for the "modern girl." If he goes for her and chases her about the aviary, you must instantly remove her to save her life, and you may as well realize that nothing is ever likely to change his hostility.

The only two policies to try are to put the cock and hen in adjoining aviary compartments, keeping them there for many months until he shows signs of friendliness, when you try him in with her; *not* vice versa. The other plan is to clip the feathers of the tip of his wing so that, while he can still get about reasonably well, he cannot fly fast enough to catch her. It may happen that when he has moulted out he will tolerate her presence and even eventually change his views about her, but as a general rule there is only one thing to be done with a misogynist cock and that is to get rid of him. A cock that has been tamed and kept in a cage is generally useless as a breeder, and a hen is little better. Although he shows nothing but hatred for the human race, his close association with them is likely, in some curious way, to have unfitted him for domestic life. Contrary to what one would expect, he is often afraid of a hen, and she, surprised and annoyed at his cowardice, has neither respect nor regard for him, so that the foundations for a happy marriage are entirely absent.

A perpendicular hollow tree trunk makes the best nest. The entrance hole should be six feet from the ground and the nest about two feet below the entrance, which should not be too large. If the trunk has no natural bottom, it should be filled to the required height with earth, mould, or peat, with some soft, decayed wood on top.

If a trunk is unobtainable, it should be imitated by a "grandfather clock" nest box, the interior of which is made climbable by tacking on a strip of wire netting. Individual hen parakeets of many species may, however, show an objection to a nest which has a deep layer of soft material at the bottom, and if a hen is found not to be settling well or to be burying her eggs, the only thing to do is to give way to her whims and provide a nest box with a concave wooden bottom hung up like a nest box for Budgerigars.

Rosellas should be given two nests, as they are double brooded, and the hen lays her second clutch before the young of the first nest have flown. The cock will attend to both establishments, but if you keep the hen waiting for her first family to vacate their home, she may drop into moult and not lay a second time. April is early enough to put in the nests as egg-binding may occur if the nights are very cold. Always remove parakeet nests at the end of the breeding season.

As the time for nesting approaches, the cock Rosella begins to feed his mate. At first she is coy and rather frightened of him and keeps as far away as possible during the operation, but later she drives him off if he pesters her with offers of nourishment when she is already satisfied. She is never, however, really master and it is only out of courtesy that he gives way to her and puts up with her tantrums. Should his temper be roused by the sight of a rival she usually knows better than to get in his way, for if he be denied the opportunity of getting to grips with the enemy he may vent his rage even on her. When the pair are house-hunting the cock goes first and, stopping at every possible, or impossible, hole he comes to, he makes a great fuss, whistling and waggling his spread tail from side to side. As soon as his mate is attracted he makes way for her and allows her to examine the place herself. Rosellas at liberty begin to look at holes in this way quite six months before the eggs are laid; as soon, in fact, as the moult is over.

From four to six eggs are the normal clutch, but far larger numbers have been recorded. The hen alone sits, being fed by her mate when she comes off the nest. The cock continues to feed his family for some time after they fly, but they must be removed the moment he begins to tire of them. Young birds, well reared, will breed at twelve months of age.

Rosellas, when in good condition and kept in pairs, are exceedingly pugnacious and quite unsafe as companions for other birds. They especially hate their own and nearly allied species, objecting a little less to parakeets of other genera and much less to birds of other orders. A case has been recorded of a hen Rosella and a hen Pennant sharing the same nest, but such an occurrence is very extraordinary and as a general rule people who boast of having kept a number of pairs of broadtails safely in the same aviary are only advertising their own incompetence. The birds must have been so low-spirited through bad management that they had not the heart to fight. Unmated cocks are less quarrelsome than paired ones and will often agree with bachelor companions of their own sex. Unmated hens are also much milder in temper than married ladies.

Incubation lasts just under four weeks and the young birds are a long time before they fly.

The Rosella makes a prettty liberty bird, and though not really quite large enough to be safe from owls, may survive a long time in a garden well planted with evergreens.

A cock whose mate is confined in an aviary will never stray so long as he can see and hear her, but should she fall ill or die he must be caught up at once. This rule applies to all birds kept at liberty that are not tame pets, fond of human beings.

The Rosella can be bred at liberty, but pairs are less easily managed than cocks. With broadtailed parakeets it is the male bird that decides the movements of the pair, not the hen, as in the case of Barrabands and their allies. The cock of a liberty pair should be a steady bird, well used to aviary life, and it is desirable that he should have nested in an aviary in the garden where he is ultimately to be released. He should first be let out alone and, when he has learned his way about, his mate should be gently driven out when he is at the aviary. Never leave her to find her own way out or she may not discover the exit until he has flown out of sight and the pair will then miss each other and both will be lost. When a pair of Rosellas is kept at liberty the chimneys of the house should have a moveable wire covering placed over them as they exercise a fatal fascination for broadtails. If this precaution is neglected and a bird is missing, a search of chimneys and empty rooms into which chimneys lead may reveal the misguided explorer before it is too late.

Rosellas can also be trained as day-liberty birds out of the breeding season, but their pugnacity makes it impossible for them to share a roosting aviary with other companions.

When free, Rosellas are sometimes inclined to be mischievous for the short period in early spring when fruit buds are swelling, but not towards the buds of common trees. They also eat a few ripe apples in autumn, but have not the wasteful destructiveness of Ringnecks and only a rather hypercritical neighbour is likely to object.

Young birds bred at liberty are rather independent and inclined to stray, so a brood is better caught up when it can feed itself. Unfortunately our English trees do not seem to satisfy the requirements of breeding broadtails very well. Only a place with plenty of old oaks and elms is likely to suit them if the omnipresent starling has not appropriated every possible hole. Artificial boxes are occasionally patronized, particularly those fixed beneath the eaves of the house.

The Rosella Parakeet has a graceful, dipping flight and when at liberty feeds a good deal on the ground. The call-note is a rapid "Chak chak, chink chink chink!" and in addition each bird has two or three musical whistled phrases of four or five notes. While there is a certain family resemblance between the whistles of different Rosellas, there is also much individual variation, as in the song of thrushes.

North of the Darling Downs in New South Wales a pretty race of the

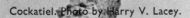
Cockatiel. Photo by Harry V. Lacey.

1. Greater Sulphur Crested Cockatoo; 2. African Grey Parrot; 3. Finsch's Amazon
Parrot; 4. Yellow-Naped Amazon Parrot; 5. Blue and Yellow Macaw; 6. Blue-Headed
Parrot; 7. Blue Fronted Amazon Parrot; 8. Roseate or Rose Breasted Cockatoo;
Scale: $\frac{1}{4}$ actual size. Drawing by R. A. Vowles.

Cloncurry Parrakeets.
Photo by Horst Mueller.

Lutino Indian Ringneck Parrakeets. Photo by Horst
Mueller.

A male of one of the many subspecies of *Trichoglossus haemotod* bearing a great resemblance to Swainson's Blue Mountain Lorikeet. Photo by Horst Mueller.

Lesser Sulphur Crested Cockatoo. Photo by Horst Mueller.

Rosella occurs, described by Gould as the Yellow-mantled Parakeet. The edges of the feathers of the mantle are golden yellow instead of pale green and the general plumage is more rich and brilliant. Single cocks are imported at long intervals, but hens are rarer.

The Rosella interbreeds freely with all platycercine parakeets. Hybrids with its nearest allies, the true platycerci, are fertile and of considerable beauty. Hybrids with the barnardius parakeets are often patchy and unattractive and favour the latter in appearance. Among the crosses recorded are those with the Pennant, Yellow-rump, Mealy Rosella, Stanley, Yellow-nape, Redrump and, most extraordinary of all, Barraband.

The Rosella should be fed on a seed mixture of two parts canary, one part millet, one part hemp, one part sunflower, one part oats and one part peanuts, together with chickweed and other green food and fruit, especially apples, cherries, and gooseberries. A branch of any non-poisonous deciduous tree is also much appreciated, the buds and bark affording both food and amusement.

In the Tring Museum there is a beautiful colour variety of the Rosella which is red, white, and yellow with no other markings.

Mealy Rosella
Platycercus palliceps

Distribution	Northern New South Wales, Queensland.
Adult male	Crown of head very pale yellow deepening towards the base of the neck. Feathers of central portion of upper mantle golden yellow with blackish markings, becoming paler and tinged with bluish green lower down. Wings various shades of violet, blue, and blue-green, the first-mentioned colour predominating. Central tail feathers dark blue; lateral ones paler blue. Cheeks and throat whitish; breast, rump, and underparts pale blue. Sub-caudal feathers red. Bill bluish white. Total length twelve and one-half inches. Size about that of a Barbary Dove.
Adult female	Resembles the male, but is a little smaller and less richly coloured and has a smaller head and beak.
Immature	When leaving the nest the entire plumage is covered with a faint greenish wash rendering the blues and yellows less vivid and the markings less distinct. Subsequent plumage changes like those of other members of the family. Bill, as in all young platycerci, at first yellowish white, but quickly assuming the adult hue.

Like many Australian broadtails the Mealy Rosella is a variable species. In the northern part of its range a pretty race occurs which is known as the Blue-cheeked Parakeet (*Platycercus amathusiae*). It differs from the more commonly imported form in having a paler head, paler and more greenish edges to the feathers of the mantle, a yellower upper breast and large dark blue cheek patches. Intermediate forms are common, as are individuals showing more or less reddish feathering on the head.

In its general character and needs the Mealy or Moreton Bay Rosella, resembles its red cousin. It is, however, more delicate when first imported, often arriving in very bad condition and needing warmth and care until it is through its first moult, after which it becomes as hardy as its allies.

It is a pugnacious bird, with a special dislike of Bluebonnets, and it and the Brown's Parakeet are the only species capable of inspiring that fierce little termagent with something like dread.

The Mealy Rosella is double-brooded and a free breeder in captivity. I have also bred it at liberty, though it is scarcely large enough to be safe from Brown Owls, and starlings will sometimes dispossess it of the hole it has selected.

A very ancient male I kept loose in my garden gave an amusing display of cunning and pertinacity in the pursuit of his love affairs. Although in a state of perpetual moult and minus the greater part of his toes, his heart was young and his brain keen in spite of his physical infirmities. He aspired to the hand of a hen Brown's Parakeet in one of the aviaries who was also desired by a cock of her own species, an old bird, but less decrepit than the Mealy. Many were the battles that raged between them, but though he fought until he could scarcely fly, the Mealy was always worsted by his rival. After a while I happened to release a bachelor cock Pennant, a big powerful bird in the prime of life. The Mealy was exceedingly civil to the newcomer, treated him with mingled deference and friendliness and showed him 'round the garden. He also introduced him to the hen Brown's and her successful suitor who was by no means pleased to see the Pennant and got the worst of the encounter which followed. This was exactly what the Mealy wanted. Time and time again he started a quarrel with the cock Brown's and left the Pennant to finish the battle. The tables were very thoroughly turned, for now it was the Brown's who had no chance against a younger and far larger enemy. More than once I intervened only just in time to save his life and at last the day came when he disappeared and we found his dead body some weeks later. The Mealy had got rid of one opponent, but only, it seemed, by substituting a more redoubtable one in his place. However, he effected by guile what he could not accomplish by force.

The Pennant quite liked the hen Brown's, but he was not indifferent to the interests and amenities of a free life. It was dull to sit all day on the top of an aviary when you could be amusing yourself in the tree tops and discovering all manner of dainties. Consequently he was often absent and while he was away the Mealy was assiduous in his attentions and offers of food to the captive lady. Soon the Pennant began to find that he was coldly received, for the more attentive suitor had gained greater favour. A broadtail is too proud a gentleman ever to waste his courtship on an unresponsive object, so he soon became as indifferent to the Brown's as she was to him. The Mealy had won! He even, by bullying a cock Stanley I had at liberty, obliged me to put him in the aviary with the Brown's. Alas, for the fickleness of the female heart! Not long afterwards she grew tired of the age and infirmities of her companion and began to treat him so badly that I had to take him away to save his life. So the poor old Mealy, like many an elderly human lover, having schemed and worked to the uttermost and even descended to crime for her sake, found himself rejected and threatened in the time of victory by the one for whom he had dared so much!

Hybrids have been produced with the Red Rosella, Bauer's Parakeet, Redrump and Bluebonnet; and a "four-cross" hybrid — the result of a union between a Redrump and Rosella hybrid with a Mealy Rosella and Bluebonnet — a good refutation of the foolish statement that all hybrids between distinct species are sterile. A pretty cross should be Mealy Rosella and Pennant.

Brown's Parakeet
Platycercus venustus

Distribution	Northern Territory, Northwest Australia.
Adult male	Breast and rump pale yellowish cream, each feather having a slight dark edging at the tip producing a scaly effect, the marking becoming heavier towards the throat. Head black; cheek patches white with more or less dark blue on the lower edge according to sex and race. Feathers of mantle black with pale cream edgings. Wings violet with a longitudinal black patch near the shoulder. Central tail feathers violet; lateral ones paler blue. Under tail-coverts red. Bill pale bluish grey. Total length twelve and one-half inches. Size slightly less than a Barbary Dove.
Adult female	Resembles the male but has a smaller head and beak and is a little less richly marked and coloured.
Immature	Resembles the adults, but the black and blue areas are smaller and less richly coloured and the markings are less distinct.

Like its near relative the Mealy Rosella, the Brown's Parakeet is subject to erythrism, specimens being often seen with a certain amount of red on the head or breast.

As to the beauty of this bird, opinions are rather sharply divided.

Some people, of whom the writer is one, consider it one of the most lovely of the genus; others do not like it and call it "odd."

Its character and needs differ little from those of its allies. Records of successful breeding are extremely few, partly because Brown's Parakeet is rarely imported; partly because the few that arrive are usually females; and partly because, like its fellow-countryman the Hooded Parakeet, it has an inveterate habit of moulting in summer and coming into breeding condition in October. It may, however, moult a little earlier each season, until finally you get a July or August nest, which has some chance of succeeding. If permitted to do so, Brown's will nest twice in the same year.

When acclimatized, the species is reasonably hardy in a favourable climate and can be wintered without artificial heat, but when there is a strong and bitterly cold wind blowing, or when sleet is falling, it is wise to keep the birds shut into the aviary shelter; otherwise they will sit in exposed parts of the flight until ill with the cold before they will seek the protection at their disposal.

Cock Brown's are of rather uncertain temper and on a railway journey should be packed separate from their hens as they are liable to kill or injure them. Misogynist cocks, who refuse to tolerate the presence of a particular hen, or of any hen, are also not unknown.

Brown's Parakeets are not large enough to be entirely safe from Brown Owls. I have kept cocks at liberty, where owls are not numerous, but when the hen is allowed to fly loose with her mate it is impossible to restrain the pair from unseasonable efforts at reproduction.

Two cock birds of this species I allowed to fly in the garden had a curious habit, when taking wing in a perfectly leisurely way, of substituting the alarm note for the usual flying call note. The effect of their progress to the tune of "Hawks! Guns! Murder!" was most upsetting to the rest of the collection, who never became used to the Brown's cry of "Wolf!"

Hen Brown's when in breeding condition and anxious for the cock to feed them, utter a plaintive note like the call of a Bullfinch. When this cry is heard eggs may shortly be expected.

Pennant's Parakeet (often, Crimson Rosella)
Platycercus elegans

Distribution	Queensland, New South Wales, Victoria, South Australia.
Adult male	General plumage crimson; feathers of mantle black with broad crimson edges. Cheek patches violet; wings violet with a blackish patch near the shoulder; flight feathers blackish with dark blue outer webs; central tail feathers dark blue; outer tail feathers paler blue; bill bluish horn. Length fourteen and three-quarters inches. Size about that of a pigeon.

Adult female Similar to the male, but has a decidedly smaller head and beak.

Immature General plumage dark green; forehead red; cheek patches blue; a little red on the throat. Some blue in the wings and tail, but less than in the adult. During the first winter a certain number of the body feathers are moulted and replaced by others, more or less crimson or black-marked, a change which has led many Australian naturalists into the error of supposing that the birds take some years to attain mature dress. Like all broadtails, however, both sexes of the Pennant assume full adult plumage with the first complete moult, which takes place when the birds are a little over a year old.

Like nearly all its allies, the Pennant is a variable bird, local races differing considerably in size, in the amount of black in their plumage, and in the degree of the brilliance of the crimson.

In its general character and requirements, Pennant's Parakeet resembles the Rosella. In mixed company it is not quite so aggressive as other broadtails, but this only amounts to saying that it is the least pugnacious of a very pugnacious family.

For its size it is by no means noisy, its whistling notes being usually uttered in a rather low and soft key. Under favourable conditions it is double brooded and young birds, well reared, may nest when a year old and still in immature plumage.

A cock Pennant, whose mate is confined in an aviary, makes a charming liberty bird during the winter months. He is too big to be molested by owls and his gorgeous plumage is a great ornament to the garden.

The Adelaide Parakeet, formerly regarded as a distinct species, is now classed as a variety of the Pennant. It differs from the latter in having the crimson replaced by pinkish brick colour, bronze green, and tawny yellow; the first-mentioned hue predominant on forehead, breast, and underparts and the two latter on the upper surface. In some races of the Adelaide the sexes are coloured alike; in others the hens are almost as red as Pennants, although the red is of a duller and more brickish hue and there is a little green on the mantle and on the upper surface of the tail. Many years ago a bitter controversy raged in avicultural circles owing to a foreign bird enthusiast happening to get hold of a normal cock Pennant and a hen Adelaide of this red type and maintaining in consequence that all the authorities were quite wrong who asserted that the sexes of Pennants are alike in colour, as indeed they usually are. Young Adelaides in first plumage are of a more yellowish bronze colour than young Pennants of the same age, though not so yellow as young Yellow-rumps. The Adelaide appears to be single brooded.

Some Adelaides, which I kept at liberty at my old home, survived and bred for ten years in a perfectly wild state without any artificial feeding before they finally dwindled and died out.

A cock Pennant in my collection developed a very strong attachment for the cock Rock Peplar of a breeding pair which occupied the adjacent aviary. Although the Pennant had a wife of his own, with whom he had nested, when he and the Rock Peplar were at liberty together, he much preferred the company of his male companion. The Rock Peplar did not return his friendship and was rather bored than otherwise by his constant attendance.

In Australia, Pennant's Parakeet is sometimes known as the "Crimson Lory."

At the onset of the moult the red in the plumage of this bird, as in that of all other broadtails, fades suddenly to a brickish hue. The change is as quick and remarkable as the change in the foliage of trees when the autumn frosts begin.

A pair of Pennants which bred at liberty in the writer's garden produced young which left the nest in the crimson plumage of the adult. Another aviculturist had a pair which had, in every brood, some young which were almost entirely crimson and others which were green. It would appear that the Pennant is nearing that stage in evolution, already reached by the lories, when the primitive, sombre dress of the juvenile is discarded, male, female and young being all alike and all brilliantly coloured.

Yellow-rumped Parakeet
Platycercus flaveolus

Distribution
: Interior New South Wales, Victoria and South Australia adjoining.

Adult male
: Crown of head, neck, breast, abdomen, and rump pale straw yellow with a slight greenish tinge; a red band across the forehead; cheek patches dark blue. Feathers of the mantle dark brown with broad straw yellow edgings. A blackish patch on the wing near the shoulder. Remainder of the wing pale blue, with a brownish tinge on many of the larger feathers. Central tail feathers dark blue, sometimes tinged with bronze. Lateral tail feathers pale blue. Bill bluish at the base, horn coloured at the tip. Total length thirteen inches. Size about that of a small pigeon.

Adult female
: Similar to the adult male, but the red frontal band is broader and less clearly defined, the crown of the head is darker, the central tail feathers are much tinged with bronze green, and the feathers of the throat and upper

	breast are shot with reddish brick colour. The head and beak are also smaller.
Immature	General colour yellowish bronze green, paler and yellower than a young Adelaide of the same age. Red frontal band and blue cheek patches present, much as in the adult, but blue areas of the plumage reduced and dark markings practically absent. During the course of the first winter a certain number of brighter and more heavily marked feathers make their appearance and full adult plumage is assumed with the first complete moult, when the bird is a little more than a year old.

Like nearly all the Australian broadtails the Yellow-rumped Parakeet is a variable species; some adult males have a certain amount of brick red on the upper breast, a feature found in all hens; for a female bird of the pale yellow type, unmarked with any red on the breast, appears to be unknown. Probably a fuller study would reveal the fact that in a certain part of its range this bird merges into the Adelaide Parakeet and through the Adelaide is linked up with the Pennant. Indeed it is more than likely that the Adelaide is simply a Pennant X Yellow-rump hybrid, now breeding on its own, to type.

The Yellow-rumped Parakeet is a rarely imported bird which does not differ in its character and requirements from the Rosella. It is a free breeder and under favourable conditions will nest twice in a season. In size it is larger than the Rosella, but distinctly smaller than the average Pennant. The clutch of eggs numbers four or five.

Barnard's Parakeet
Barnardius barnardi

Distribution	Interior Queensland, New South Wales, Victoria and South Australia.
Adult male	Throat, neck, breast, abdomen, rump, and forepart of crown pale blue-green. Chin pale blue. Frontal band dull, dark red. A large triangular patch at the back of the head dark bluish green washed with brownish olive. Mantle rich dark greenish blue. A large patch of yellow on the lower breast. Wings pale blue-green. Under wing-coverts and bend of the wing cobalt blue. Flight feathers blackish with blue outer webs. Central tail feathers green becoming darker and bluer at the tip. Outer tail feathers various shades of blue and pale blue. Bill bluish. Total length thirteen and three-quarter inches. Size about that of a pigeon.
Adult female	Differs from the male in having a smaller head and beak

and in being usually much, though occasionally only slightly, paler and duller than a cock of the same race.

Immature   Resembles the adult, but the plumage is paler and tinged with a faint greenish wash, dulling and softening the blue areas. A partial moult of the body feathers during the first autumn and winter leads to the assumption of a brighter intermediate plumage. Full adult dress is assumed with the first complete moult.

Barnard's Parakeet is another variable species. Besides *B. barnardi* already described, the South Australian *B. whitei* is often imported, a smaller, darker and less handsome bird with the breast patch inclining to orange. The pale green Cloncurry Barnard *B. macgillivrayi* with no red frontal band is very rare in captivity. *B. crommelinae* is at present only known by the type specimen, a female living in the writer's collection. She is a very blue bird with no yellow on the breast and the collar reduced to two small yellow patches on the sides of the neck.

In its general disposition and needs this very beautiful broadtail resembles the Rosella. It is a bad traveller when not properly cared for and the few that have survived the dirty and careless methods of transport too often employed by dealers, have of recent years, proved almost invariably to be females.

Barnard's Parakeet is double brooded and its nesting habits do not differ from those of its allies. A cock in breeding condition is very lively, sometimes checking his flight is such a manner as to give his progress a jerky appearance and continually spreading his tail and uttering his loud, musical, whistling calls.

At liberty the Barnard is safe from owls and a cock whose mate is confined is perfectly hardy and a good stayer if not released before he has actually paired with her. Some years ago I bred a number of Barnards at liberty, but the young were inclined to wander and did not materially increase the population from year to year.

In captivity, or indeed at liberty in this country, individual cock Barnards are apt to display the most curious and at times irritating peculiarities of disposition. One very beautiful male in my possession was tame, that is to say he had no fear of humanity. He took no interest in the society of females of his own race, but devoted his life to the persecution of mankind. For this purpose he stationed himself at the lodge gates and, swooping down upon passers-by, endeavoured to seize them by the nose! As he was only too successful in attaining his object I was soon obliged to get rid of him. Another cock I bred myself was remarkable for his jealous disposition and the strength of his views on a wife's duties to her home. He was paired to a rather weakly hen who was subject to egg-binding and had to be removed from the aviary for treatment. Instead of being overjoyed at her return, as the average cock broadtail would be, he used to fall into a passion of rage with the hen, for, as he apparently believed, deserting her nest and husband. Had the two been left together he would certainly have killed her and it was always necessary to turn him loose until his anger cooled, which did not happen for some days. On the last occasion I substituted for his mate a new hen, also in breeding condition. Although he clearly disliked her, his behaviour was totally different from what it had been on former occasions. Instead of keeping close to the aviary and trying to get at the occupant, he wandered about the garden calling for his proper mate, and eventually he strayed in search of her and was lost. It was evident that his bitter resentment at his wife's supposed wrongdoing sprang from a very great love that would not readily be consoled for her loss.

A third cock hated all broadtailed parakeets, but showed the greatest friendliness to all parrot-like birds of other orders, regardless of condition and sex. His greatest friend was a hen Guilding's Amazon Parrot nearly three times his size. He was perfectly civil to a cock Layard's Parakeet that shared her aviary, but desired to murder a Many-colour. One would imagine that in a previous incarnation he had been a philanthropist who was very badly treated by his relations!

A fourth cock, soon after being separated from his first mate, took a profound dislike to all hen Barnards, but remained friendly with cocks and other broadtails. The following year he became a hater of all broadtails, like his predecessor, though he did not object to non-platycercine parakeets.

In Australia Barnard's Parakeet is sometimes known as the Bulla-bulla.

Red-capped or Pileated Parakeet
Porpureicephalus spurius

Distribution   Southwest Australia.

Adult male   Cap dark crimson; cheeks bright greenish yellow; mantle and wings green; under wing-coverts, outer edge of wing, and portion of flight feathers blue. Rump yellow with a greenish tinge. Central tail feathers green, darkening towards the tip. Outer tail feathers blue and white. Breast purple. Vent and under tail-coverts red. Bill bluish horn and peculiarly long and narrow. Total length fourteen and one-half inches. Size about that of a pigeon.

Adult female   Very variable. Some hens, except for a few green feathers on the cap and a duller shade on the cheeks, have the same plumage as the male. Others, even sisters in the same nest as the bright form, never acquire a plumage very different from the immature, save that they are a little more purple on the breast.

Immature   Head and upper parts dull, dark green, slightly paler on the cheeks; bastard-wing, primary coverts, and outer edge of flight feathers blue; rump greenish yellow. Middle tail feathers bronze-green. A narrow bar of red across the forehead. Throat and foreneck dusky grey with a slight reddish tinge on the breast. Abdomen pale, purplish blue. Lower flanks and thighs apple green, the feathers margined with red. Under tail-coverts similar but paler and inclining to yellow. Adult plumage is acquired with the first complete moult when the bird is a little less than a year old.

The Red-capped Parakeet is one of the many Australian species which appear threatened with early extinction, partly through the reprisals of orchard-owners whose fruit it damages and partly through the cutting down of trees in its rather limited range.

Previous to 1914, I had several untamed individuals and during recent years I have had some hand-reared specimens. Both lots of birds agreed in being hard to acclimatize and very liable to chills, but in other respects the difference was very striking. The wild birds were the most nervous, unsteady creatures I have ever possessed, though not for that reason unwilling to go to nest and sit steadily. They did well on the usual parakeet seed mixture, both in cage and aviary, and were easily confined by ordinary wire netting. The hand-reared birds, on the other hand, were excessively cheeky, inquisitive, and familiar. They required netting of cockatoo strength to keep them in and only with the greatest difficulty could they be prevented from getting over-fat and dying of apoplexy. Not only was it necessary to restrict them to plain canary with one or two peanuts, but not more than a dessertspoonful of seed could safely be allowed to each bird when it was not moulting or breeding. This, with unlimited fruit and green food, I found the most satisfactory diet for *tame* birds, but the timid ones could be given sunflower quite freely!

The Red-capped Parakeet is an extremely lively, restless creature, constantly on the move. If it is necessary to confine it during the process of acclimatization the cage should be as large as possible and it should have turf and a branch to tear up and exercise its beak. As already indicated it is very liable to chill until it has passed through its first moult, vomiting being a common sign of illness. Ultimately it may become reasonably hardy, but it should have a warmed shelter in winter and should not be allowed out on days that are particularly inclement.

If threatened with an attack of apoplexy the bird becomes dull and inactive but sits with its plumage tight and unruffled and does not puff its head feathers as when suffering from cold. It should be caught up and fed on fruit only for several days, and when it is returned to the aviary its seed must be more strictly rationed.

The Red-capped Parakeet has a peculiar clucking call "Clririk! clor-clor! Clririk!" The male bird when displaying raises the feathers on his head, spreads his tail, throws it up slightly above the level of the back and lets it fall again; but he never waggles it from side to side like a Rosella. A tame cock is an amusing, sociable fellow and, although he does not like being touched, he will get quite fond of his human friends. In mixed company this species is spiteful and unfriendly, nor will pairs tolerate the presence of their own kind.

Pileated parakeets have been bred in captivity both in Europe and the U.S.A., but they are not the easiest of birds to rear. Unlike most parakeets, they are often extremely intolerant of having their nests inspected and will desert their young immediately if this error should have been committed. They are also at times addicted to plucking their young in the nest, cocks as well as hens being offenders in this matter — a most unusual occurrence. The cause and cure of this tiresome vice, which is often hereditary, are at present alike unknown, but it is most likely to make its appearance in aviaries which are too small and where the birds are not given green branches to chew up and are supplied with too monotonous a diet. Pileated Parakeets, when rearing young, should be supplied with milk sop made with wholemeal bread and sweetened with sugar. This is indeed a useful extra for most parrot-like birds, when breeding, and even Budgerigars will take it freely.

Many years ago I kept a single cock Pileated Parakeet at liberty during the autumn and a considerable part of the winter. Ultimately it strayed in search of a mate, but this is an almost universal habit with untamed parakeets when their owners are foolish enough to leave them in a state of freedom with no companion of the opposite sex within reach.

XIX

The Smaller Broadtailed Parakeets

Redrump
Psephotus haematonotus

Distribution   Interior South Queensland, New South Wales, Victoria, and South Australia.

Adult male   Head, neck, upper breast, and lower part of the rump bright bluish green. Mantle darker and duller green tinged with brown. Wings bluish green, a small yellow mark near the bend of the shoulder; bastard-wing, primary coverts, and flight-quills deep blue on the outer webs. Upper part of the rump scarlet; abdomen and thighs pale yellow, fading into bluish white under the tail; flanks slightly tinged with green. Under wing-coverts dark blue. Central tail feathers green turning darker and bluer at the tip; outer tail feathers blue with long white tips and brown on the inner webs. Bill bluish horn. Total length eleven inches. Size about that of a thrush.

Adult female   General plumage greyish brown, tinged with green, slightly paler on the under surface and greener on the rump and cheeks. One or two red feathers are occasionally present on the back.

Immature   Young males in first plumage are much browner than adults, but are still sufficiently green to be easily distinguishable from females; they have also a small patch of red on the rump. Full adult plumage is assumed early in the first winter by, if I am not mistaken, a complete moult.

The Redrumped Parakeet is said to congregate in large flocks in its native land, a sociable habit it appears, like the large broadtails, to discard completely when imported into England.

The species is totally unsuited to cage life and soon pines away in very close confinement, but it does quite well in a small aviary or even a large

142

flight cage which enables it to use its wings. It is a graceful and attractive little bird, spending a considerable amount of time on the ground, where it runs about with great activity.

It is a very free breeder, producing two or more families in a season and frequently needing to be restrained from too late nesting by the removal of the box or log. It is less intolerant of a dry artificial nesting-site than many Australian parakeets and will often rear quite strong young in a box placed under cover. The hen alone sits, being fed by her mate who also assists in attending to the young. He, however, grows tired of them rather quickly after they have left the nest and they must be removed the moment he shows the slightest inclination to drive them off.

The Redrump is a spiteful bird in mixed company and will often bully parakeets much larger than itself.

The principal call-note is a musical whistled phrase of six notes or less.

Redrumps are rather subject to septic fever, but are not likely to give trouble when reasonable precautions are taken to ensure cleanliness in the aviary and to quarantine newly imported birds. In a wild state they are occasionally subject to a curious epidemic, which causes their flight feathers to fall out like French moult in Budgerigars, without otherwise affecting their general health. Locally they have been temporarily exterminated from this cause.

The Redrump makes a charming liberty bird in those few districts which happen to be free from Tawny Owls, the green cock and his brown mate making a delightful picture as they run about the lawn. If the cock be released for some days before the female is allowed to join him the pair will stay extremely well and nest in their owner's garden, if suitable accommodation be provided and the usurping Starling kept at bay. The young also, if the sexes are equal, will not wander from their birthplace. Where Brown Owls are present, however, Redrumps can only be kept as day-liberty birds and their pugnacious disposition prevents them from sharing a roosting aviary with their own species or with other parakeets. When a cock Redrump is released for the first time care must be taken to see that he does not lose touch with his mate, either through her aviary being placed too far from the tree he is first likely to settle in, or through her ceasing to call and getting out of sight in the aviary shelter. Once, however, he has come down on the top of the aviary and found her inside, there is no cause for further anxiety, although, assuming that he is allowed to roost out, it may be prudent, if the hen has been shut into the shelter for the night, to release her at daybreak on the next morning and not leave him alone for the first few hours after sunrise. If an accident should overtake one of a pair of Redrumps at liberty the survivor must be caught up immediately, or a new mate provided; otherwise it will certainly stray and be lost. A yellowish form occurs in confinement.

The Redrump has produced hybrids with the Rosella, Many-colour, Bluebonnet, Paradise and Hooded Parakeets.

A pair of Redrumps in the writer's collection was given some Bluebonnet eggs to hatch, their own eggs being infertile. Two young Bluebonnets lived to leave the nest, though one died a few days later. The survivor was a hen, and the cock Redrump divorced his wife and married her immediately. On the removal of his foster-child the Redrump refused for the rest of his days to console himself with any hen, either Redrump or Bluebonnet. In this he was very abnormal, for a cock Redrump, though a faithful and devoted husband as long as his mate is alive, is usually very ready to take another bride as soon as he is sure he will never see his first partner again. This cock, however, led a bachelor existence at liberty for many years, either driving away, or fleeing from, every female I provided for his approval. One day he had a desperate encounter with a rat which attacked him when he was feeding on the ground. He managed to beat off his assailant, but was so severely mauled that his recovery seemed doubtful. He did get well, however, and lived for a year or two longer, until another rat caught him at roost in the ivy and this time ended his career.

The Redrump should be given a seed mixture of two parts canary, two parts millet, one part hemp, one part oats, and one part sunflower. Chickweed seeding grass, and other green food are essential, but fruit is not much relished.

Many-coloured Parakeet
Psephotus varius

Distribution   South Queensland, New South Wales, Victoria, South Australia and West Australia.

Adult male   Head, throat, cheeks, and breast brilliant, glittering, bright grass green. Back of neck and mantle darker and duller green. A yellow band across the forehead; and a small yellow bar on the wing; a portion of the remainder of wing bright bluish green; bastard-wing, primary coverts, and outer edge of the flight feathers rich, deep blue. A cinnamon or almost blood-red patch at the back of the head. A band of yellowish green across the wing and an ill-defined one across the tail-coverts. Base of the tail green, shaded with blue on the middle feathers towards the tips. The outer tail feathers are crossed by a black band, becoming pale blue or white towards the tips. Under wing-coverts bright blue. Belly and under tail-coverts pale yellow with a considerable quantity of bright scarlet in the region of the thighs. Bill bluish horn. Total length

	eleven and one-half inches. Size about that of a thrush.
Adult female	General plumage greenish brown, merging into rather pale green on the lower breast and abdomen. A dull, red patch on the back of the head and a rather brighter red bar on the wing. Rump shaded successively with dark green, pale green, dark green, olive, and dull, pinkish red. Base of central tail feathers green, remainder dark blue; outer tail feathers blue shading into white.
Immature	Males in first plumage bear a considerable resemblance to the opposite sex in their comparatively brown plumage and red wing-bars. They are, however, always sufficiently green to be easily distinguishable. Full mature dress is assumed by a complete moult which begins in the first autumn and is completed by about mid-winter.

This very beautiful parakeet has been given a bad reputation for delicacy by some of the older writers on aviculture. Owing, it was believed, to the lack of some essential item in its captivity diet, it was liable to die in the most disappointing fashion from what was called "cerebral haemorrhage." Under certain conditions Many-colours do undoubtedly leave this terrestrial sphere with disconcerting frequency and suddenness, but the cause of the trouble has nothing to do with diet. Like Bluebonnets, they are highly sensitive, not only to ordinary septic fever, but also to a form of septicaemia which produces symptoms, as well as a post-morten appearance, easily mistakable for cerebral haemorrhage or apoplexy. In favourable climates and in movable aviaries Many-colours may be little more trouble to keep than Redrumps. But in unhealthy districts they are hardly worth the worry and expense they entail, and it is quite useless to try them in fixed aviaries with earthen floors. Even in the most favoured localities the movable, or the concrete-floored, aviary is really a necessity if initial success is not, after a few years, to be succeeded by failure. Of course there are some people who do not seem to mind this; they are quite pleased with themselves if a bird whose natural period of life is thirty or forty years, has managed to survive with them for three and breed for two; while if it has lived for six seasons they are quite sure that it has died of "old age." It may be pointed out, however, that even a very small species like the Budgerigar, will, under favourable conditions, live to be twenty at least; a medium-sized parakeet should survive at least as long as its owner: while a parrot or cockatoo should have a good chance of being in a position to receive an invitation to his funeral. The writer has kept hundreds of parrot-like birds, most of which were adult on arrival, over a period of more than fifty years. In only four cases has old age been the main cause of a bird's death and in three others a contributive cause. Remember, therefore, not to be in too great a hurry to put down to "old age" casualties really due to mismanagement, or to unpreventable illness or accident.

When properly acclimatized the Many-coloured Parakeet becomes indifferent to cold and will run about happily among ice and snow. It should, however, be shut into a snug shelter at night, partly because, if allowed to roost in the flight, it will almost certainly kill itself by flying against the wire in a nocturnal alarm.

Under favourable conditions this species is double brooded, but if one good family of four or five is reared in a season there is no cause to feel dissatisfied.

In general disposition and habits the Many-colour closely resembles the Redrump and its food should be the same.

The call of the Many-colour bears a striking resemblance to that of the nuthatch and is therefore neither loud nor unpleasing.

Pairs of Many-colours do not stay at liberty quite so well as Redrumps, being neither more nor less reliable in this respect than Rosellas. When they can be induced to remain in places free from Brown Owls they are most delightful, have the Redrump's charming habit of spending a considerable part of the day feeding on the lawn and garden paths, which latter, incidentally, must not be treated with weed-killer where parakeets are turned loose.

A cock Many-colour can be trained as a day-liberty bird but he will not share a roosting aviary amicably with other parakeets. As he and his mate have rather feeble voices, special care must be taken that he does not lose touch with her when first released. It is wise to place the hen's aviary at the foot of some trees of medium height and, choosing a calm day, to drive the cock gently into a compartment of an aviary flight immediately adjoining hers. An easily-discovered exit should then be opened in the cock's compartment and he should be left to find his own way quietly out. If left completely undisturbed his first flights will be of short duration and will carry him to no great height or distance. Once he realizes that the aviary still contains his mate and that he has only to fly on to the roof to find her, he will never go more than a few hundred yards from her home.

The Many-colour interbreeds freely with the Redrump and has also been crossed with the Hooded Parakeet producing a hybrid said to be indistinguishable from the extinct (?) Paradise Parakeet.

In Australia the Many-colour is sometimes known as the Mallee Parrot.

Hooded Parakeet
Psephotellus dissimilis

Distribution   Northern Territory.

Adult male   Head, moustachial feathers, and centre of back of neck sooty black; mantle and upper part of the wings dark,

9. Blue Wing Parrotlet; 10. Lineolated Parrakeet; 11. Tovi Parrakeet; 12. Petz' Conure; 13. Yellow Fronted Amazon Parrot; 14. Green Cheeked Amazon Parrot; 15. Spectacled Amazon Parrot; 16. Golden Crowned Conure. Scale: $\frac{1}{4}$ actual size. Drawing by R. A. Vowles.

Blue, or Mealy, Rosellas. Photo by Horst Mueller.

sooty grey. A large yellow patch on the wing; flight feathers blackish brown with a tinge of dull green on the outer edge of the primaries. Throat, cheeks, breast, and greater part of the rump pale blue merging into bright bronze-green near the root of the tail. Central tail feathers bronze-green becoming blackish towards the tips. Outer tail feathers bluish green with a black band near the basal portion. Under tail-coverts soft orange-salmon colour. Bill greyish white. Total length twelve inches. In size somewhat smaller than a thrush and more slender.

Adult female   General colour yellowish olive green with a pronounced pale bluish tinge on the cheeks, lower breast, abdomen, and rump. Central tail feathers bronze-green. Under tail-coverts soft orange-salmon colour.

Immature   Resembles the female. Adult plumage is assumed by a complete moult which begins when the birds are about nine months old or possibly not until the second year.

In a wild state this beautiful parakeet has the rather peculiar habit of breeding in the nests of termites or white ants, making a burrow into the side of the nest and hollowing out a chamber at the end. In consequence its instinct makes it very reluctant to make use of wooden nest boxes, and with good reason, for the young reared in such quarters are weakly and never make good birds.

In the bird-trade the Hooded Parakeet is universally miscalled the "Golden-shouldered," a title which properly belongs to its rare near relative *P. chrysopterygius* with the yellow frontal band.

In unhealthy districts it is so delicate as not to be worth keeping, but in healthy ones it is not particularly hard to preserve in good health. In Bedfordshire, where the climate appears to suit it, I have successfully wintered it out-of-doors, not only in aviaries of more than one type, but even at complete liberty. The chief difficulty with this species is its strong objection to adapting itself to our seasons. While the majority of Australian parakeets, with the exception of its fellow-countryman the Brown's, fall in line with our summer at once, the Hooded obstinately persists in moulting in May and coming into breeding condition in October. It is, however, quite useless to yield to its desires, as in an outdoor aviary the young have no chance of survival in late autumn and the hens are almost sure to get egg-bound; while nestlings bred in a heated birdroom are so lacking in stamina as to be not worth the trouble of rearing.

The only thing is to be firm and season after season remove all nesting facilities at the end of August. This will cause the birds to moult earlier and earlier and ultimately patience will be rewarded by a July nest. For breeding accommodation a very large mound of earth mixed with turfs should be raised in the aviary flight. About two or three feet from the ground a more or less horizontal burrow should be made into the side of the mound with the hand and arm, and as much earth as possible scooped out with the hand at the end, so as to form a chamber for the nest. The admixture of turfs with the earth will give a more stable consistency to the mound and prevent the roof of the chamber and passage from crumbling and falling in. There should be some overhead shelter to keep heavy rain from falling directly on the top of the mound, but some moisture soaking in from the edges is all to the good.

P. dissimilis resembles the Redrump in disposition and should receive the same food. No parakeet suffers more quickly from the effect of very close confinement, and even six months in a cage on hard perches will produce overgrown and deformed bill and toenails, wry tail feathers and a general sad disfigurement. It is essential, therefore, while a Hooded Parakeet is being acclimatized, to keep it in a flight cage and give it a twiggy branch for a perch.

Occasionally young Hooded Parakeets are imported which appear healthy and in good condition but lack flight and tail feathers. On no account, however, should a Hooded Parakeet be purchased which is unable to fly, as the disease is as incurable as the "French moult" in captive Budgerigars to which it seems to be allied.

The call of the Hooded Parakeet resembles the word "Chissik" or "Chillik!" When courting, the male bird puffs the feathers on his lower breast so that they stand out separately, and performs graceful short flights around the hen, holding himself upright and alighting and walking with a great deal of dignity and swagger.

As a liberty bird the Hooded Parakeet is a glorious creature, the male, with his big yellow wing patches and graceful dancing flight, looking like some enormous butterfly. He is scarcely less attractive when running about feeding on the lawn. Naturally, however, only in owl-less districts can he enjoy complete freedom and if it is necessary to shut him up at night the same precautions must be observed and the same methods of training followed as advised in the case of the Many-colour. Cock Hooded Parakeets pair readily with female Redrumps and in some ways a Redrump makes a better companion for a liberty Hooded than a hen of his own species as she is less likely to get into trouble through searching for a substitute for termite mounds, or through trying to propagate her kind during inclement weather.

A tame Hooded makes an attractive pet with strong likes and dislikes for his human acquaintances.

XX

Grass Parrakeets and Their Allies

Blue-winged Grass Parrakeet
Neonanodes ehrysostomus

Distribution   Tasmania, Victoria, New South Wales.

Adult male   Head, neck, breast, mantle, and rump olive green, the head sometimes showing a pronounced golden tinge. Frontal band dark, vivid blue; moustachial area and minute feathers 'round the eye yellow. Abdomen and under tail-coverts pale yellow, the former sometimes showing an orange patch. A large part of the wing dark, brilliant blue, the blue being sometimes partly concealed by the overhanging green feathers of the mantle. Under wing-coverts dark blue; flight feathers blackish. Central tail feathers greenish blue; lateral ones partly yellow. Bill bluey horn. Total length eight and seven-eighth inches. Size about half as large again as a Budgerigar.

Adult female   Resembles the male, but the frontal band is much less fully developed and is sometimes practically absent, the blue wing-bar is duller and interspersed with greenish feathers and there is never an orange patch on the abdomen, nor a pronounced golden tinge on the crown.

Immature   Resembles the female, but the frontal band is absent and the blue area on the wing is smaller, duller, and tinged with olive green. Adult plumage is assumed by a complete moult during the course of the first winter.

The Blue-Winged Grass Parrakeet is a summer visitor to Tasmania, returning to the adjacent mainland of Australia after breeding.

As much confusion exists with regard to the various species of Grass Parrakeets, which are constantly mis-named by trappers and dealers, the following notes may be of service to enable aviculturists correctly to identify the birds that may come into their possession.

Blue-winged Grass Parrakeet — General plumage olive green; frontal band

149

of vivid dark blue and a broad wing-bar of the same colour. Occasionally an orange patch on the abdomen.

Elegant Grass Parrakeet — General plumage golden olive; frontal band dark blue with a pale turquoise upper edging; a *narrow* dark blue wing-bar, also with a pale turquoise upper edging. Occasionally an orange patch on the abdomen.

Orange-bellied Grass Parrakeet — General plumage rich grass green. Frontal band and a narrow wing-bar dark blue. Orange patch on the belly.

Rock Grass Parrakeet — General plumage dull brownish olive; frontal band and narrow wing-bar dark blue, sometimes merging into paler blue but never showing the brilliant turquoise of the Elegant. Yellow area on the abdomen restricted and not bright.

Hen Turquoisine — Differs from all the above-mentioned species in having a decided tinge of blue on the cheeks as well as on the forehead.

Hen Splendid Grass Parrakeet — Differs from the hen Turquoisine in having a considerable amount of very pale turquoise mixed with olive in the wing, the hen Turquoisine having the lower part of the wing a uniform soft blue.

Although the grass parrakeets appear to be getting scarcer, the Blue-wing is the least uncommon of the six species and, although not imported freely at the moment, was for a period not uncommon on the bird market. With characteristic apathy, however, our aviculturists took but little interest in them and made no serious effort to induce them to breed under conditions likely to secure the continuance of the race and of those brought over the great majority have already perished from mismanagement and neglect.

The Blue-wing, like all the members of its genus, is a delightful little parrakeet, possessing a quiet, yet brilliant, beauty. It is harmless to other birds and innocuous to growing plants; it can be handled safely without gloves, its weak bill being unable to pierce the skin; while its low, sibilant call would not offend the most sensitive ear.

Although unsuited to very close confinement, the Blue-winged Grass Parrakeet will live well in a flight cage, provided that every part is kept scrupulously clean. For successful breeding, however, a roomy aviary is a necessity, small fixed aviaries with earthen floors being responsible for a high percentage of infertile eggs and degenerate young useless for stock purposes. In unfavourable climates the Blue-wing, like all the grass parrakeets, is hopeless as an aviary bird, but in healthy ones it will live well enough, especially if the aviary shelter be slightly heated during the winter.

The Blue-wing has an inveterate habit of killing itself by flying against the roof of its cage or aviary when suddenly frightened, for which reason it is necessary to provide the cage with a false floor of canvas and the aviary with a false roof of string netting carefully watched to see that it remains taut. In order to prevent the birds from biting holes in the string netting and getting between it and the wire, smooth boards about a foot wide may have to be fastened to the sides and end of the aviary immediately below the juncture of the string netting and the wire. Grass parrakeets are poor climbers and the smoothness of the wood, by depriving them of foothold, makes it impossible for them to reach and bite the netting above them. Not all pairs, however, are string-biters.

Blue-wings are extremely sensitive to septic fever infection and, when kept or transported in dirty cages, to eye disease and to wasting and incurable form of enteritis. The eyes of a healthy grass parrakeet should be as round and bright as boot buttons, the slightest inclination to close the eye or blink with undue frequency being a sure sign of the approaching onset of contagious conjunctivitis. Nothing is more disheartening and maddening than this wretched complaint. Frequently it does not make its appearance for weeks, or even months, after the bird's arrival. At first it seems but a trifling ailment, the parrakeet continuing to feed and its general health remaining unaffected. Indeed, I have seen birds actually play during the first stages of the ailment, though the hand of death was as surely on them as if they had been suffering from a severe attack of pneumonia.

Eye disease may take the best part of a year to run its course, but the writer has never succeeded in curing a single bird of the genus under discussion. Among perfectly useless remedies may be mentioned all forms of boracic, rose water, and zinc ointment. Contagious conjunctivitis, deadly and vexatious as it is, is a wholly unnecessary scourge. It never appears when birds are kept in pairs in clean cages or travelling boxes, the perches of which are washed daily and the floors at frequent intervals.

When suffering from any form of chills a grass parrakeet makes a bad patient with no great power of resistance. In very desperate cases, when the bird is obviously going down in spite of an even temperature of eighty-five degrees Fahrenheit, good results may sometimes be achieved by forcible feeding of the patient every two or three hours with raw egg beaten up in half a cup of milk and administered drop by drop from the end of a small paintbrush. If the bird's strength can be maintained until after the disease has passed its crisis, there is a chance that it may begin to feed again and in time pull through. During the process of feeding the parrakeet should be wrapped in a handkerchief and every care be taken not to soil its plumage unduly. The first meal should be a very small one or vomiting may ensue.

When displaying, the cock Blue-wing draws himself up to his full height, depresses his shoulders to show the blue on the wing, brings up food from his crop, and utters a call resembling the syllables "Scroop-tew." Breeding pairs should be kept separate and care must also be taken that the hens, who are the stronger sex, do not injure males who are strange to them and to whose presence they may at first object. The hen lays four or five eggs and is usually single brooded, her mate playing the same part in the domestic menage as a cock broadtail. Young Blue-wings are not exacting in their nursery requirements and will do well in a log or box hung up in the aviary. The nest should not be too steep to enter, as Blue-wings are not great climbers; but neither should it be too large, nor should the nest be practically on a level with the exit, or the young may scatter and get chilled or fall out before they are properly fledged.

Young birds will breed when twelve months old if given the opportunity of doing so, but it is prudent not to allow the hens to nest before they are two years old, as, for some reason, they are very apt to die when not fully mature, either while laying or during incubation.

The Blue-wing should be fed on a seed mixture of two parts canary, two parts millet, one part oats, and one-half part hemp and sunflower, together with plenty of chickweed, seeding grass, and spinach beet. Blue-wings are liable to sun-stroke and in hot weather there should be plenty of shade in the aviary flight. A few leafy branches thrown on the roof are a good protection. The species is also known as the Blue-banded Grass Parrakeet.

Elegant Grass Parrakeet
Neonanodes elegans

Distribution	New South Wales, Victoria, South Australia, West Australia.
Adult male	General plumage golden olive; frontal band dark blue with a pale turquoise line on the upper edge. Forepart of the cheeks, throat, abdomen, and thighs golden yellow, an orange patch being sometimes present on the abdomen. Lower edge of the wing dark blue with a line of pale turquoise above it. Primaries mainly black. Central tail feathers bluish green; outer tail feathers yellow. Bill bluish horn. Total length ten and one-quarter inches. Size about half as large again as a Budgerigar.
Adult female	Similar to the male but duller and less golden in colouring; duller also in regard to the frontal band and blue areas of the wing.
Immature	Differs from the adult as does the young of the Blue-winged Grass Parrakeet and has similar plumage changes.

Although none of the green grass parrakeets can be described as tough, hardy and long-lived birds, the Elegant has done better than any other member of the group outside its native country, and is fairly well established as an aviary bird. Some English fanciers have wintered it successfully in outdoor aviaries which have had no artificial heat. But, since losing a fine cock from inflammation of the lungs when a warm April day was followed by an extremely cold and foggy night, I have given my Elegants moderate heat in the shelter during the more inclement months of the year. The treatment should be the same as that recommended for the Blue-winged Grass Parrakeet. The species is often double brooded.

Turquoisine Parrakeet
Neophema pulchella

Distribution	Southeastern Australia.
Adult male	Green. Upper breast yellow tinged with green; lower breast golden yellow, sometimes with a tinge of orange on the abdomen. Forehead brilliant dark blue merging into turquoise; cheeks and part of the lower wing-coverts, turquoise. Under wing-coverts, lower edge of wing, and greater portion of flights dark blue. A bar of maroon-red near the shoulder. Outer tail feathers yellow at the tip. Bill dark brown. Length eight and one-half inches.
Adult female	Olive green; abdomen yellow. Forehead, cheeks, and under wing-coverts tinged with blue. Lower part of wing and outer webs of flights blue. Outer tail feathers with yellow tips.
Immature	Resemble the female, but from the first young males show rather more blue on the face and may have a speck of red on the wing. Adult plumage is assumed by a moult which begins when the birds are about five months old, or less.

This lovely little bird, eclipsed only in splendour by its relative, the Scarlet-chested Grass Parrakeet, was well-known to aviculturists during the middle of the last century and was described by them as hardy and prolific. As a matter of fact, as a species, it is neither; its reputation having been doubtless gained by the circumstance that it goes to nest readily several times a year and that individual pairs have sometimes been wintered without artificial heat. Although, as I have just said, it goes to nest readily, that does not mean that the majority of pairs can be relied upon to produce large numbers of offspring. A few may do so, but they are rare treasures and on no account should they be overworked. If experience has shown that even the hardy Budgerigar should not be allowed to rear more than two broods in a season, the need for preventing parent birds from exhausting themselves by raising too many families is infinitely greater in the case of this delicate grass parrakeet. It may go against the grain to throw away third-round Turquoisine eggs; but, if you have no lovebirds available as foster parents, that is the only wise course of action to follow if ultimate disaster is to be avoided. Lovebirds, as I have already hinted, make tolerably successful foster parents for grass parrakeets, but I have never had any luck with Budgerigars in this matter as the average pair refuse to feed any nestling which, like a baby Turquoisine, is hatched with a long covering of white fluff.

Turquoisines are extremely temperamental birds and, while a few pairs will live together in harmony, some are given to indulging in violent and dangerous brawls, the hen being occasionally the aggressor, but more often the cock. A good many cocks, indeed, are not only wife-beaters, but also wife-murderers and need the most careful watching; while others are liable to kill their offspring as soon as the latter leave the nest.

If it is necessary to take the young birds away rather soon they should be placed in a roomy flight cage with the top covered, if it be of wire netting, so that they do not fly up in sudden alarm and crack their skulls against it; an accident very likely to occur with all species of grass parrakeets, both in flight cages and in aviary flights. The cage and perches must be kept scrupulously clean and the floor of the cage thickly covered with dry sand on which plenty of seed and attractive green food is at first scattered. Only when the birds are well accustomed to the cage, and feeding well, can the seed be offered in a dish. Young grass parrakeets suitably housed in this way and kept at a comfortably warm temperature will usually feed themselves adequately almost immediately after they have left the nest. But if they should appear slow in doing so, and especially if there is only one in the brood, it is not a bad plan to put in with them one or two steady young Budgerigars, not long out of the nest, but feeding themselves freely, in order to help the Turquoisines to feed by their example.

When the young birds are steady and feeding well, they can be returned to a suitable aviary. At first they should be confined in the shelter and later driven into it at night until they roost there of their own accord. The usual precautions should be taken to prevent them from cracking their skulls against the roof, or end, of the flight. When they first leave the nest, young Turquoisines are often extremely nervous and dash wildly about, hitting themselves violently against the wire netting. For this reason, when they are expected to leave the nest, it is a good plan to tie plenty of leafy branches against the wire netting at the end of the flight. This precaution is indeed desirable when almost any brood of parrakeets is expected to leave the nest. The aviaries which I myself find most satisfactory for grass parrakeets have the back and end of the flights boarded up on the outside and a hard floor of tiles or concrete.

Another trouble with Turquoisines is that the young are more likely to die in the nest than in the case of any other species of parrakeet. Although it is desirable to remove the corpses if only a part of the brood should perish, it is equally necessary to avoid disturbing the birds by too many inspections. Very often by applying one's nose to the entrance hole of the nest box without actually opening it one can gain some idea as to whether all is well inside or the reverse!

Breeding pairs of Turquoisines should be kept out of sight and hearing of other members of their species; otherwise the excitable and irascible temper of the cocks is likely to be aroused. Difficult as Turquoisines are apt to be towards their own kind, they are not, however, as a rule spiteful with birds not nearly related to them.

In winter, as I have already intimated, the shelter of a Turquoisine's aviary should be kept at a comfortably warm temperature, and this is especially necessary in the case of young birds. Males of the latter will not agree together once they start to moult into adult plumage at the age of a few months. Turquoisines should be fed on canary seed, millet, including spray millet, and oats. Hemp should not be given to them except in very small quantities when they are actually rearing young as it is very liable to induce feather-plucking, a vice to which the species is somewhat prone. An abundant supply of chickweed, seeding grass, and spinach beet should always be available.

Hybrids have been produced with other species of green grass parrakeets; but, strange to say, they are usually, though not invariably, sterile.

Turquoisines, when imported or kept under dirty conditions, are extremely prone to eye disease; and also, it must be admitted, are capable of developing most of the other ailments to which parakeet flesh is heir! For this reason it is useless to attempt to keep them in fixed aviaries with earthen floors to the flights. Like other members of the family, they make bad patients, having little resistance to disease and the chance of their recovery is remote unless they are taken into the bird hospital at the very first sign of illness. When sick, they do not as a rule put their heads under their wings, but partly close their eyes and slightly puff their plumage.

The late Mr. Astley had a tame, talking Turquoisine, which it is not surprising that he describes as a most delightful pet.

Splendid Grass Parrakeet
Neophema splendida

Distribution   Southern Australia.

Adult male   Green. Face dark, brilliant blue; remainder of head turquoise blue, mixed with green at the back of the head. Upper breast green at the sides with much red and orange-red in the centre; abdomen and under tail-coverts yellow. A considerable amount of very pale turquoise on the wing. Under wing-coverts rich dark blue. Flights blue with a green tinge to the edge of the outer webs and dusky inner webs. Tail feathers green with dusky inner webs; outer ones largely yellow. Bill black. Length eight inches.

Adult female   Dull olive green; a little blue on the forehead and cheeks. Some orange on the abdomen. Thighs and under tail-coverts yellow. Some very pale turquoise mixed with green in the wing. Flights bluish. Under wing-coverts turquoise mixed with green.

The few skins of this gorgeous little parrakeet which the writer has examined do not agree very closely with the coloured plates in works of reference. The cocks have not the clean-cut blue head and clean-cut round crimson patch on the breast seen in the pictures. The blue on the rear of the crown is mixed with green, and the breast patch is straggly and irregular in form.

The female, instead of being a replica of the male without the red breast patch, is of a much duller green and has scarcely more blue on her face than a hen Turquoisine. She can, however, be readily distinguished from the latter by the very pale turquoise mixed with olive in her wings. The hen Turquoisine has the lower part of the wing of a uniform, soft blue, not very pale and with no admixture of green in the blue area.

This matchless avian gem, the most gorgeously coloured of the small parrakeets and, indeed, one of the most brilliantly plumaged birds in the world, has quite a romantic history. Very rarely seen since it was first described by Gould, it was, for a long period, believed to have become totally extinct. Rather miraculously, however, not very many years ago it turned up again in reasonable numbers in its native land; and, which is perhaps even more remarkable, it is being bred there in captivity in considerable numbers. It has also been bred both in Europe and in the U.S.A. None of the green grass parrakeets can be described as tough and hardy birds; all require care, and all, even when they receive the attention which, in the case of the species under consideration especially, they so richly deserve, are a bit too liable to disappoint their owners by an untimely death. As grass parrakeets go, however, the Splendid is by no means one of the hardest to keep and rear. Its food requirements are simple — canary and white millet seed, oats, spray millet, a little hemp and sunflower during the breeding season, and green food in the form of chickweed, seeding grass, and spinach beet. It goes to nest readily; indeed, at times, almost too readily in that a breeding pair must not be allowed to rear more than two broods in a season if their health and stamina and that of their offspring is not to suffer. It may go against the grain to throw away the eggs of so valuable a bird but this should always be done if a third lot of eggs make their appearance and foster parents in the shape of lovebirds are not available.

I have never, myself, known Budgerigars to rear the young of any parrakeets which are not hatched naked and without down, but others have had a different and more fortunate experience.

Adult pairs of Splendid Grass Parrakeets must be kept separate from their own kind and from other members of their genus; but they are not, as a rule, spiteful with less nearly-related birds. They cannot, however, safely be kept in a crowded aviary as they are likely to develop eye disease or pick up infection from the dirt of such quarters.

All the grass parrakeets have very weak, gentle voices, that of the Splendid being musical and singularly deep in tone for so small a bird.

When courting the cock trips about 'round the hen and takes occasional short flights, but he seems well aware that he is beautiful enough not to need any extravagant antics for the better display of his good points. When recommending a nest to his mate, he hangs on to the entrance hole and goes through the motions of a bird having a bath!

Splendids are much less temperamental than Turquoisines. The cocks are rarely wife-beaters and married couples do not indulge in dangerous and unseemly brawls. Some cocks, however, very quickly grow tired of their young once they have left the nest and the latter must be carefully watched and removed even, it may be, when they are only out of the nest a day or two, if their male parent is seen to be getting tired of them. It is a good plan, until they are steady and feeding themselves freely, to place them for a time in a roomy flight cage with the top covered so that there is no risk of their cracking their skulls against the roof in a sudden alarm. Plenty of seed should be scattered on the floor of the cage, as well as a seeding grass. In the case of very young birds, never put seed in one dish only, as they may not find it. If they seem slow in feeding themselves the presence in the cage of a young Budgerigar which has just begun to feed freely, may help to get them started. All young grass parrakeets, when first leaving the nest, are apt to be very nervous; for which reason before they fly it is well to fasten a number of branches against the wire netting at the end of the flight so that they do not crash against it. I also strongly advise an inner lining of string netting to the roof of the flight.

Young Splendids are not very easy to sex in nestling plumage but, like Budgerigars, they moult into adult plumage or something like it, quite early and long before they are twelve month's old.

If there are no hens with them, cock Splendid Grass Parrakeets will often agree together, even after they have assumed adult plumage; a thing which Turquoisines will never do.

Bourke's Parrakeet
Neopsephotus bourkii

Distribution   Interior New South Wales and South Australia adjoining.
                 Interior West Australia.

Adult male   Head and upper surface greyish brown. Feathers of the
                 lower part of the wing edged with pale buff. Some greyish
                 white 'round the eye and on the moustachial feathers and
                 cheeks. Upper breast rose pink marked with greyish
                 brown with increasing faintness towards the abdomen.
                 Lower breast and centre of abdomen rose pink. Under
                 wing-coverts, under tail-covers, thighs, and sides of the
                 rump pale blue. A bluish tinge at the bend of the shoulder
                 and in well-coloured specimens some lavender-blue on
                 the forehead. Degenerate aviary-bred males may lack the
                 blue forehead. Central tail feathers and flights dark grey-
                 ish olive. Outer tail feathers white with a slate blue area
                 not visible in the living bird. Bill dark horn. Total length
                 nine and one-half inches. Size about half as large again
                 as a Budgerigar.

Adult female   Resembles the male but is more slender and has a smaller
                 head and beak. The upper part of the breast is more
                 heavily marked with greyish brown and there is never
                 any blue on the forehead.

Immature   Much resembles the adult but duller and browner.

An Australian observer writes of this parrakeet: "It usually frequents
open and sandy country, interspersed with small clumps of prickly acacia,
Neelia, or other small bushy trees, which usually grow in groups. During
the day it lives in these and feeds under the shade of them on various seeds;
the small, hard, black seeds of the Neelia tree being its favourite food.
They are rarely in flocks of more than six or eight. They have the peculiar
habit, no doubt a protective one, of coming to water after dark or before
dawn."

Although usually referred to as a grass parrakeet, this desert species
is totally distinct from the green grass parrakeet and has no near relatives.
Although it shares with the green grass parrakeets an unfortunate fondness
for cracking its skull against the unprotected roof of an aviary flight, it is,
on the whole, a much hardier and more easily-managed bird than the
members of the genus Neophena and is now well established in captivity.
If provided with a dry and cosy shelter it can, in England, be wintered
without artificial heat. It is a very attractive species and has much to
recommend it. The soft browns, pinks, and blues of its plumage present
an unusual and lovely harmony of colour. Its voice is a gentle musical
chirrup and in flight its wings also make a musical whistling sound. It

is not in the least destructive and, while breeding pairs will not agree together, it is quite inoffensive towards other birds, including the green grass parrakeets. If kept sufficiently dirty it *can* develop eye disease, but possesses considerably more resistance to the ailment than the green grass parrakeet and will sometimes recover. In captivity it is often double brooded, but the production of a third brood should be discouraged.

As a rule the cock is a good husband and father, but I have known individual males who would bully their hens badly in their anxiety to make them start another nest before the young of the first nest were fully reared. A plain seed mixture of millet, canary, and oats should be provided. If hemp is given to breeding birds, care should be taken to see that it does not bring the cocks into too high condition, with the results already described. When feeding young the species should be provided with seeding grass, chickweed, and spinach beet, but, no doubt on account of its desert habitat, it is not as fond of green food as most of the other Australian parakeets.

I have known Bourkes kept on the colony system in a large aviary and allowed to nest too often, to produce young suffering from French moult, exactly like Budgerigars.

Some Bourkes make good foster parents to the young of grass parrakeets, but certain pairs will stop feeding when the green feathers of their foster-children appear.

The display of the cock Bourke is very graceful and pretty. He moves about 'round the hen, every now and then, as he reaches a new position, making a slight curtsey and drawing himself up to his full height. Occasionally, he raises his wings above his back after the manner of a bird stretching in order to show the blue on his flanks. When on the ground, Bourkes move by a series of dainty, tripping runs.

Budgerigar
Melopsittacus undulatus

Distribution   Australia.

Adult male   Wild form — green. Forepart of crown yellowish, white. Rear of crown, hind-neck, upper part of cheeks, mantle and smaller wing feathers, pale straw colour tinged with green and barred with blackish colour. Lower part of cheeks and throat yellow. A small patch of dark blue on each cheek below which are three black spots. Flights dull brownish green with large yellowish white and greenish white spots near the base. Tail long and blue-green in colour. Bare skin 'round nostrils rich dark blue. Bill bluish lead colour. Iris straw colour. Length seven and one-half inches.

Adult female   Similar to the male but with very pale blue cere when not breeding: otherwise dark brown or cream cere.

Immature   Markings fainter. Breast paler and abdomen with a bluish tinge. Forehead with faint, dark bars. Iris dark. Cere pinkish lilac. Adult plumage is assumed after a few months.

The Budgerigar is the only member of the parrot family which in a true sense can be said to have been domesticated. It is exceedingly prolific, even under conditions which would discourage breeding in any other members of the order of birds to which it belongs, and it is extraordinarily adaptable. Its merry and amusing ways, which, in many respects, are peculiar to itself, and the readiness with which it can be tamed; endear it to a vast number of bird lovers, rich and poor. Last but not least, it has shown a capacity for producing colour variations, unique in the animal kingdom. Budgerigars are now bred in, literally, hundreds of colours and combinations of colour, including one of singular beauty which occurs in no other living bird, i.e., the combination of snow white and sky blue which nature, without the aid of human art, only seems to provide in inanimate forms.

In a wild state the Budgerigar is gregarious at all seasons and very uncertain in its movements, sometimes staying in a district for a year, or for a portion of a year, and then vanishing for several seasons, to occur in great numbers elsewhere. It breeds in colonies and a trace of its original social instincts is still found in the unwillingness of some, but by no means all, pairs to go to nest when they are out of sight and hearing of members of their own kind. Though very gregarious, hens have very strong views about the ownership of their nesting sites and will fight energetically, and at times murderously, with other members of their sex in defence of them. Cocks are a good deal less pugnacious and also less physically capable of inflicting a hard bite. In captivity, provided an aviary is not overcrowded and at least two, and preferably even more, nest boxes of the same type are provided for each female, the fighting when the boxes are first put in does not usually have very serious consequences; especially if the hens have been associated together before breeding is allowed to begin. It is a very different matter, however, if a hen should take a fancy to a box already occupied by one who has eggs or young. If she insists on pressing her claim there may then well be a fight to the death. For this reason it is most unwise to introduce new hens in breeding condition into a colony where other hens are already nesting. For no matter how many spare boxes may be available, the perverse creatures will, more often than not, insist on pestering the ladies already in possession of homes, until the latter see red and serious trouble occurs. Although quarrelsome over their nests, hen Budgerigars do not, as a rule, display much jealousy over their mates, whose morals they seem to regard as being beyond hope! The morals of the cock Budgerigar of the domesticated strain, unlike I think, those of the wild bird, are, it must be admitted, indeed conspicuous by their absence. A cock will pair with any hen who will give him the least encouragement, but he will only help in feeding the young of his first, or "official," wife, his other lady friends being left to bring up their families single-handed! This, in point of fact, they are quite capable of doing; although, as the strain of bringing up a brood alone is naturally greater, they must not be over-taxed in this way. If a hen Budgerigar is rearing a brood single-handed, she should on no account be provided with a mate until her brood is fully reared. If a new cock is given her too soon he may prove spiteful towards young who are not his own, or he may induce the hen to go to nest before the last of the young of the first brood have flown. In which case they will be neglected and starved. Odd cock Budgerigars in an aviary do not usually do much harm but they require watching, as individuals may worry the breeding pairs unduly. Normal cock Budgerigars, whether members of breeding pairs or otherwise, are usually tolerant and unselfish in their attitude towards all young birds, making way for them at the feeding place. Strange to say, the dominance of the young cocks over those who are fully adult tends to persist indefinitely. And in much the same way, very young hens are often able to hold their own with those that are fully mature.

The morals of hen Budgerigars, though not always beyond criticism, are decidedly better than those of cocks. If it is desired in colony breeding that two particular birds should be mated, this end can often be secured by putting the couple together, alone — but within sight of others of their species — and providing them with a nest box. When the hen is seen to be on affectionate terms with her mate and to be going into the nest box, the couple can be returned to the aviary and are likely to keep together. As already pointed out, however, the transfer must be made when all the birds are first being put up for breeding and *not* after some pairs occupying the aviary have already laid their eggs. A hen Budgerigar always shows her acceptance of a suitor by "rubbing noses" with him with a circular motion. If she pecks at him or remains unresponsive to his advances, she has not accepted him, even if she allows him to feed her now and then.

Occasionally, though rarely, two hens will form an attachment for one another and abandoning their usual jealousy, will decide to share a mate and nest box, bringing up a joint brood in common. Hen Budgerigars usually begin incubation with the laying of the second egg and sit for just under three weeks, the young remaining in the nest for a month. More often than not the eggs do not hatch together, but one by one, at intervals of two days, so that there is a great difference in size between the eldest member of the family and the youngest. The habit is an entirely natural one and it is rare, if the birds are properly managed, for the youngest member of the family to be either smothered or starved, even though an inspection of the nest box might lead one to anticipate that such would be his fate. The normal clutch of eggs is six, but larger numbers are not uncommon. It is usual for people who wish to breed birds to show quality, and to be certain of their pedigrees, to keep their pairs separate, in flight cages or small aviaries; but although the reasons for this policy are thoroughly sound, the older and more natural method of colony breeding need not necessarily be discarded. A young Budgerigar on first leaving the nest should, if well reared, be able to fly strongly; if not always very accurately. If it cannot do so, it is a sign of some constitutional weakness.

For the first day or two it will probably sit about rather quietly, depending on its father for food, but after that it will soon begin to look after itself. If really strong and well fed by their parents all the time they have been in the nest, most young birds will, at a pinch, feed themselves adequately even from the time they fly, provided they are kept warm and that food, plainly visible, is always before them. Usually it is a good plan to leave young birds in the parents' aviary for a week or ten days after they have flown. But if, for any reason, it is necessary to take one out earlier it should be placed in a cage, the whole bottom of which is sprinkled with seed and well covered with dry sand. The presence of a slightly older companion will sometimes encourage a very young bird to start shelling seed for itself. As a rule canary seed is selected in preference to millet for the first venture. If for any reason, a young bird leaving the nest for the first time should be starved and weakly, and should not begin to take an adequate amount of food of its own accord, it may be necessary to recourse to hand feeding.

Whole meal bread should be chewed up; well-moistened with milk and heated to blood heat, for young Budgerigars will not swallow food which is at all cold and clammy. The bird should then be taken in the hand and small morsels of the warm, semi-liquid food should be placed against the side of its beak with the aid of a camel-hair paintbrush. When very hungry it will soon begin to feed, but care and patience will have to be taken to make sure that it receives an adequate amount in the course of its earliest meals. A similar policy may, of course, have to be adopted in the case of young birds which have to be taken from the nest owing to the illness, or death, of their mother.

If a brood should be getting their feathers and be able to dispense with maternal warmth at night, the cock alone may rear them successfully if the hen should fall ill. Care should, however, be taken to see that he is doing his duty and that their crops are full at nightfall. Smaller nestlings may have to be given foster parents. Most Budgerigars are very obliging in taking on the care of strange nestlings, if the latter are about the size of their own or a little younger. But care should be taken to see that all is well if the foster child is old enough to show feathers of a very different colour from those of all the other occupants of the nest.

In general, Budgerigars are very tolerant of inspection of their nests, but a great many people disturb them unnecessarily and at times with disastrous results. It is especially desirable to leave hens quiet and undisturbed when they are actually laying and if later inspection of the nest boxes can be made when the hen has come off the nest of her own accord, so much the better. It is quite unnecessary to be constantly cleaning out nest boxes containing young birds, for nature has so arranged that the droppings of those whose parents are properly fed, are dry and inoffensive and do not soil the feet or plumage. Hen Budgerigars normally start to lay again before the youngest of the first family has left the nest. This is a perfectly natural procedure and it is rare for the young birds to damage the eggs or for the hen, having grown tired of them, to ill-treat them. Some hens always make a practice of moving to a new nest for a later brood; others invariably use the same nest. If the hen moves to a different nest the cock will continue to care for the young of the first nest until they have flown. If there is any danger of the aviary becoming overcrowded, young birds are best removed to new quarters when they are about ten days out of the nest and if it is ever desired to show them, it is a good plan at this period to cage them for some days. This makes them steady and confiding, and the effect of such a steadying is not subsequently entirely lost when they are turned into another aviary.

Although some fanciers say that the sexes should be kept separate out of the breeding season and as far as possible from one another, I have never, myself, found that any harm results from keeping them together. It is the presence of nest boxes rather than the companionship of the opposite sex which acts as an incentive to breeding and in an aviary without boxes the hens will not usually become jealous or quarrelsome. The cocks will even tend to show more interest in, and appreciation of, the company of members of their own sex and there will be no serious fighting, nor will many eggs be laid from the perch. In an aviary where breeding is on the colony system it is a good plan, in addition to supplying a large number of boxes, to place partitions at the side of each box so that a hen sitting outside the nest she has chosen cannot see her neighbours. This arrangement prevents a good deal of jealousy and fighting, as some hens, especially when boxes are first put in, get so excited and possessive that they cannot bear to see another female anywhere near them occupying a box. In a few days, however, when a hen has definitely decided on the box she prefers, she will grow less intolerant of her neighbours and more ready to respect their rights.

Budgerigars start to come into breeding condition at an extraordinarily early age. Hens out of the nest box themselves little more than eight weeks will start prospecting for nests and, not very long afterwards, will begin laying, if allowed to do so. Orthodox breeders insist that birds should not be allowed to go to nest before they are fully twelve months old, but unless a person aims at producing winners for the show bench, I should say, judging from my own experience, that they may be allowed to breed at a considerably earlier age if they are through their first complete moult, vigorous, and well grown. After all, no one regulates the age at which wild Budgerigars shall begin to breed in Australia; nor the number of nests they shall be allowed to have, and yet the species is in no danger of extinction.

Orthodox breeders also consider that birds should not be allowed to have more than two nests in twelve months, and this advice is normally wise. In breeding birds for the show bench they also recommend that not more than four eggs shall be left in the nest; the remainder of the clutch, if valuable, being given to foster parents.

Breeders with indoor accommodations often arrange for their birds to nest during the winter, a little artificial heat being provided if required, and also artificial light to give the birds a twelve hour "day." Experience has shown that a longer period of artificial light is not beneficial; in fact, rather the reverse. When the birds are kept in outdoor aviaries in a climate like that of England, they should not be given their nest boxes before the middle of February. Nor should they be allowed to start nesting after the middle of August. Young birds which leave the nest later than October, and those which are hatched in outdoor aviaries in mid-winter, are usually rickety and suffer from breathing troubles which cannot be cured even by bringing them into a warm room.

There are many different patterns of Budgerigar nest boxes, but whatever the type chosen it is essential that the portion to receive the eggs should be concave and not flat. No material is really necessary inside the box, but I have found that a handful of very soft decayed wood, well crumbled up in the hand, is usually popular with the hens and is very seldom thrown out. I am not myself in favour of sawdust, which is apt to get into the young birds' beaks.

Cock Budgerigars which enter the nest a great deal while the hen is sitting on eggs are usually a nuisance as they are apt to disturb her and cause the eggs to be broken. They are best removed if pairs are kept separate, but when the birds are bred on the colony system this particular trouble is almost unknown, as the cocks have more to occupy their attention.

Some persons find the sexing of young Budgerigars difficult. In the case of the non-red-eyed varieties, however, the pinkish lilac, which is characteristic of both sexes when they first leave the nest, is replaced within a very few weeks in the case of the cocks by a more uniform and decided blue; while the hens' ceres get paler and duller and become suffused with cream or brownish tints. Red-eyed birds such as lutinos and albinos are much more difficult to sex; for the ceres of the cocks, even when fully adult, are never blue, but pinkish, slightly suffused with bluish white. The ceres of the hens on the other hand, when they are in breeding condition, assume the dark brown tint characteristic of the female of other varieties. Incidentally, the dark brown skin of the ceres of a breeding Budgerigar usually flakes off when the bird goes out of breeding condition and her appearance when this is happening should not be mistaken for the disease known as "scaly-face."

Budgerigars differ from other birds in having no regular moulting season; in frequently moulting at least two or three times a year; and in being willing and able to breed successfully even when they are in full moult. The advice given by experts that pairs should not be put up for breeding when they are showing signs of moult may be sound enough if the pairs are kept separately, but if they are being bred on the colony system there is not the slightest need, when the correct time of year arrives, to delay putting in the nest boxes because the birds happen to be moulting. A healthy hen Budgerigar inspired by the sight of a nest box and the presence of female rivals who may wish to take it from her, will stop moulting immediately, rush into breeding condition and start to lay not very many days later than her sisters who do not happen to be moulting at the time. Moulting cocks are equally ready to undertake domestic duties and it is quite a common thing for such birds, even if not moulting when first put up for breeding, to have a heavy and complete moult when nesting operations are in full swing without either their fertility or their interest in parental duties being in the slightest degree affected.

Budgerigars should be fed on canary seed, white and Indian millet. The latter is the ear, commonly known as "spray millet," is a great delicacy and useful for taming birds, but it is rather expensive. Some oats may be added to the mixture, especially when young are being fed. Chickweed is the best green food and seeding grass, especially rye grass. Care should be taken to distinguish seeding grass from grass in bud or in flower which has no feeding value. In winter when green food is scarce Budgerigars can sometimes be induced to eat sliced carrot. They are always more ready to make experiments in new foods when they are feeding young than at other times. Spinach beet is a useful green food and much appreciated by the birds, but is should be given in rather strict moderation to those which have young in the nest or it may cause digestive disturbances in the latter and "wet nests." Chickweed, however, will never do this and can be given ad lib. Milk sop, made with whole meal bread and slightly sweetened, is also appreciated by breeding birds. It should, of course, be changed daily and on no account allowed to become sour or stale. A Budgerigar aviary should have a hard floor of tiles or concrete with a pitch which causes all rainwater to run off immediately. If it collects in pools the birds will drink the water contaminated by their own droppings. The shelter should be cosy and draught-proof and also well-lighted. It is a good plan to shut the birds into the shelter when they are first introduced into the aviary so that they can find the food there and get into the habit of entering it to roost. A number of thin perches should be arranged fairly near the roof and if they are to be permanent it is a good plan to have an arrangement whereby the ends rest in two strips of slotted board running parallel with each other, from which they can easily be lifted out for cleaning or in the event of it being necessary to use the catching net to capture them. The floor should be thickly covered with dry, gritty sand and a dish of similar sand, changed occasionally, should be kept in the flight together with a dish of agricultural lime well-slaked in water so that all burning properties have been removed. A piece of clean turf regularly changed is also appreciated by the birds, which eat a considerable amount of the soil. Another very useful feature in the aviary, usually omitted, is a good supply of the twiggy branches of non-poisonous, deciduous trees from which the birds derive an infinite amount of exercise and amusement in nibbling the bark and buds. I myself prefer to hang the nest boxes in the aviary flight and not in the shelter, providing such protection from wind, weather, and vermin as is necessary for the birds' safety and comfort. It is a good plan to cover over a wide portion of the centre of the aviary flight and arrange some side protection as well, placing under the covered portion plenty of natural branches on which the young birds can sit and roost in comfort when they have left the nest and before they have found their way into the shelter. When breeding is in operation, seed should be available and plainly visible in the flight as well as in the shelter for the benefit of inexperienced young birds which have not yet discovered the latter. Nest boxes in the aviary flight should have adequate protection from the hot sun as well as from the wind and wet. Fanciers living in hot climates have, indeed, found that it is desirable to avoid breeding during the warmest months of the year. One advantage of breeding in the flight rather than in the shelter is that boxes hung up in the former are less likely to become infested with red mite, a most serious pest which is believed, by some, to be one of the principle causes of "French moult."

It is very important to see that the perches in a breeding aviary are securely fastened at the ends and are not thick, smooth or slippery; otherwise satisfactory mating will be hindered and many infertile eggs will result.

The colour breeding of Budgerigars is now a highly elaborate science and those anxious to master it are advised to obtain one of the many publications written by those who have made a special study of the question. For the benefit of beginners in the fancy I will here confine myself to a few brief and elementary observations. Some colour varieties are what is known as "dominant" over others and some are "sex-linked." As an example, if a cock green Budgerigar of green ancestry for several generations is mated to a lutino hen of the common recessive (the opposite to dominant), sex-linked type, all their young will be green. The daughters, moreover, will be just what they look like — ordinary green — and of no more value for breeding lutinos than any other hens. The sons, on the other hand, though in appearance pure greens, have a capacity for producing some lutino daughters and, if they are mated to lutino hens like their mother, a capacity for producing, in addition to lutino daughters, some sons which are also lutinos. Lutinism, characterised by yellow, unmarked plumage and red eyes, especially noticeable when the birds are young and easily seen, even in tiny nestlings, are sometimes described as being the albino form of birds of the "green series," while snow white birds with red eyes, are referred to as albino forms of the "blue series."

Opaline Budgerigars are birds which have the ground colour of the plumage of the wings the same as that of their breasts and rumps, while the colouring of the cap — yellow in a bird of the green series and white in the case of a bird of the blue series — shows a tendency to spread over the greater part of the head. An ordinary cobalt Budgerigar, for example, has the ground colour of the wings dark grey with blackish markings and whitish edges to the feathers. The head behind the white cap is greyish white finely barred or striated with darker colour. In an opaline cobalt, on the other hand, the ground colour of the wings is cobalt and not grey, and the greater part of the head is whitish. In birds of show type the area between the shoulders should be as free as possible from dark markings, but it is difficult to breed birds completely without markings in this part of the plumage which are also not more lacking in markings on the wing than is considered desirable. The various opaline forms have a characteristic silky texture to their plumage and are often of very great beauty.

Some varieties of Budgerigars are what are known as "colour hybrids," that is to say two birds of the same colour mated together will never, no matter what their ancestry may be, produce offspring all of which are similar to themselves. Cobalts are "colour hybrids," and two cobalts mated together will produce, sometimes in the same nest, cobalts, mauves, and sky blues.

As a pet, the Budgerigar possesses almost all the virtues of the larger parrots without any of their vices. It is lively, friendly, and amusing and, when at liberty in the room, though it may occasionally nibble papers, it lacks the strength of beak to do any serious damage. By reason of its small size few of the noises it makes are loud enough to be irritating; while its capacity for learning to talk in a low, husky, but often perfectly clear, tone is very great indeed.

If an indoor pet bird is required, by far the most satisfactory is a young cock taken a few days after it has left the nest and as soon as it can feed itself properly. As at this age it is difficult to sex birds with certainty by the colour of the cere, one practical and quite useful test which may be applied is to take the bird in your hand — or preferably to get someone else to do so! If it gives a sharp bite it is certain to be a hen, but if it bites little, or not at all, it is likely to be a cock. Hen Budgerigars rarely make satisfactory pets as they are neither healthy nor happy when they are not allowed to breed. A common, stupid, and reprehensible practice is to give a pair of untamed Budgerigars in a very small cage as a present to a child or other person. Kept in this way neither bird will get really tame and both will suffer from lack of exercise and die of premature old age. If you *must* have two birds, it is far better to get two cocks and on no account should the cage be less than two feet in length by one foot three inches in width by one foot six inches in height. Even a cage of this size, however, will be more of a prison than a home to birds of such great activity if it is not possible to let them out for exercise.

A single cock, taken young and thoroughly tamed, is therefore infinitely preferable, as he can be let out for exercise in the room. He will not miss the companionship of his own kind and will, indeed, make a much better pet if he never sees them, as he will then transfer all his interest to human beings. As most Budgerigars do not learn to bathe in a dish, like a canary, a pet bird should have access now and then to a quantity of clean grass or leaves, soaking wet in some shallow vessel of considerable size. In this he will take a bath by rolling about after the manner of his kind in a natural state. A pet bird should be discouraged from running about on the floor 'round his owner's feet, being driven up with a gentle flap from a cloth or handerchief if he starts to do so. Otherwise there is a grave danger that he may one day be trodden on. Great care must also be taken when the bird is at liberty in the room that, in following a person who is going out, he does not get pinched in the door. care must also be taken to see that he gets an adequate night's rest and is not kept active and awake too long in a room where there is artificial light.

When teaching him to talk, repeat the same sentence constantly in the same tone of voice, at times when he is able to give you his whole attention, and always repeat the entire sentence and not merely a part of it. Tame talking Budgerigars, once they have learned a number of words, will re-arrange them to suit their own fancy, sometimes with most amusing and unexpected results.

Although some fanciers consider that a hen Budgerigar is past her best for breeding after her third season, a cock kept as a pet and allowed adequate exercise, should live quite as long as a dog or cat and even attain the age of twenty years in some cases.

As liberty birds, Budgerigars make a most delightful addition to a country garden, and destructive as they are to shrubs when confined in an aviary, they will do no damage whatever when free. Success, however, will only be achieved if the following rules are strictly adhered to.

The aviary for liberty Budgerigars should be placed near the lower branches of a tree and it is all to the good if close beside it there is also an evergreen shrub with spreading branches and rather scanty foliage. The aviary should be divided into two compartments, one for the breeding birds and those flying at liberty, and one where the hens are kept confined during the period of the years when it is desirable to prevent them from nesting. Nest boxes should be hung up nearly all 'round the aviary flight at the top. They must have some overhead and side protection from wind and weather, and, as already recommended, a considerable portion of the centre of the flight must be covered over with some rain-proof material. The wooden framework of the aviary flight should be on the inside in the case of the top of the aviary; but on the outside in the case of the sides, as it will then serve a useful purpose by encouraging young birds to alight on it when they are trying to find their way home. In addition to the seed in the shelter, seed must also be provided in the flight in a box about fourteen inches square and about eighteen inches below the top of the aviary flight. Immediately over the centre of this feeding box a circular exit hole about five inches in diameter should be made in the roof. Across the exact centre of the exit hole a detachable ladder of little perches should be hung from hooks, the bottom rung of the latter being just above the level of the seed in the feeding box while the top rung is exactly three and one-half inches below the edges of the exit hole, *neither more nor less*. A cross-piece of stout wire attached to a moveable metal frame should be made to fit closely into the exit hole, its purpose being to exclude hawks, the smaller Budgerigars being able to pass easily through the four sections.

A downward-pointing funnel of wire netting, also moveable and having a metal frame made to fit the exit hole exactly, must also be provided, the funnel being slightly less than the diameter of the exit hole at the base, but tapering until it is just large enough to allow a Budgerigar to pass easily through at the tip. The purpose of this funnel is to keep birds that return to feed in the afternoon confined in the aviary for the night, and therefore safe from owls.

If the aviary be a large one containing a considerable number of birds, it is a good plan to have another feeding box, rather longer than the first and on a much lower stand, placed fairly near the side of the aviary. Exactly opposite the middle of this feeding box there should be another inward-pointing funnel of wire netting longer than the first and leading in from the side. This funnel can be a fixture. Its shape should be different from that of the downward-pointing funnel and should somewhat resemble the nostril of a nose; that is to say, the opening should be on the under side and not at the end, but, unlike the nostril, it should be on the under side *only near the tip*. The funnel is thus constructed in order to enable young birds seeking entrance to the aviary, as some do, through the side and not through the top, to find their way in. The reason for the opening not being at the tip of the funnel and only at the end of the under side is to prevent birds from finding their way easily out again through the funnel in the reverse direction. If the whole of the tip or the whole of the under side were open, inquisite birds climbing about on the funnel would soon find their way out. Opposite the entrance to the funnel there should be a wooden platform or alighting board. It is indeed quite a good plan to have other fixed inward-pointing funnels at any place in the side of the aviary where young birds are observed to alight on the outside framework and persistently seek entrance.

If it should be feared that four-footed vermin might find entrance through the funnel, it is possible to make the lowest alighting platform so wide and carried so far the whole way 'round the climbable portion of the aviary, that no rat or mouse can get past it.

When the aviary is in working order and the birds are going in and out, the daily routine is as follows. At five p.m. in the middle of the summer and at one p.m. in midwinter place some steps or a short ladder against the side of the aviary opposite the tall feeding stand. When you have climbed to the top, take out the cross-piece of wire and lay it on one side; next unhook the ladder and lay it against the side of the feeding box in such a position that it will not impede birds feeding or entering, nor allow them easy access to the tip of the wire netting funnel; then put the latter into the entrance hole. The following morning reverse the process, taking the funnel out of the entrance hole and putting it on one side and putting the cross-piece of wire and the ladder once more in place. If the weather should be rainy, the seed on the feeding box will get wet, but that is unavoidable and, if the box be cleaned out weekly, no harm will result. It is safe, when the weekly clean-out takes place, to put the seed from the tall stand onto the larger and lower stand, if there is one, and leave it there for another week before removing it altogether. Be very careful to make sure that the birds never run completely out of food on the stands, for if they do the absence of feeding companions will no longer attract those at liberty to the right place of entry. Inexperienced persons, if such should have to be put in charge of the birds, are very apt to mistake seed husks for seed and to fail to make allowance for the growing food demands of increasing numbers of young birds still in the nest. If for any reason it is inconvenient to put the funnel in at the correct time, there is not the slightest objection to putting it in much earlier. Indeed, if there be a special reason for doing so, there is no objection to keeping the birds confined for several days or even a few weeks. Do not release liberty birds when it is snowing; when there is thick fog; or when snow or hoar frost cover thickly even the slender branches of the trees, as such conditions are apt to confuse birds of tropical origin. There is, however, no reason why they should not be released in cold, but settled, winter weather, provided the trees are reasonably free from snow and that all snow has been removed from the neighbourhood of the entrance hole of the aviary. Budgerigars, incidentally, can stand a considerable degree of cold, but they should not be exposed to temperatures in any way approaching zero or their feet will suffer from frostbite.

When a start is being made with an aviary of liberty Budgerigars, stock from a tested "homing" strain should, for preference, be obtained. Birds which have shown a disposition to stay well in one part of the country and not lose their heads when first released, will behave equally well in a new home, provided that they are properly managed. If birds of a homing strain are not obtainable a start must be made with ordinary stock which are known to have been bred in large outdoor aviaries. Birds of show type which have been bred in cages or very tiny aviaries are less suited for flying at liberty. They are apt to be heavy and clumsy; not sufficiently alert to avoid natural enemies; and stupid about finding their way back. New birds, whether of a homing strain or otherwise, should be confined in the aviary until the young of the first round are *just* beginning to leave the nest, when the exit hole can be opened for the first time. If you are making a start with birds of a non-homing strain you must not expect very striking results your first season. When the exit hole is opened some of the cocks and an even larger number of the hens will not go out at all. A few cocks will go out and stray and a rather smaller number will go in and out and behave sensibly. Practically all the young birds, however, will find their way out and, for a time, return sensibly; but as the weeks go by a good many even of these will also stray. A certain percentage, however, will remain and the young hens as they become sexually mature will start to take an interest in nest boxes. If this happens before August fifteenth, you can if you like, allow them to rear one brood before removing them to the hens' "resting" aviary. Such early breeding might horrify the orthodox, but in point of fact it does the young birds themselves no harm whatever from the standpoint of future breeding, and the young they rear if sometimes a little on the small side will often be quite satisfactory birds for your purpose. The young birds of your own breeding which have survived the danger period from the standpoint of staying will be the foundation of your homing stock and the percentage of stayers will tend to improve about twenty-five percent with each succeeding generation.

As the prettiest show with new Budgerigars is provided by the young birds a few weeks out of the nest, since the old ones when busy with family duties do not leave the aviary so much, it is desirable to extend breeding over as long a period of the year as possible; having regard, of course, to the weather conditions and hours of daylight in the district in which you live. There is, however, in this connection a problem to overcome with liberty birds which does not arise in the case of those permanently confined in an aviary. As already pointed out, it is undesir-able to allow breeding Budgerigars to exhaust themselves by rearing too many large families. If, however, you put your birds up for breeding at the beginning of February and transfer all the adult hens to the resting aviary when they have reared their second lot of young by the end of June, serious trouble may ensue, for you will have disturbed what is an all-important factor in an aviary for liberty birds, i.e., the breeding psychology of the inmates. A cock Budgerigar, unlike a male of the larger parakeets, is not sufficiently attached to his mate to desire to remain in her vicinity throughout the year, when she is not in breeding condition. If all the breeding hens are removed from the liberty aviary during the summer months and confined in another department, a curious change comes over the other birds. The cocks get wild and restless and start straying, and even the young hens bred early in the year will not, when they reach the normal age, start coming into breeding condition and occupying boxes in the aviary, but will share in the general restlessness and also begin to wander. It is, therefore, essential to depart from orthodox practice with regard to the number of nests allowed so as to maintain the breeding atmosphere in the aviary until late September or October. In order to prevent the overtaxing of the constitutions of the breeding birds, it is, however, possible, by the removal of eggs, to reduce the number of young which they are allowed to rear to two, and this is the policy which must be followed. It is the feeding of a large brood, rather than lay-ing and incubating eggs, which taxes the strength of parent birds and the feeding of two youngsters is quite a light task for a pair. Indeed I am inclined to think that a hen keeps healthier and happier when engaged in light parental duties than when sitting about in an aviary with nothing to do and indulging in a series of moults merely to pass the time! If desired, the number of eggs in the first clutches can be reduced as well. During the winter when the days are short and wild food is no longer abundant, there is little risk of Budgerigars straying. Moulting birds, also, do not stray and most Budgerigars have a moult in October, regardless of the number of times they may have moulted earlier in the year.

For flying at liberty those colours should be selected which provide the most striking and attractive display against a natural background of trees or sky. It is also desirable to select those varieties which show pure and bright colours when in nestling plumage — for the reason already given, that it is the young birds which are the most active and the most often seen in flight. Yellows, cobalts, white and yellow-wings, and opaline blues are among the most attractive colours. Greens are not so good; neither are olives, greys, or mauves, which latter are grey in their first plumage. Among my own homers I have some red-eyed birds, i.e., lutinos and albinos, but although their colours are attractive I think they are hardly as suitable for flying at liberty as are the dark-eyed birds because their eyesight is inferior and they are more likely to lose their way or get caught by hawks.

For flying at liberty a different type of Budgerigar to the show type is desirable and one which, except in colour, approximates more nearly to the wild form. In a liberty bird the qualities most desirable — in addition of course to the homing propensity — are activity, intelligence, alertness, hardiness, prolificacy, and good temper in mixed company. Details of form, carriage, or shade of plumage can be ignored, for when a bird is seen in flight it does not matter if its wings are long or short; if its skull is flat or round; or if its spots are large or small. Show birds, as a result of selective breeding and breeding under very artificial conditions, are getting more and more a type of their own and not a good type for liberty work. They are slow both in flight and wits; easily lose their heads and their way when they first find themselves at liberty; and the hens, not being used to social life when they are breeding, are often quarrelsome and interfering and, like many human beings, incapable of protecting the virtue of minding their own business!

With regard to the problem of straying, birds which leave their home may be divided into two classes. There are those which go away, not because they do not know their way back, but because they have a wandering disposition. These are as useless to the breeder of a strain of liberty Budgerigars as is the pigeon which does not bother to return, even when it has the strength to do so, to the owner of a stud of racing homers. Some Budgerigars, however, which have lived all their lives in aviaries stray when first released because, like many larger parrots under similar conditions, they are upset by the strangeness of their surroundings and are afraid to fly *down* and in consequence, by the time they have learned to manage themselves in the air, have lost their bearings completely. Such birds, if reported to their owner directly they are seen, may often be recaptured with the aid of a decoy bird — preferably a fairly tame and steady cock — in a cage, and another empty cage containing seed, with a door at floor level. As soon as the strayed bird is located (very likely it will be feeding on the ground), walk quietly up to it with the two cages; but do not approach it so nearly that you drive it up into the air. If you can, however, set the decoy bird, with the other cage alongside it, and the door open, down within sight of the wanderer. If all goes well the latter, attracted by the appearance and call of the decoy, will approach its cage and, being probably rather hungry, will be attracted by the dish of seed put inside the door of the other cage and soon enter. When it has done so, walk quietly up from the same side as the open door and when you are very near, attempt to close the latter so gently and quietly that the bird merely flies up onto the perch or side of the cage and does not flutter about wildly, finding the open door before you can close it. When a decoy is used, be careful not to leave it unattended in a place where it may be attacked by a cat or dog. When your capture has been brought back, you can with safety return it to the aviary without any special pre-cautions. By this time it will have learned to find its way about when free and, if it has any aptitude as a liberty bird at all, it will give no further trouble even if it should again get out.

If the owner desires to make his birds more steady and familiar than ordinary aviary birds, he can have a little door made in the front of the flight and just inside it a bracket with a number of very stout pieces of wire across it. Sitting on a chair outside the aviary and putting his hand holding a bunch of spray millet through the door, so that hand and the seed rest on the bracket, he can encourage the birds to come and feed. This they will soon do if they have learned that spray millet is a delicacy, but are not given so much of it in other parts of the aviary that they are already satisfied. With a little patience, birds can later be trained to feed from the millet held in the hand when they are free in the garden outside the aviary, but it is as well not to encourage them to become as wholly fearless as ordinary pet birds, for, if they should come to feel that they have not an enemy in the world, they may lose their natural alertness which is a protection against predators.

In England, the only serious enemy of liberty Budgerigars is the Sparrow Hawk and occasionally, though more rarely, the Kestrel. Adult birds of a good homing strain are usually too swift and wary to be caught, protecting themselves, either by a lightening get-away as the hawk descends on them, or by not leaving the shelter of the aviary when they have reason to suspect that their enemy is about. Young birds, not long out of the nest, are, however, liable to be taken and even old ones may be so greatly scared by the repeated visits of a hawk that they will desert their home. The best remedy for the visits of a Sparrow Hawk is, of course, the gun. Birds of prey are fairly regular in their time of hunting, and if the hawk should be observed one day at a particular hour success is most likely to be achieved if it is waited for at about the same time on following days. If shooting should be impractible, the Budgerigars can be kept confined for some days until the hawk gets tired of paying fruitless visits. A good scarecrow is also sometimes effective, but it must *be* a good one. The ordinary coat and hat on a stick are perfectly useless, and the figure must not only bear lifelike resemblance to the human frame, but particular attention must be paid to its face. It is the face of their enemy which birds most quickly observe, as any sportsman who has shot driven game will have noticed. A bright, fluttering object hanging from the scarecrow's hand or arm is also useful, and it should be so constructed that it does not lose its mobility in wind or rain.

The ailments of Budgerigars are, for the most part, similar to those of other parrakeets. As with the latter, the rate of sickness is much higher in summer, especially during wet, muggy, and changeable weather, than it is in winter. Enteritis due to chill, is probably the most frequent ailment, the sick bird ruffling the small feathers of the wings, puffing those of the head and breast, and sitting with its head "under its wing" and both feet on the perch. The eyes are also half-closed and vomiting may occur in some cases. Very young birds, only a day or two out of the nest, will sometimes sit with their heads "under their wings" and both feet on the perch; but, if they are well, the feathers of the crown and breast will be held fairly tight and their eyes, when they are gently disturbed, will look round and bright.

Birds suffering from pneumonia have a habit, when taken into the hospital, of sitting with their wings slightly spread and every few moments extending them a little at the shoulder and then drawing them in again. Patients suffering from this serious ailment which do not seem to be making any progress at the usual hospital temperature of eighty-five degrees Fahrenheit may benefit by an extra five, or even ten degrees, of heat.

Coccidiosis is usually a hot-weather disease. Affected birds do not often put their heads "under their wings," but partially close their eyes and fly less briskly than healthy birds, when disturbed. The droppings at first are dark in colour and not yellowish like those of birds suffering from enteritis. Individuals vary greatly in respect of the severity with which they take this disease. If the correct treatment is given, about half the sick birds may be expected to recover, some quickly and easily, and others only after a long and severe illness.

Budgerigars, when kept under filthy and neglected conditions, can develop psittacosis, but there is not the slightest danger of this from any bird which has been kept under clean and proper conditions, and has not been brought into contact with diseased individuals.

Hen Budgerigars will sometimes become egg-bound if they attempt to breed when rather out of condition, especially if the weather be very cold. Heat treatment will always bring relief but the birds should not be allowed to go to nest again for several weeks. Their eggs, if valuable, should be given to foster parents. When an egg-bound hen is in the hospital room or cage, some thick sand or soft material should be placed under the perch if it is desired to save the egg.

Plucking of the young is not very uncommon in hens breeding in rather close confinement. The cause and cure of the trouble are unknown and, as it is often hereditary, birds showing the vice are best got rid of.

French moult is a disease rarely seen in any parrakeets other than Budgerigars. In mild cases the flight and tail feathers are dropped before, or immediately after, a young bird leaves the nest. For a time it continues to grow feathers which are not properly developed and fall out, but eventually, without any special treatment, normal feathers are produced. Post-mortem examination shows an abnormal condition of the liver. The worst examples of the disease have all their feathers more or less seriously affected, and are incurable.

The precise cause and nature of the ailment is still a matter of much controversy even among experienced fanciers. In the opinion of the writer it is a deficiency disease of rather obscure origin. It appears most commonly among birds kept in rather close confinement and allowed to rear too many broods. It is more frequent in hot than in cool weather and in establishments where the supply of green food is scanty than in those where it is generous. It may, however, occur where a generous and varied supply of other foods is given to the birds with the object of avoiding diet deficiencies. Although the contrary has been stated, it seems certain that it is not caused by any parasite living permanently on the bird and experiments appear to show that it is not hereditary nor contagious. The theory that red mite, which attack the birds only at night and normally leave them in the daytime, is, anyhow, one important cause of French moult, may have a considerable amount of justification.

Definite claims have been made that hybrids have been produced between Budgerigars and one or two species of lovebirds, but no skin or good photograph of such a cross seems to be in existence. Budgerigars will pair readily both with Bourkes and with green grass parrakeets, but in all cases known to the writer the eggs have been infertile, even where normal mating has been observed.

XXI

Kings, Crimson Wings, and Polyteline Parakeets

King Parakeet
Alisterus scapularis

Adult male   Wings and mantle dark green, each wing having down the centre, longitudinally, a narrow strip of pale green which at times may be almost hidden by overlapping feathers, but is very conspicuous when the bird is displaying. Head, neck, breast, and abdomen scarlet; rump very dark blue merging into black; tail blue-black on the upper surface. A very thin strip of dark blue on the nape where the red joins the green of the mantle. Upper mandible red with a black tip. Iris pale and yellow. Total length fifteen inches. Size about that of a wood-pigeon.

Adult female   Head, nape, mantle, wings, and upper surface of the tail dark green, upper rump blue merging into green at the edges and towards the tail. Throat, neck, and upper breast dull green with a reddish tint showing through. Abdomen scarlet; sub-caudal feathers scarlet blotched with green. Beak blackish with a trace of yellowish red on the culmen and lower mandible; iris duller and paler than the male's. The light green wing stripe is absent or rudimentary in most females, but in a few is fully developed. Size very variable, some hens being nearly a third larger than others.

Immature   Much resemble the females in first plumage, but young males soon begin to show some red in the upper mandible. At the first complete moult they assume a patchy mixture of green and scarlet in those areas which eventually become wholly scarlet. Full plumage is gained with the second complete moult when the bird is in its third year.

The King Parakeet is a fairly enduring, but sluggish and unhappy cage bird. Its disposition, however, does not unfit it as a pet and there

177

is a case on record of a lady who trained a King to be quite an intelligent and amusing companion with some talent for mimicry. She allowed her bird a considerable amount of liberty in the room, but no one who does not intend to take this trouble should keep a King in close confinement.

In healthy climates the King makes a hardy aviary bird, indifferent, when acclimatized, to the severest cold. In unhealthy ones, however, the hens, especially, may give a good deal of trouble. As it is susceptible to tuberculosis, septic fever and coccidiosis, and feeds a good deal on the ground, a moveable aviary or one with a hard floor is desirable.

The King Parakeet goes to nest quite readily if provided in the open flight with a large, hollow, perpendicular tree trunk about six feet high. The nest should be almost at ground level, as Kings like a *very* long descent, and the interior must be made climbable with wire netting. The courtship of the King Parakeet is elaborate and amusing. When a pair in good condition is introduced to one another they show great excitement. The cock puffs the feathers on his head; draws his body plumage tight; displays his green wing-bar to the fullest extent, shakes his head, gives his wings a quick, shivering flip; makes a nibbling motion with his beak; and, after uttering his "Crashak! crashak!" call loudly, goes off into a singular kind of song in a minor key interspersed by sounds not unlike those of a hen announcing the arrival of her egg. All the while his eyes blaze with contracting pupils, and from time to time he scratches his head violently; the access of the tender passion apparently sending blood to his brain to such an extent as to cause irritation! The hen responds by also puffing her head feathers, drawing tight her body plumage, contracting the pupils of her eyes and joining her cries to those of her lover. When courting a hen confined in an aviary, a cock at liberty will sometimes indulge in an aerial form of display, flying about in a figure of eight with his plumage set as when displaying on a perch, and keeping up his chirruping song as he goes.

When in breeding condition and about to lay, the hen King invites the cock to feed her by a noise and up-and-down motion of the head similar to that of a hen Barraband or Rock Peplar under the same circumstances. Out of the breeding season the cock is a faithful, but somewhat domineering husband who expects his mate to get out of his way. The hen King alone incubates and the cock helps in feeding the young. Four to six eggs are usually laid, and cases of a double brood are on record. Hen Kings, well reared, may breed at a year old; cocks probably not before they are two years old at earliest.

Cock Kings, while not exactly murderous, are of a rather bullying disposition towards other parakeets. With birds of different orders they are usually trustworthy.

The King Parakeet should be fed on a seed mixture of one part canary,

Leadbeater's Cockatoo.
Photo by Horst Mueller.

Rose Breasted Cockatoo.
Photo by Horst Mueller.

Rock Pebbler. Judging from the greater depth of yellow in its coloration, this bird probably comes from that part (Victoria) of the species' range in which the population shows the brightest yellow. Photo by Horst Mueller.

A pair of Golden Shouldered Parrakeets, male at left. Photo by Horst Mueller.

one part millet, one part oats, one part sunflower, one part hemp, and one part peanuts with fruit and green food ad libitum. When rearing young an extra dish of sunflower and peanuts should be provided.

Pairs of Kings are not very satisfactory at liberty. They are apt to stray and even when they have stayed through a breeding season and the hens have apparently laid and incubated, no young have appeared; probably English trees are not suited to their requirements. There is, however, no finer liberty bird than a cock King whose mate is confined and it is a great pity that owners of country estates do not give their gardens in winter time the ornament of one or more of these noble parakeets. Continually in the picture with his graceful, sweeping flight and brilliant plumage; utterly indifferent to cold and wet; never straying to any distance; and well able to defend himself from owls; the King has the added recommendation of being harmless to trees and shrubs unless a ripe apple or the swelling buds of fruit trees in early spring should tempt him — at which time he can, if necessary, easily be confined for a few weeks. Cocks at liberty do not quarrel, so you can have as many loose as you choose to provide with hens and aviaries. As with most parakeets, however, you must not expect adult cocks to stay if there are no available females for them to visit.

A cock King, intended for liberty, should be trained to the use of a feeding box. This is a large rectangular wooden box four feet by two feet by two feet with a wire netting bottom, made to rest on the wire top of an aviary flight and so constructed that only a bird trained to do so will enter it to feed, whereby an enormous wastage of seed stolen by sparrows, etc., is avoided. In the front of the box in the right-hand corner, rather low down, seven inches from the bottom, is the entrance hole, eight inches by seven inches. Towards the back of the box, near the corner furthest from the entrance hole, is fixed a bracket holding the food dish and in the back of the box, just behind this, is a door which can be opened to take out the dish and replenish the seed. Immediately on the right of the bracket holding the food dish is fastened a tongue of wood projecting forwards parallel with the food dish and just, but only just, long and wide enough completely to hide the food dish from a bird which may chance to look in at the entrance hole. Out of the entrance hole a perch projects about a foot, one end being firmly fastened to another perch which runs at right angles to it, right across the front of the interior of the box, and six inches from the front. This long perch passes just in front of the front end of the wooden tongue and when the tongue is passed another perch at right angles leads up to the food dish. A trained bird, entering the hole, walks along the inside perch past the end of the tongue to the food 'round the corner which he cannot see, but which he knows from experience is there; but a hungry sparrow who chances to put his head in at the opening, seeing nothing but a rather uninteresting wooden interior, is not encouraged to make further investigations and fails to discover the secret.

Since the box rests on the top of an aviary flight, the sparrow is never attracted by spilled seed underneath, nor is he able to see that the box contains a food dish by getting immediately underneath and looking up through the wire bottom. In order to train a parakeet in an aviary it is necessary to put, on a strong bracket in front of the aviary flight, a box exactly like the feeding box but minus the front, the tongue, and the wire bottom. The first day the food dish should be put just inside the box which at this stage resembles a model of an open-fronted shed. The second day the food dish should be removed to the back of the box to the position it will occupy when the final stage is reached. Next day and for several subsequent days one board should be added, thus gradually building up the front until it is completely closed, with the exception of the entrance hole. Finally the tongue is put in and it is a good thing to fasten it in such a way that you can swing it 'round towards the left a few inches at a time until it completely hides the food dish from the entrance. At first is should only partly obscure it, or the bird may think that the food has been removed and refuse to enter. At every stage in the training it is necessary to observe by the appearance of the seed whether the pupil is keeping pace with the alterations in his dining room; for if you go too quickly he may stop visiting the box and starve. When the bird has learned to go past the end of the tongue to the invisible dish beyond, let him have a week to get thoroughly used to this venture of faith; then put a feeding box on the top of his mate's aviary flight and turn him loose one calm morning before he has breakfasted. The calls of his hen will soon bring him down to the aviary once the first excitement of liberty has worn off and if, in due course, you see him enter the box you may know that all is well. If he is slow in entering the box make the seed vessel apparent for a day or two.

During hard frost a dish of water should be kept by the feeding box, and if the hen's aviary cannot conveniently be placed in a sheltered spot near tall evergreens, it is well to have a second feeding box on a stand of wire netting on a wooden frame in such a situation that the cock may find and learn to use it before severe weather sets in. In ordinary weather he can use a box standing on an aviary in a fairly open position; but if a blizzard should be raging, it is wise not to force him to face the open in order to reach his food, as he may get confused in the white, whirling storm and be swept away down wind. I have never lost an Australian King in snow, but I have seen them rather badly puzzled by the hurricane and stinging flakes. When snow has fallen the whole of the feeding box and the frame of the aviary near it should be swept clear first thing in the morning, and if necessary swept again twice during the day. Especially during the short days of winter, or when a bird is newly released, take care that he is not kept away from his food for hours at a time by people working or playing games so close to the box that he is afraid to visit it.

When you wish to catch the cock in order to return him to his mate, remove the seed dish from the box or boxes and put it on a stand close in front of the hen's aviary. As soon as he has found it, put an inward-pointing wire funnel in the small door in the front of the hen's flight, and place the seed in the mouth of the funnel. When he has fed there, put it inside at the end of the funnel and he will pass quietly through into captivity. If you have many parakeets at liberty you will need to watch from a distance the final stage of the operation to see that you do not trap the wrong bird. Early morning is the best time to entice the cock in, as he is bound to come soon for his breakfast and you have less waiting about and less general interference with the feeding arrangements of other liberty birds.

In addition to the calls already mentioned, both sexes of the King Parakeet have a long-drawn whistle, "Eeng, eeng, eeng," repeated, many times in succession, at short intervals.

Hybrids are said to have been produced between most of the members of the King — Crimson-wing — Barraband group. They are often of great beauty, especially the Barraband X Crimson-wing, but always steril.

Crimson-winged Parakeet
Aprosmictus erythropterus

Distribution	New South Wales, Queensland, Northern Territory, Northwest Australia.
Adult male	Head and neck very brilliant apple green; breast, abdomen and lower rump slightly paler green; mantle black. A large patch of very rich crimson in the wing; upper rump deep ultramarine blue; outer webs of flight feathers and upper surface of tail dark green. Bill small and of a light, carroty red with a yellowish tip. Tail somewhat square in shape and of medium length. Total length thirteen and one-half inches. Size roughly that of a pigeon.
Adult female	Somewhat resembles the adult male, but the green areas of the plumage are paler and duller; the rump is a paler blue; the black mantle is lacking; and the red patch on the wing is reduced to a narrow strip on the lower edge. Size usually a little larger than the male.
Immature	In first plumage resembles the female, but the extreme tip of the tail tends to be more salmon-pink and less yellow. In second plumage the young male has some black

on his mantle and a broken patch of red and green on his wing. Adult plumage is assumed in the third year at the second complete moult.

The Crimson-winged Parakeet makes a tolerably enduring, though not a particularly happy cage bird. In close confinement it is usually rather silent and, if tamed, fairly gentle, though not affectionate towards its owner.

An adult male is a gorgeous ornament to an aviary; no living bird shows more striking contrasts of rich colouring, yet somehow there is nothing gaudy or crude about the whole combination. The lovely pale green of the head and breast goes perfectly with the sooty mantle and with the wonderful wing patches, which fairly glow and blaze in their intense crimson, either in sunshine or shadow; while the opening of the wings in flight gives an added glimpse of beauty as the blue of a no less marvellous depth and richness comes into view.

The Crimson-winged Parakeet is exceedingly susceptible to coccidiosis, tuberculosis, and also to the form of septic fever which causes spots to appear on the liver, but safeguarded from infection by diseased companions and kept in a clean aviary, a few birds are hardier or less subject to ailments. Mr. Seth Smith in his article on the Crimson-wing in "Parrakeets," speaks of the cruelty of keeping birds which hail from hot climates in exposed outdoor aviaries in winter. While agreeing with his general argument I cannot help feeling that in selecting the species under consideration to give point to his remarks he made an unfortunate choice, for the Crimson-wing is decidedly less sensitive to low temperatures than any of the true broadtails. The cock of my breeding pair has been at liberty and never ruffled a feather, nor looked in the least puffy, through a spell of the most appalling winter weather. First biting east winds; then continued torrential rain; then a raging blizzard with deep snow; then a cold, foggy thaw and more rain. His son, a rather late-hatched bird, though shut up at night in an unheated aviary shelter, has, by his own choice, spent the greater part of each day in the open.

Sad to relate, when tested by the standard "handsome is as handsome does," the cock Crimson-wing is an undoubted failure, for he is often a wife-beater, a bully, and a coward. Making but a poor show in combat with a courageous adversary, he is decidedly aggressive towards timid companions and he may give his long-suffering mate a thin time. Individual cocks vary enormously in disposition; some are scandalously promiscuous in their amours; others are at least faithful. The worst are incorrigible hooligans, but even the best can hardly be termed polite. You can never tell what will happen when you introduce a healthy cock to a female. Sometimes he will pursue her furiously about the aviary with open beak and torrents of Billingsgate. In more hopeful cases he will mingle the pursuit and the abuse with a certain amount of display and if really in love with the lady he will do more showing off then cursing, though he will never entirely·forego the latter exhibition of masculine talent. The display of the Crimson-wing is curious and is of two kinds. Sometimes he will slightly depress his shoulders so as to show the blue patch on his back, draw his plumage very tight and with contracted pupils and blazing eyes take two or three long strides in a rather drunken and uncertain gait. At other times he will fly to and fro, uttering a kind of song, repeatedly gathering and chewing up bits of green stuff. On very rare occasions during the early days of their married life, a cock Crimson-wing may feed his hen, but he never perseveres in the attention sufficiently to be of any real service to her when she is actually engaged in domestic duties. If the cock is very spiteful when the two birds are put together and gives the hen no peace at all, it may be necessary to remove him and only let him associate with her for a few hours a day when she appears to be near laying. Strange to say the eggs will usually prove fertile, even though you may never have observed the least sign of friendliness. And the cock's incessant and savage persecution of the female when she comes off to feed may later have rendered his permanent separation necessary. Another good plan is to cut the tip of the cock's wing, enough to curtail his activity, but not sufficiently to deprive him of all power of flight. In some cases the hen will stop in the middle of the pursuit and invite the cock to pair with her. He will do so after first pulling out some of her feathers, and he may then become moderately quiet and amicable.

The mildest and most dramatic cocks always indulge in a good deal of chasing and swearing when the nest is put in, but when one has had a little experience of Crimson-wing ways one can easily tell when serious trouble is to be feared. A *really* good cock will not interfere with his hen unduly, and may even feed her and help in feeding the young before and after they leave the nest. I have noticed that the offspring of such good fathers are less liable to be rickety than others. In fairness it must also be added that even the worst wife-beaters who have refused all share in the care of their offspring will not molest them when they meet them after they have flown. One of my most disreputable cocks even extended this tolerance to the young of allied species of parakeets. On one occasion when he was engaged in a flirtation with a hen King, a young cock Barraband settled on the aviary beside him and walked up to him. I expected to see him fall upon the rash youngster, as he treated adult Barrabands with scant courtesy, but instead I witnessed a comical exhibition of a conflict of emotions. Jealously impelled him to attack the intruder, but his one virtue — a sense of duty of forbearance to the young — held him back. So it ended in a compromise; he walked 'round and 'round the Barraband with his beak open, anathematizing him to the full extent of his very generous vocabulary, but he never touched him and eventually the young bird moved off unharmed.

In the matter of nesting sites the needs of the Crimson-wing are identical with those of the King. Dryness and a wooden floor are fatal to the young, and they must have a long climb down almost to ground level. I have more than once seen a brood, reared in a dry artificial box, so rickety on leaving the nest that they could hardly crawl, let alone fly; their bones being so brittle that the slightest tap would break them. Yet after some months on the damp earth in the open air they improved amazingly and became quite tolerable specimens.

The Crimson-wing lays from four to six eggs and is not infrequently double brooded. May is early enough to put in the tree trunk as there is great risk of egg-binding if the weather be very cold.

Pairs of Crimson-wings seem to stay well at liberty, but they range widely and have an inveterate habit of going down chimneys on every possible occasion. Only cocks and young birds can therefore be released with any great measure of safety. Unfortunately, the Crimson-wing comes within the category of birds which the Brown Owl regards as a desirable addition to his menu, so where this curse of controlled-liberty aviculture exists, Crimson-wings can only be released for the day. The method of training is the same as that for the Rock Peplar, but owing to the bullying disposition of the old males, only young birds can with safety be allowed to share a roosting aviary with other species of parakeets. Being very cunning and intelligent, it is necessary at the final stage of training to make the wire funnel rather extra long or the Crimson-wings may learn their way out as well as in. At liberty they make a delightful show. The flight, though less rapid than that of the polyteline parakeets, is extremely buoyant. A bird descending suddenly from a height comes down with a wonderful series of plunging drops with a slight pause between each, as though he were suspended and checked by an invisible line. An old cock wheeling sideways against a background of grey sky is, too, a sight not easily forgotten. A Crimson-wing whose mate is confined never strays and seldom gets into trouble, but if he should fail to appear in the roosting aviary one evening a search of the chimneys is desirable, as occasionally, though not often, one comes across a bird who, even when alone, cannot always resist exploring these fascinating apertures.

Crimson-wings should be fed on a seed mixture of two parts canary, one part millet, one part oats, one part hemp, one part sunflower, one part peanuts, with fruit and green food. When they are feeding young an extra dish containing hemp, sunflower, and peanuts only should be at their disposal; likewise milk-sop.

The usual call note resembles the word "Crillik!" and when startled

and on the wing they make a noise like "Etz! Etz! Etz!" In Australia the
bird is known as the Red-winged Parrot or Bloodwing.

Barraband's Parakeet
Polytelis swainsonii

Distribution	Interior New South Wales, Victoria, South Australia.
Adult male	General plumage brilliant, glittering green; flight feathers bluish green; hinder crown tinged with blue; tail long and pointed, under surface black; upper surface green; forehead orange yellow; cheeks and throat buttercup yellow; a scarlet crescent across the foreneck immediately below the yellow. Bill red. Iris yellow. Total length sixteen and one-half inches. Size about that of a small pigeon.
Adult female	General colour a green much less vivid than that of the cock and somewhat paler on the breast. Flight feathers bluish green. Sides of face, chin and throat greyish green. Thighs bright red. Under surface of tail showing broad, pink edgings to the feathers. Bill pink; iris yellowish brown.
Immature	Resemble the female, but cocks from the time of leaving the nest often show a distinct yellowish tint in those areas of the plumage which are yellow in the adult and a distinct pinkish tint where the red crescent will appear. Some very forward birds show a few yellow feathers when not more than six months old. Towards the end of their first winter young males begin a very slow moult into adult plumage, which is not completed until the following October. Females may breed when a year old, and moult at the same time as the adults and equally quickly.

Barraband's Parakeet is credited by an Australian writer with the qualities of an attractive pet, being gentle and docile, showing fondness for its owner and sometimes learning to talk. From my knowledge of the species I should certainly expect a tame cock Barraband to be a charming companion, but I would not attempt to keep him very closely confined, partly because caged birds are said to be subject to fits and partly because their cry is too loud and penetrating for a room.

As an aviary bird the Barraband is delightful and in a healthy district perfectly hardy and indifferent to cold. In unhealthy places imported birds are very difficult to acclimatize and apt to die in summer and autumn, so for such localities good specimens reared in Europe are greatly to be preferred. Barrabands are quite easy to breed in large aviaries, but in small fixed aviaries the cocks are often sterile and young males reared in such quarters are invariably useless for stock purposes. Their nesting requirements are similar to those of Rock Peplars, but if a natural tree trunk is unobtainable, a tall grandfather clock imitation in boards usually does equally well, provided it is stood in the open aviary flight and has no wooden bottom.

The hen Barraband alone sits, but the cock helps her in feeding the young which may usually be left with their parents a long time without risk of injury. Only one lot of eggs, from four to six in number, are laid in a season. Occasionally a pair of Barrabands may indulge in a little mild squabbling if the hen is unreasonably slow in taking to the nest. Such delay in taking up her duties fills the cock with anger and distress, and he will attempt to force her to attend to business. The strange thing is that this annoyance on the part of the male bird, which is sometimes shown by other species of parakeets as well, is not appeased by the hen being sufficiently in breeding condition to invite pairing, and it is very seldom irrational. For, if there be no nest in the aviary, the cock hardly ever displays anger and unrest. Hen Barrabands, when in breeding condition, invite their mates to feed them by the same calls and gestures as hen Rock Peplars.

Few parakeets are less destructive to growing shrubs than the Barraband and few are more amiable with other birds. Even adult pairs in breeding condition may not quarrel seriously, but as a twenty-four foot aviary is hardly large enough for two pairs, and a more extensive one is difficult to move, it is, on the whole, better to keep pairs separate when nesting. The only thing that will make cock Barrabands fight seriously is a misunderstanding due to one getting an erroneous idea that another is making advances to his wife. When really angry they strike with their claws as well as bite, and while they are slow to lose their tempers, they are even slower to forgive a real, or fancied, injury. They are very devoted to their hens and very jealous, and appear to observe quite a high code of mortality, a strong cock never attempting to rob a weaker one of his mate. Some years ago I had two bachelor cocks at liberty, an old and a young one, the former being the master. When I obtained a hen I put her out on the verandah in a cage and the younger cock was the first to find her and pay her attentions that were very well received. Some days later I introduced her to the old cock when the young one was not present. He, too, was delighted and his advances were encouraged by the hen. After a time the young cock arrived on the scene and I expected a fight in which he would be worsted, but to my astonishment the old bird gave way to him with scarcely the least show of protest; yet the same evening in the roosting aviary it was the old cock who was master as before. I tried the experiment several times, always with the same result. The old cock wanted the hen and she was quite kind to him, but the other fellow had met her first and he was too much of a gentleman to overcome his weaker companion's right by an exercise of superior force. Finally I gave the hen to the old cock, and when the three birds met again some months later it was the young cock who accepted the inevitable and made no attempt to drive away his rival and regain possession of his former sweetheart.

The courtship display of the Barraband is of a lively and varied character; sometimes he will fly in a very slow and laboured fashion around the hen, bowing as he alights with contracting pupils and uttering a great variety of calls. When very excited he will puff his head feathers, draw his body plumage tight, partly spread his wings, and race to and fro around the hen in a series of rapid hops, "scroogling" at the top of his voice. If the object of these attentions is favourably impressed she crouches motionless with puffed head feathers and partly spread wings. It is noteworthy that with the Barraband, as with many other parakeets, the full courtship display is not in any sense a preliminary to actual pairing. It takes place months before the birds are in full breeding condition and is not repeated at a later date.

Young cock Barrabands begin to chuckle and croon to themselves after the manner of the adults a few months after leaving the nest. As hens seldom utter more than the ordinary call note the habit is an indication of sex.

Barrabands do best on a diet of canary, millet, oats, hemp, and sunflower. Fruit and green food must also be provided. They are particular as to the quality of their apples and will usually only take the best dessert kinds, rejecting those that are at all soft or sour. In giving apples to rather dainty and weak-billed species it is a good plan to give a whole one at a time, chipping a bit of the skin off the top with the finger-nail. If they reject the fruit, or grow tired of it before it is consumed, it can be given to a less dainty bird. Even broadtailed parakeets usually need to have an apple "started" for them by the breaking of the skin.

Cock Barrabands make delightful day-liberty birds, their flight being as rapid and beautiful as that of the Rock Peplar. The system of training and management should be the same as for their larger ally. Only mated adult birds and birds of the year can be released with safety. On no account should a hen be let out with her mate, an unmated cock with a male of the year, even though both be home-bred and liberty-trained birds. It is also very dangerous to let cock Barrabands out in a fog or during a snowstorm as both types of weather confuse them, and they are liable to lose their way. Should snow start to fall after the birds have been released, the wire funnels should be put in at once to recapture them as soon as possible in the roosting aviary. By a "mated" bird is meant one that has actually paired with a hen. The presence of an unpaired female in an aviary and even the fact that a bachelor cock has been paying her some attention will not always prevent him from straying if he has another bachelor companion to go off with. Properly mated birds can, however, be released with absolute safety, as they will never willingly desert their wives and yearling cocks are equally safe if unaccompanied by bachelor brothers a year older. As the Brown Owl appreciates a Barraband as an especial delicacy it is very desirable to take every precaution to get the birds into the roosting aviary each night. Be careful never to leave spilled seed outside the aviary or the birds will feed on it and not come in. It is also desirable to arrange the hens' aviaries in such relative position to the roosting aviary that the cocks will not be worried by being unable to see their mates, as this is inclined to encourage them to stay out. It is also necessary to try to prevent jealous misunderstandings. If you have two cocks at liberty and put a hen's aviary on each side of the roosting aviary, all will be well; but if you put both hens' aviaries on the same side, one beyond the other, the following scene may occur:

Cock A (to his wife in the further aviary) "Hullo! darling."

Cock B (whose wife is in the nearer aviary, flying up angrily) "What do you mean by calling my wife 'darling'!"

"I wasn't speaking to your wife, you fool!"

"You were; if you can't behave like a gentleman, get out!"

"I won't get out; calling your wife 'darling,' indeed! I'd as soon call a Black Cockatoo 'darling'!"

Then the two angry gentlemen fall upon each other and fight with all the bitter tenacity of righteous indignation; nor is the quarrel easily forgotten.

With young birds Barrabands are singularly gentle and borbearing and will usually give way at the seed dish to any youngster, whether it be one of their own offspring or a stranger.

The most remarkable recovery of a strayed parakeet I ever had was that of a Barraband, a bird of the year bred in France and not long trained to fly at liberty. Not having at that time learned the danger of allowing Barrabands out in falling snow, this young cock was released on the morning of a day which soon developed into the worst blizzard that had occurred for years. About ten o'clock in the morning the raging northeaster blew down a large cypress tree with a crash, scaring the Barraband up into the sky. Though well able to negotiate the wildest storm in clear weather the stinging flakes confused him and he would not face them; he was swept away seaward to the southwest, over the Solent to the Isle of Wight, where he was seen a few days later, not much less than thirty miles away. The weather remained exceedingly severe for some days after the snowstorm, the frost continuing, and the wind blowing with unabated violence. Nine days later the Barraband came home, apparently not a penny the worse for his adventures, having crossed a not inconsiderable branch of the sea on his return journey. His endurance was all the more remarkable in that a Barraband, unlike a broadtailed parakeet, has usually little power of picking up a living, even in summer, if it strays beyond reach of artificial feeding. In Australia the species is usually known as the Green Leek.

Barrabands, unfortunately, are exceedingly subject to eye disease when newly imported. Fully half of those brought over contract the complaint. This wretched ailment would, however, never occur if dealers would pack the birds singly, or in couples, and keep their travelling boxes scrupulously clean. Barrabands, especially hens, are also subject to paralysis of the legs, caused apparently by the birds over-eating themselves on dry seed after a period of starvation due to fear or other causes. Many newly caught birds perish in this way and sometimes further losses may occur directly after arrival. I once lost a pair of acclimatized birds from the same cause. They had strayed and were caught and returned to me in a starving condition. A day later both became suddenly and permanently paralyzed. In the ordinary course of events, however, eye disease and paralysis are unknown among acclimatized birds properly cared for.

Black-tailed Parakeet or Rock Peplar
Polytelis anthopeplus

Distribution	Interior New South Wales, Victoria, South Australia, South West Australia.
Adult male	General colour pale yellow with a slight olive tinge including the head, rump, sides of face, throat, and entire under-surface. Darker and more olive on the crown and hind-neck; mantle and scapulars oil green; bastard-wing, greater upper wing-coverts, and primary coverts bluish black, the inner greater coverts on the apical portion red with a maroon tinge and tipped with yellow. Flight feathers dark blue-black on the upper surface. Beak red; eyes hazel. Length seventeen inches. Size about that of a pigeon. Individual males vary greatly in colour. Those from Victoria are the purest yellow; others from New South Wales being almost as olive as hens. The colour of the tail is, however, a certain guide to sex in all forms, when adult.
Adult female	Olive green in those areas where the male is yellowish; body plumage otherwise very similar. Tail feathers bronze-green above and broadly margined with pink on the under surface.
Immature	Resemble the female but young cocks begin to show a sprinkling of yellowish feathers during the course of their

first winter. They assume adult dress with the first complete moult when about a year old. During the first autumn a number of body feathers are moulted.

This charming parakeet deserves to be far more widely kept by those who can afford to make adequate provision for its needs. Young birds are easily tamed and make attractive pets, becoming very sociable and possessing some power of mimicry. A cock in my possession whistles the tune, "We Have No Bananas To-day," right through and tries to talk in a hoarse, indistinct voice. Another in the possession of a friend imitates perfectly the cooing of a dove. The natural cry of the Rock Peplar is almost impossible to describe in print. As parakeet calls go, it is not unduly loud nor unpleasant.

Being very active and one of the most marvellous fliers among living birds, the Rock Peplar is unsuited to cage life; nor does it usual survive many years in a small fixed aviary. In a large aviary, however, it is apart from liability to coccidiosis, as healthy and hardy as anyone could wish and if given reasonable care until through its first moult, it is utterly indifferent to the cold and wet of the most inclement winter. It is also quite a free breeder and, not being in a hurry to commence nesting operations before the weather is warm, it is hardly ever troubled with egg-binding. The hen incubates, but the cock assists her in feeding the young. The hen Rock Peplar at all times of the year usually keeps her husband very much in order, and although she is really fond of him once she has accepted him as her mate, she may, out of the breeding season, accord rather a rough welcome to a strange male, particularly if he be not in very good health and spirits at the time of the introduction. When in breeding condition and near laying the female continually invites the male to feed her by crouching close to him on the perch, moving her head up and down and uttering a low, hoarse noise. He is by no means an ardent suitor and usually takes a great deal of persuasion before he will respond to any of his wife's solicitations. It always strikes me as rather a pity that Nature should have arranged that hen broadtails should be married to husbands who almost pester them to death with continual offers of food when they are already satisfied, while polyteline ladies who want to be fed all day long can only with the greatest trouble induce their mates to bestow on them the most casual attention!

It occasionally happens that a cock Rock Peplar, although in perfect health, will even refuse to pair for a season, although he may have bred quite satisfactorily the year before and will do so again the year after. Some cocks have a strange and tiresome peculiarity; they are so madly anxious to have a family that they drive their hens into the nest the moment it is put in and keep them prisoners until they lay, but so great is their haste and anxiety that they quite forget to pair and the eggs are always infertile! Hen Rock Peplars are rather particular about their nesting sites and no young parakeets are more intolerant of an artificial element in their early environment than their offspring. A wooden box with a wooden bottom is usually sure death to them, causing either pneumonia or rickets. They must have moisture and there must be no hard material between them and the earth. The best kind of nest is a natural hollow tree trunk about five or six feet in height, stood out in the flight under the open sky. If it is a mere empty cylinder of wood, boards should be nailed across the top to form a roof. The entrance hole should be cut immediately below the roof with a perch for the parakeets to alight on, and if the interior is very smooth, a strip of wire netting should be tacked up to assist the birds in climbing. The bottom of the trunk should be filled with a few feet of damp mould from the interior of some old and decayed tree. If a natural tree trunk should prove absolutely unobtainable it may be imitated with boards. On no account should it have any bottom; however much mould may separate the young birds from the wooden floor.

I had one very tiresome hen who for years refused to look at any kind of nest and would lay her eggs in the open flight. Usually they came to grief, and on the only occasion when she hatched young she insisted on moving them about, carrying them by the beak and inflicting considerable damage in the process. The last year I had trouble with her she was mated to a Princess of Wales's x Crimson-wing Hybrid. The hybrid was a sensible bird and did everything in his power to try and coax her to take to one of the two nests I had provided. At times he even attempted force, but as she was stronger than he, he could not accomplish much in this direction beyond giving her a sly nip and chasing her when she took wing. I even covered the floor of the aviary flight with wire netting, but all to no purpose. In due course the eggs arrived on the ground, and when others were added after the removal of the wire the hen started moving them to a fresh site each day, breaking one after another in the process. The rage and disgust of the poor hybrid was comical to witness. He stood as near his erratic spouse as he dared and flapped his wings and whined and cursed and snapped his beak, and called her all the names I wished to call her, though restrained by the fear of being overheard by my aviary attendant. When the last egg had been disposed of the idea occurred to me to fix a slanting wooden funnel, about eight inches wide, four feet long and lined with wire netting, to the entrance hole of one of the nest logs — a portion of a natural tree trunk, bottomless, and resting on the ground. Although the Rock Peplar had firmly declined to have anything more to do with this log after a few inspections of the interior, she took to it almost immediately the funnel was in, laid a second clutch and incubated with exemplary patience. It was interesting to observe that at the beginning she used to descend the funnel tail first. Some particularly fussy hens insist on an entrance shaped like a chimney pot and will look at nothing else, while many insist on a long descent like a King.

Rock Peplars lay from four to six eggs and in this country are usually single brooded. Incubation lasts just under four weeks. Young birds, well reared, will sometimes breed at twelve months of age.

Freshly imported Rock Peplars are unfortunately very subject to eye disease due to the often dirty conditions under which they are kept in dealer's shops and on the voyage. Intending purchasers should have nothing to do with a bird that shows an inclination to rub or close an eye, or with one that has any swelling of the eyelid or unusual bareness in that region. He should also be careful to inspect both sides of the parakeet's head, as if affected in one eye only, it will always keep the healthy eye towards the observer. Unfortunately, disappointment may result even when every precaution is taken at the time of purchase, since contagious conjunctivitis sometimes has a period of incubation of several weeks and even of a few months. The Rock Peplar should be fed on a seed mixture consisting of one part canary, one part millet, one part oats, one part hemp, and one part sunflower, together with a few peanuts, green food and fruit. Many individuals appreciate mealworms or a small piece of cake as a tit-bit.

In mixed company the species is usually harmless to other birds and it is not very destructive to growing shrubs.

Cock Rock Peplars make charming day-liberty birds, although where Brown Owls occur, they cannot with safety be allowed to roost in the open. Their flight, when they are going their fastest, is marvellous, providing a spectacle quite unequalled by any British bird I have had the chance to observe. The aerial play of young Rock Peplars just released from the aviary is particularly beautiful. They circle 'round and 'round, twisting and swooping with great rushes so swift that the eye can scarcely follow them. And still going at full speed will dive in and out of the branches of thick trees in such an apparently reckless fashion that one wonders they are not dashed to pieces every second. Old cocks are more sedate and spend a lot of time on the top of their wives' aviaries, but they also in moments of playfulness or alarm will give a fascinating display of wingmanship, though never leaving the immediate vicinity of their homes.

The process of training Rock Peplars to fly at liberty is as follows. Obtain a true pair and when they have actually mated and made some attempt at nesting in an aviary it will be perfectly safe to rely on the cock's affection for his wife to prevent him from straying at any time of year if he is a wild-caught bird. Aviary-bred ones may, however, lose their heads and their way. The next step is to construct a roosting aviary of the type described in an earlier chapter and place it alongside the other. Put the cock in the roosting aviary and place the food dish on the bracket in the front of the flight near the little entrance door. Keep the cock shut up for some days until he is thoroughly used to feeding on the bracket and then, choosing an evening when there is promise of a calm day to follow, remove the food dish and any seed that may be spilled on the ground below it. First thing next morning, open the small top door in the front of the aviary flight and drive the cock gently out through it before he has anything to eat. When he is out, close the top door, open the little door by the bracket and put the food dish back on the bracket. At eleven o'clock if it is winter, or twelve o'clock if the days are fairly long, put an inward-pointing wire funnel (it should not be too long or narrow at this stage) into the little door by the bracket if the cock has not yet come home, as he will probably have done. Next day repeat the process, with the exception of the evening removal of the food, and continue to do so until the cock has learned his way out, as well as in, through the door by the bracket. When the cock is thoroughly used to the funnel it may be wise to lengthen it a little until it projects a few inches beyond the edge of the bracket; otherwise there is some danger that he may learn his way out by travelling along the funnel the reverse way. Eventually too, it is a good plan to start feeding inside the shelter of the roosting aviary; or a swarm of wild birds will come in after the seed on the bracket and the aviary will be filled with a voracious flock of sparrows, tits, and chaffinches. Do not remove the dish on the bracket the moment you start feeding in the shelter, but merely cease to replenish it so that for a time there are husks to tempt the bird to enter until he is ready to do so without any visible encouragement.

Winter is just as good and safe a time to accustom a bird to day, or to complete, liberty as summer, provided, of course that it is acclimatized. Never, however, let out a Rock Peplar, even a trained one, on a day when snow is threatening, particularly if it be accompanied by wind; and if snow starts to fall after the birds have been let out, put the funnels in at once so that they may be recaptured as soon as possible. Utterly indifferent as they become to cold, and splendidly as they breast any hurricane when the atmosphere is clear, falling snow seems to blind and confuse them and they flutter helplessly in the air and are swept away.

When you have young birds to train — they can be turned out as soon as they are entirely independent of their parents — first remove the old cock, whom we will assume is already a trained bird, from the hen's aviary to the roosting aviary, so that he may resume his life of partial freedom. For several days feed the hen and her family from a dish on the bracket in the front of her aviary placed in the same position as the training dish in the roosting aviary. One calm evening move a young cock into the roosting aviary occupied by his father and take away the food in that aviary. Early next morning drive the two birds out through the top door before they have fed, put the food dish on the bracket of the roosting aviary, and proceed as when you were training the old cock. Also temporarily remove the food dish from the bracket on the hen's aviary to the shelter, or the youngster at liberty, on returning home hungry, may waste his time trying to get into the wrong aviary.

As soon as the first young cock knows his way about, you can proceed to educate his brothers, one by one. It is very unsafe to allow cocks and hens out at the same time unless the hens are quite babies only a few weeks out of the nest. Probably hens could be allowed their freedom so long as their male relatives were confined, but I have not tried the experiment, nor do I know if tame hens, when once they have bred in a place, can be trusted not to stray when loose with their mates. Certainly they are not dependable stayers before they have nested, although there is less risk of losing tame birds than wild ones, should they stray, as they will allow themselves to be caught when hungry and an advertisement will usually lead to their restoration to their owner. Young cocks can safely be flown at liberty for about five weeks, after which they must be caught up until a year or more, later when they have entered fully into the responsibilities of the married state.

Adult cock Rock Peplars will share a roosting aviary quite amicably with Barrabands, but as the breeding season approaches they are apt to grow intolerant of each other's presence and have to be separated and returned to their wives. It is fatal to try to force a bird to roost in an aviary where he knows he will be bullied and harried. Sooner or later he will prefer the apparently lesser evil of sleeping out hungry and an owl will complete the tragedy. Never, therefore, overcrowd your roosting aviary, but make sure that every bird can regard it as a place of rest and comfort.

Viscountess Grey of Fallodon has been very successful in hand-rearing young Rock Peplars and the birds so raised were perfectly delightful at liberty, as they would, when loose in the garden, fly up to a person, even a stranger, and alight fearlessly on his head or shoulders. The advice she gives in the Avicultural Magazine as to the management of the young birds is so valuable that it is worth quoting at some length, as it could no doubt be followed with equal success with many other species of parakeets. Lady Grey recommends the use of a light wickerwork basket fourteen inches long, six or seven inches wide and six inches deep, closed with a lid with a stick that runs through the wicker staples. Two squares of mackintosh (rubber sheeting) should be prepared for the bottom of the basket and a dozen flannel squares for loose lining. Take the young birds you intend to rear while they are still in down with the feathers in quill, and the colour just showing. Put one rubber square in and lay one of the flannel squares in the basket loosely. Have more of the flannel under the birds than over them. There should be one light "flap-over" of the flannel to

A Black-Capped Lory of the genus *Domicella*. Photo by Horst Mueller.

Senegal Parrot, Photo by Horst Mueller.

Scarlet Macaw. Photo by
Albert Gommi. Reproduced
with permission of the
copyright owner, the
Champion Paper and Fibre
Company.

Upper: Nyassaland Love Bird. *Lower:* Black-Cheeked Love Bird. Drawing by R. A. Vowles.

cover them, but as they get older they will cease to need it. It is essential that they should be in a warm hole with air 'round them, rather than folded closely. They must be able to potter about inside the flannel-lined basket. Between the wall of the basket and the flannel keep a fresh bit of brown bread in a wisp of tissue paper so that it keeps clean and may be always handy. Bite up a little into small bits and moisten it well in your mouth until it is of a soft, porridgy consistency. Lift the bird you want to feed and holding it carefully in both hands, place its bill between your lips, sideways. If it does not feed at once touch its bill with your lips lightly but be careful not to close your lips over its nostrils. Brown bread, mouth-moistened till it is almost fluid is enough at first, but as the birds get older mix it with little mouthfuls of bitten and peeled apple, chewed lettuce, or grape pulp. Even from the first, small drinks of warm water are good and later are essential. The birds will let you know when they are hungry by calling for food. For the first four or five days feed every three hours, but when their feathers are grown four meals a day will suffice, the first given about seven a.m. When the young are a month old a millet spray should be hung in the basket. Allow the birds to have plenty of exercise as they grow older and let them walk about and stretch their wings, but be very careful not to let them have a fall. Do not hurry over the feeding; to feed three takes about twenty minutes. Change the flannel square repeatedly and if their feet should ever get clotted with dirt stand them for a minute or so in a soap dish of warm water. A camel-hair paintbrush is a good implement to use as an alternative to mouth-feeding.

One of the most remarkable displays of intelligence that I have ever seen in a bird was shown by a Rock Peplar I once owned. Foolishly, as it ultimately turned out, I put the poor fellow's mate in an aviary at some distance from the roosting aviary so that he could not see her when he was confined in the latter. This separation made him anxious and worried, and though for a long time he had used the entrance funnel without hesitation he ultimately came to realize that when the funnel was in he could not get back to his wife after feeding. He would therefore fly up to the roosting aviary and look at the little door where the funnel was put. If the funnel was not in position, he would enter without a moment's hesitation and go to the shelter at the back to feed. But if the funnel was in he would only pass through it when exceedingly hungry; otherwise he would go back to the hen and roost out in the trees when darkness fell. Had he ever been frightened or hurt in the funnel, or had he become shy of the aviary as a place of irksome restraint at all times, there would have been nothing remarkable in his behaviour, but it was extraordinary that he should have grasped the fact that a particular placing of a small piece of wire netting — an object which he knew by experience was in itself harmless — changed the whole aviary from a convenient feeding place into an irritating prison. Alas! His cleverness and devotion proved his undoing, for, finding the funnel in place, he roosted out one night too often and a brute of an owl devoured him during the hours of darkness.

Princess of Wales's or Queen Alexandra's Parakeet
Northipsitta alexandrae

Distribution	Central Australia, Northern South Australia, interior of North and Midwest Australia.
Adult male	Hind-neck, mantle, scapulars and innermost secondaries pale olive green. A large patch of pale yellowish green on the wings. Outer webs of primary quills bluish green with narrow yellow edgings. Rump lilac blue. Middle tail feathers golden green and of great length. Lateral tail feathers blue-grey on the outer webs, deep rose pink on part of the inner webs. Crown pale lilac blue. Some poorly coloured males (usually aviary-bred) have a slate blue crown and rump like the female. Chin, throat, and foreneck, lower flanks, and thighs rose pink. Breast and under parts mother-of-pearl. One primary in each wing has a curious prolongation or spatule at the tip, which not infrequently gets broken off some months before the moult. Length sixteen inches. Size of body roughly that of a Barbary Dove.
Adult female	Resembles the adult male but lacks the spatule on the primary and has the crown and rump bluish slate colour. Tail also somewhat shorter.
Immature	Resembles the female, but the rump and head are even more dull and slatey and the tail is shorter.

By reason of its comparative rarity in confinement, the soft beauty of its unique colouring, the elegance of its form and the friendly and fearless nature of its disposition, this lovely bird has always been the joy and pride of its fortunate possessors and the envy of the less fortunate majority whose collections it has never graced. A wandering native of remote desert regions, it is wont to appear unexpectedly in a particular locality, rear its young and then vanish, to be seen no more for, perhaps, as long as thirty years. One observer writes, "They travel in flocks, from one pair up to almost any number; are very tame, feeding about the grass near the camp and seem in no way afraid of people, cattle, or horses." Another Australian naturalist notices their habit of perching along the thick limb of a tree after the fashion of a nightjar.

I have had specimens so wing-stiff from close confinement that it was obvious that they had survived many years of cage life, but a cage is a poor prison for so lovely and active a bird. As pets they have much to recommend them, though it must be admitted that in a room their voices are unpleasantly shrill and penetrating. No parakeet is naturally so fearless of mankind nor so easily tamed and, while it dislikes being touched and handled, as do all species which have not the habit of caressing their mates, none is more delighted by being spoken to and noticed by its owner and none will give him a devotion more free from cupboard love. Almost any Princess of Wales will come up and display to you if you cluck and chirrup to him for a few moments and tell him he is a pretty bird. Aviary-bred young, instead of being desperately timid, will be sitting on your arm and feeding from your hand before other young parakeets will be even reasonably steady and tolerate your proximity without trying to break their necks in blind panic against the wire.

I once had a magnificent old cock who was very tame and devoted to men, though he had not much use for ladies and still less use for birds, including the females of his own species. He whistled a bar of "Tom, Tom, the Piper's Son," and used to say "Kiss little Cocky; kiss little Cocky boy." After spending two winters in an unheated outdoor aviary he fell a victim to pneumonia one showery May. We took him into the heated hospital, but it was in vain. Even when he was dying, if a friend went to visit him and express sympathy he would still try to pull himself together and make a feeble effort to show off. It was an interesting, as well as a very touching sight, for the moment a parakeet falls even slightly ill it never by any chance displays to a female companion. Poor Cocky's devotion to human beings was something deeper than mere sex instinct, urging his friendly little soul to an expression of love, even when his body was failing in pain and weakness.

Although now and again one comes across a weakly specimen that needs a good deal of coddling, the Princess of Wales's Parakeet is quite reasonably hardy and when adult can be wintered out-of-doors without artificial heat. Birds of the year, however, should have some extra warmth in their aviary shelter during their first winter, as they moult when about four months old, completely, if my memory is not at fault.

The food should be the same as that of the Rock Peplar and mealworms are often appreciated as an extra. A natural perpendicular hollow tree trunk makes the best nest and it should not be put into the aviary until the nights are warm. Six eggs form the normal clutch and if the first lot fail to hatch the hen will often lay a second time. A large aviary is desirable as the cock birds are very apt to be sterile in cramped quarters and on stale ground. Male Princess of Wales's Parakeets vary considerably in disposition. Some are faithful husbands and good fathers, feeding their mates and their young. Others are the very opposite. My first cock was a sad rake. When the breeding season approached he used to fall in love with every hen parakeet within sight of hearing except his lawful spouse. Rosella or Ringneck, King or Crimson-wing, it made no difference to him; he wanted to lay his heart at the feet of each and all. Only by concealing all his neighbour's wives from his ardent gaze was it ever possible to bore him into paying some casual attention to his own hen and even when he did, which was by no means always, he never thought of feeding her or giving her the least help with the rearing of their offspring. Many hen Princess of Wales possess, unfortunately, a maddening habit of breaking their eggs, and others lay an excessive number but refuse to incubate. No remedy is known for either vice.

The Princess of Wales's Parakeet is gentle in mixed company and agrees fairly well with its own kind, although some cocks prove to be too bullying in disposition to be desirable companions for others of their sex.

Hybrids have been reared with the Barraband, the Crimson-wing, and the Rock Peplar. The Barraband Hybrid, bred by the late Mr. Astley, was a very striking bird with an entirely red breast. My Crimson-wing hybrid is also of great beauty. He is slightly larger than either of his parents and has a yellowish green wing patch edged with crimson on the lower side. He has also a considerable amount of red colouring on his breast and a lovely blue rump. He took three years to attain full plumage, but mated when twelve months old, although so far he has proved sterile. He is an intelligent bird and a great mimic of other parakeets' calls and he has some of his father's friendliness for humanity.

Hen Princess of Wales's Parakeets, when well reared, will breed at twelve months old. Whether cocks ever breed before they are two years old is uncertain.

XXII

Lories and Lorikeets

Purple-capped Lory
Domicella domicella

Distribution   Ceram and Amboyna.

Adult   Rich crimson, darker on the back. Some golden yellow showing at the base of the neck. Cap violet. Upper part of wings olive-brown; remainder green; flights with large yellow spot on the inner webs. Tail red with darker brownish tips to the feathers. Bill orange-red. Length twelve inches. Tail fairly short.

Immature   Said to show more green on the back.

The Purple-capped Lory is a member of a small group of the brush-tongued parrots which are distinguished by their rather stout bodies and comparatively short tails. Their plumage is of great richness and brilliance, red usually predominating. They are extremely active, climbing, hopping, and bounding about. In a wild state they live in pairs and in confinement they are very intolerant of the company of other parrots, though they may be a trifle less vicious towards their own species than towards others. Males of breeding pairs that have lost their fear of human beings may be very savage even towards their owners, but single birds often become most affectionate and gentle, not infrequently learning to talk. They are said to stay well at liberty but can only be let out in summer, as they are unable to stand cold. They are unsuited to cage life and do best in birdrooms or outdoor aviaries with roomy and well-heated shelters. They should be fed a farina-type baby food prepared as for infants and sweetened, together with sweet grapes and other ripe fruit with the exception of orange. If rice can be obtained which contains the *whole* grain, and not the polished form usually employed for human consumption outside its place of origin, which has little feeding value, I am told by an experienced aviculturist that when boiled it makes a good ingredient in lory's food. They are inclined to be noisy but their calls are less trying than those of lorikeets. As with all large honey-eating birds their droppings are copious and frequent cleansing of their quarters is very necessary. For the floor of their shelter, sawdust is better than sand.

Purple-caps have nested in captivity, but the eggs were eaten by the male — a common vice in captive lories. Captain Smithwick describes a tame Purple-cap as the most beautiful and companionable bird he ever possessed, and one with an unequalled power of producing from his throat a wonderful range of tone and note in his mimicry. He loved being put on his back and tickled under his wings. Another bird of the same species, though very savage on arrival, became even more gentle and affectionate, though less talented.

Black-capped Lory
Domicella lory lory

Distribution   Northwestern New Guinea, Waigiou, Mysol, Salwatty, Batanta.

Adult   Cap black. Cheeks, throat, rump, upper tail-coverts, under wing-coverts, and feathers over ribs red. A narrow band of pinkish red behind the crown. Upper part of wings olive brown; lower part green. A large yellow spot on the inner webs of the flights. Lower part of back of neck, centre of mantle, and upper breast dark blue. Centre of breast blue-black. Abdomen brilliant blue; under tail-coverts slightly paler blue. Tail feathers dull green with dark blue terminal portion; a red patch near the base. Bill red. Length twelve inches.

Immature   Said to have no red band below the crown; more green on the mantle; a blue collar round the neck and the greater under wing-coverts yellow with black tips.

Black-capped Lories are far too active and make too much mess to be suited to cage life and should be allowed to fly loose in birdrooms during the winter and in aviaries or at liberty during warm weather. As already indicated the reputation for gentleness given them by the old writers on aviculture is undeserved. While it is true that nothing can be more charming than the behavior of a tame bird towards a person to whom it is attached, pairs are murderously savage towards psittacine neighbours and single specimens will fight furiously when first introduced. A pair I imported some years ago tolerated a third Black-cap in the same room, but made it very clear that all other lories must go. When sold, they went to nest in a rather small and dark indoor flight cage and successfully reared a young one. Close confinement soon told on them, however, for they plucked their baby in the nest and their subsequent efforts at breeding were abortive, while their beaks and claws became overgrown and misshapen. The young bird when newly hatched was covered with yellow down and on growing up he made a talented and affectionate pet. His father, when nesting, attacked the aviary attendant and his mistress at every opportunity.

Lories should be fed on a farina-type baby food prepared as for babies and sweetened, and on sweet, ripe fruit. Tahiti lories should be given the baby food at half-strength diluted with water.

The female has a narrower skull and beak than the male.

Chattering Lory
Domicella garrulus garrulus

Distribution	Halmahera.
Adult	Bright red. A few partly yellow feathers in the middle of the back, at the bend of the wing, and more underneath the wing. Upper part of wing olive-bronze; remainder green, a large scarlet spot on the inner webs of the flights. Basal portion of tail dull red, terminal half dark blue-green. Thighs greenish. Bill red. Total length twelve inches.

The Chattering Lory is reputed to make a clever mimic but to be of a passionate and excitable disposition. It has been bred by Lord Poltimore, one young bird being reared.

Swainson's Lorikeet (often, Blue Mountain Lory)
Trichoglossus moluccanus

Distribution	South Australia, Victoria, New South Wales.
Adult	Green. Head feathers streaky blue on a dark background. A pale yellow-green nuchal collar. A few partly orange and red feathers on the upper mantle. Upper breast fiery orange-red mixed with yellow. Centre of lower breast dark blue. Flanks orange-red and green. Thighs green, yellow, and orange. Under wing-coverts orange-red. A large yellow spot on the inner webs of the flights. Tail pointed and of medium length. Bill red with a yellow tip. Total length twelve inches. The female has a smaller, rounder, and more effeminate head.
Immature	Has a yellower breast, a narrower nuchal collar and a blackish beak.

Swainson's Lorikeet or the "Blue Mountain Lory," as it is sometimes called, is the best known representative of a well-marked sub-genus of the brush-tongued, nectar-eating parrots. Between the different species there exists a strong family resemblance and what is true of one is to a great extent true of all. With about one exception they are brilliantly coloured with a high gloss on their plumage, particularly on the head, where the feathers are lanceolate and usually more or less blue in colour.

They are extremely active birds, leaping, climbing, and flying with great swiftness. The sexes, which are coloured alike, show great attachment to each other and often play together in an amusing and puppy-like fashion, rolling over and over and pretending to bite. When courting, they perform droll and curious antics, dancing, bobbing, bowing, and squirming. Though not particularly intolerant of the company of their own species, and sometimes safe with non-psittacine birds, towards the parrot tribe in general they manifest the greatest hostility, male and female backing each other up in a joint attack which usually puts even the largest enemy to flight. They are particularly dangerous in an aviary where other parakeets are trying to breed. For ordinary conversation they possess a large repertoire of crooning, squealing, and whining noises, and when excited or alarmed the majority screech unpleasantly.

Most species stand cold pretty well but appreciate a log to roost in. They may breed at any time of year and often have two or three broods in a season. During the winter it is advisable to hang the log in an aviary shelter that can be warmed, as, although egg-binding is not a common complaint among lorikeets, it is not unknown and precautionary measures should be taken if the birds are observed to be pairing and going much into the log during the daytime. The cock feeds the hen, spends a good deal of time with her in the nest, and assists in rearing the family — that is to say, when he does not eat the eggs or kill his babies — a vice to which male lorikeets are unhappily now and then addicted. Sinners in this respect are best got rid of. The writer has tried most of the foods advised by experts for birds of this family with such complete absence of success that, however good the results they may have yielded in other hands, he has no confidence in recommending them. There is, however, one satisfactory food for every kind of lory and lorikeet that never produces fits or digestive troubles and that is a farina-type baby food prepared as for infants and well sweetened with sugar. This, together with sweet grapes (the small, hard, white kind are as good as any) will keep lorikeets in health for any period.

Lorikeets will exist for a time on sweetened malted milk or even on ordinary milk scalded and sweetened.

Lorikeets are quite unsuited to cage life, both on account of their activity; and also on account of the copious and liquid nature of their droppings, which not only fall on the floor, but are liable to be squirted through the bars. They should be kept loose in birdrooms or in aviaries; for the floors of the shelters of the latter, sawdust is a better and more absorbent material than sand. Lorikeets can easily be tamed sufficiently to feed from their owner's hand, but I have never heard of one becoming attached to its master or mistress. There should, however, be no reason why a single bird should not be rendered as docile and affectionate as a lory.

There is an interesting record of the taming of a large flock of wild Swainson's Lorikeets. "At first Mr. Gardiner had a young caged bird that enticed a wild bird, which was captured. On account of its brilliant plumage it was called 'Reddy' and, after being feasted on sugar and other dainties for about six months, was set at liberty again. Reddy, mindful of home comforts, occasionally returned with a mate and later with young ones, all of which Mr. Gardiner continued to feed with sugar and water. Then, as if imposing on good nature, scores of birds came and finally hundreds.

"When Mr. Gardiner was reading or reclining, numbers of his feathered friends would climb all over him, and were fond of running his hair through their bills. But, strange to say, the birds would not alight on his man or his man's wife, although both used to feed the birds in Mr. Gardiner's absence. Often when Mr. Gardiner was returning home flocks of hungry, fluttering lorikeets would meet him a hundred yards away from the house."

Hybrids have been produced with the Red-collared Lorikeet and Chattering Lory.

Lorikeets do fairly well at liberty if one of a pair is tame. Wild birds are disappointing, staying for a time and then leaving. The species seldom destroys growing shrubs.

Index

205